Bad Girls

WHY MEN LOVE THEM & HOW GOOD GIRLS CAN LEARN THEIR SECRETS

Bad Girls

WHY MEN LOVE THEM & HOW GOOD
GIRLS CAN LEARN THEIR SECRETS

by Carole Lieberman

Published by Cogito Media Group

ISBN: 978-2-923865-12-6

Cover design: Francois Turgeon
Text design and composition: Nassim Bahloul

Cover photo:
© Colin Anderson/Blend Images/Corbis

Backcover photo:
© Werner Amann

Cogito Media Group
279 Sherbrooke Street West
Suite#305
Montréal, Quebec
H2X 1Y2
CANADA
Phone : + 1.514.273.0123

www.cogitomedias.com

Printed and Bounded in the United States of America

Contents

Acknowledgments

I gratefully acknowledge:

My devoted parents, Sylvia and Sidney Lieberman, who taught me to believe in impossible dreams, and tried their best to teach me to be a 'good girl'. Indeed, it could be said that I was destined to grow up and write *Bad Girls* because, when I was little, my mother was always telling me "Susie Bad" bedtime stories. Susie, it seems, just happened to engage in exactly the same bad behavior that I had engaged in that day, such as throwing a tantrum in the bakery because she (and I) wanted a cookie before dinner. The stories always ended with Susie regretting her 'bad' behavior and promising never to be 'bad' again. The moral and purpose of those cautionary tales were clear. Of course, the bad girls in this book are protagonists in 'bedtime' stories of another sort, and want more than a forbidden cookie.

My beautiful daughter, Tiffany Sabrina Towers, the joy of my life and a girl of many talents – from actress to scholar to equestrian – and research editor for *Bad Girls*.

The more than one hundred men, who loved, dated or married bad girls (and the bad girls, themselves) whom I interviewed. Thank you for opening your hearts and trusting me enough to share your most intimate experiences and feelings. I hope you will find comfort and pleasure in knowing that your stories are helping others.

The visionaries at Cogito Publishing, who not only 'got'

Bad Girls in a heartbeat, but whose enthusiasm and expertise have nurtured it along the way. To Pierre Turgeon, Publisher and CEO; Francois Turgeon, Graphic Designer; and Gratia Ionescu, Acquisitions Manager, *j'envoie un grand merci.*

Michael Wright, more than an awesome publicist, a 'magician' and friend.

Ginny Weissman, an amazing friend who excels at anything she sets her sights on, including encouraging me to stop everything to write *Bad Girls*. Other special friends, who have been dear to me along this journey: Dr. Mari Edelman, Dr. Claude Lannoy, Michele Marshall Mathes, Esq., Suzanne Takowsky, and all my equestrian trainers and friends.

Dedication

This book is dedicated to all the good girls who have been wearing their heart on their sleeve... only to have it broken, and to all the men who have been preyed upon and hurt by bad girls. May this book soothe your pain and help you find the love you deserve.

Introduction

Are you wondering when it will be your turn to walk hand-in-hand into the sunset with the man or woman of your dreams? Whether you are a good girl who is discouraged by losing out to the bad girls, or a man who wants to avoid being a bad girl's prey… you are about to embark on a journey that will give you deeper insight into yourself, allow you to unravel the mysterious allure of bad girls, and help you find more authentic and fulfilling love.

Countless women have had the frustrating experience of loving a man who is oblivious to them, while being swept up in the drama of loving a bad girl instead. Everyone sees the heartbreak coming and wants to save him from it, but he won't listen.

In the first chapter, "Our Love Affair with Bad Girls", you will discover what makes bad girls tick and why otherwise smart and successful men fall head over heels for them. Ladies, you can take the 'Bad Girl Test' to find out whether your score puts you in the: Wanna-Be Bad Girl, Bad Girl, Very Bad Girl or Man-Eater category. Men, you can take the 'Sitting Duck Test' to find out how vulnerable you are to being put under a bad girl's spell.

Next, each one of the dozen dangerous damsels gets her own chapter, where she is placed on Dr. Carole's couch to be analyzed. Secrets will be uncovered from The: Gold-Digger, Addict, Sex Siren, Sexual Withholder, Married Woman on the Prowl, Commitment-Phobe, Husband Hunter and Trapper, Husband Stealer, Ultimate Damsel in Distress, Cougar, Ball-Buster and Bad Girl Scorned.

These secrets will help you crack the bad girl code, so that you'll understand what each type of bad girl wants, why she wants it, and why men fall for her.

Real stories from men on the dating front, collected through in-depth interviews of over one hundred men who have loved, dated or married bad girls, will bring to life each dangerous damsel – and the chaos they create when they're on the prowl. These men come from all walks of life, spanning a wide spectrum of ages, geographical locations, work settings, economic status, family backgrounds and relationship histories. They share intimate details and reveal what the attraction was, how far they went to 'catch' the bad girl before she caught them, and what impact the experience had on their lives.

At the end of each chapter is a list of famous bad girls – from history to headlines, and real life to reel life – who illustrate the different types. They include Angelina Jolie, Samantha from "Sex and the City", Madonna, Sarah Palin, Britney Spears, Lady Chatterley, Marilyn Monroe, Anna Nicole Smith, Alex Forrest from "Fatal Attraction", and many more.

When *Bad Boys: Why We Love Them, How to Live with Them, and When to Leave Them* was published years ago, men called foul and pleaded, "When are you going to write about bad girls?" This book grants your wish. You will recognize some of the bad girl scenarios as having happened to you or to men you know. Whether you are a man who has so far been spared the painful drama of loving a bad girl, or whether you are still licking your wounds from your last disaster, this book will save you from being trampled on by the next bad girl who's determined to put you under her spell.

And ladies, this book is the answer to your wishes, as well, because it evens the playing field. You can say "good-bye" to the sobs and self-loathing that come from losing your man to a bad girl. Each chapter provides invaluable clues to romantic success, and the last chapter, "Bad Girls' Secrets to A Man's Heart" will add to your insights. You will learn how to capture the irresistible allure of bad girls, without resorting to becoming 'bad' yourselves. From your peek inside the bad girls' book of spells, you will discover how to become man-magnets, but not man-eaters!

Happy hunting! You are all on your way to getting the love you deserve!

Chapter 1

OUR LOVE AFFAIR WITH BAD GIRLS

Just as little girls are forewarned that they'll need to kiss a lot of frogs before they find their prince, society forewarns little boys that they'll need to slay a lot of dragons before they'll win the heart of their true princess. These childhood messages, garnered from parents and peers, fairytales and fables, media and meddlers, are planted in our unconscious mind and direct our dating behavior when we grow up.

Oftentimes, these men grow up believing they are not entitled to a princess unless they accomplish some death-defying feat equivalent to slaying a dragon, such as making a ton of money, driving a fancy car, living in a mansion, displaying trophies attesting to their prowess in some sport, or being able to flash business cards with an impressive title after their name.

They believe that, unless they have achieved such accomplishments, women who are attracted to them must be inferior specimens – not real princesses. Even when some men have achieved these badges of honor, they are still caught up in the illusion that they are not good enough, and they must continue to prove their worth in order to win the woman of their dreams. These are the men most likely to embark on a self-destructive path of falling for a bad girl, while casting aside seemingly inferior princesses who actually love the man for who he is, not how many dragons he has slain.

You are about to discover why otherwise smart and successful men fall head over heels for bad girls, losing their savings, self-respect, and sanity in the process. These men are caught up in the 'knight in shining armor' fantasy. Their self-worth is intimately and inextricably bound to their ability to rescue a woman from her plight, usually a life of chaos. Whether it's by slaying a dragon, saving her from eviction or addiction, giving her her best orgasm, or being the first boyfriend who doesn't beat her up, such men are driven to chase after their damsel in distress until she's trampled all over them.

Unfortunately for these knights, there are plenty of bad girls ready to be rescued, though not nearly as helpless as they appear. In fact, many of these seemingly fragile beauties are master manipulators, lying in wait to take these vulnerable men on the roller-coaster ride of their lives.

Bad girls come in many flavors, each girl a product of her own dysfunctional childhood. Their long list of disappointments in love begins with their dads and ends with the last cad who broke their hearts. They are a complex paradox of insecurity and ruthlessness, deprivation and entitlement, emptiness and chaos. Their hard lives have hardened their hearts, especially towards men, whom they make pay for all the previous lovers who treated them badly. They use their looks, sex, and feigned helplessness as bait, while secretly strategizing how to best take advantage of the current man who is on their hook. Bad girls are the 'naughty mommies' of their man's worst nightmares.

The dirty little secret underneath the armor of such a wannabe knight is that he is really trying to 'save' or 'rescue' himself from being hurt, rejected, or abandoned. In his heart of hearts, he doesn't believe that he is man enough for a fair damsel to fall in love with him, and feels that it is only if he provides her with something she wants or needs that she will be with him. The often-repeated refrain from men who have loved bad girls is: "This white knight stuff comes from thinking I'm not good enough. I think I have to buy a woman's love or do something to earn her affection." If a man rescues her by providing what she's looking for, he hopes that it will give him some power over her and that she will be beholden and devoted to him like the happy endings in tales where the hero lifts his fair damsel in his arms and carries her off into the sunset. But tales of bad girls don't have happy endings. Instead of being forever grateful, she takes what she's looking for and moves on, when the man has no more to give, or she's bored or she spies a more vulnerable prey.

When men are busy rushing to the rescue of bad girls, they see what they want to see, focusing only on the little girl inside who seems to need protection (not unlike women who see the little boy inside bad boys and want to rescue them). But what these men don't realize is that the once sweet and innocent little girl has been crushed, overpowered, and transformed into a big bad girl who is self-absorbed with her fantasies and has cruel intentions.

Our obsession with bad girls takes us from the bedroom to the big screen. From Blanche duBois in "A Streetcar Named Desire" to Scarlett O'Hara in "Gone with the Wind," and from Carrie Bradshaw in "Sex and the City" to Alex Forrest in "Fatal Attraction," they keep us on the edge of our seats. In real life, too, there's an unending supply of bad girls who fascinate us: Angelina Jolie, Marilyn Monroe, Britney Spears, Monica Lewinsky, Lindsay Lohan, Mary Kay Letourneau, Oksana Grigorieva, Anna

Nicole Smith, Madonna, and Paris Hilton are only the tip of the iceberg. They're the women we love to hate and hate to love. But the 'baddest' of all are everyday real-life women who are surreptitiously batting their eyelashes and worming their way into the beds and hearts of good men everywhere.

What *is* a bad girl?

There was a little girl,
Who had a little curl,
Right in the middle of her forehead.
When she was good,
She was very good indeed,
But when she was bad she was horrid.

When Henry Wadsworth Longfellow wrote these words in the 19th century, he could hardly have imagined how "horrid" bad girls would become.

A bad girl is a woman whose heart has been hardened by men who have hurt, abused, or abandoned her in her past, most notably her father. To protect herself, she has taken her heart off her sleeve and locked it away, having given up hope of ever meeting a charming prince who will kiss her and make her feel loveable.

Indeed, the problem is that, because of her past experiences, she does not feel loveable and no longer expects to be loved. This pains her and causes her to feel fearful and angry. She transforms her pain, fear, and anger into a single-minded crusade to get 'something' from a man, leaving broken hearts in her wake. The 'something' she wants to get varies, depending upon which of the 12 categories of bad girl best describes her.

When a woman has had a dysfunctional relationship with her father that has made her feel unloveable, it usually propels her towards relationships with bad boys first. But at some point, after having been hurt by one or more bad boys, she gives up, throws away the key to her heart, and vindictively goes after good boys to punish them and make them pay to compensate for her past suffering.

There are 12 types of bad girls, or a dozen dangerous damsels: The Gold-Digger, The Addict, The Sex Siren, The Sexual Withholder, The Married Woman on the Prowl, The Commitment-Phobe, The Husband Hunter and Trapper, The Husband Stealer, The Ultimate Damsel in Distress, The Cougar, The Ball-Buster, and The Bad Girl Scorned. There is not a separate category for cheaters, because bad girls in these other categories can and do resort to cheating, if they start having trouble getting what they want from their man. They simply feel entitled to look for it elsewhere.

Whatever category she fits into, a bad girl is sexy, attractive, alluring, free-spirited, bold, seductive, fun, wild, exciting, flirtatious, cunning, and smart. She knows just what a man wants to hear and just what he wants her to do to make him feel cared for, adored, and like the biggest stud who ever walked the planet. Once she's enticed him into her web and extracted all she can from him, she finishes him off like a black widow spider killing the male after she mates.

Like a cat with a canary, she relishes watching men fall all over themselves as they try to satisfy her desires. She recognizes the fear in their eyes – the fear of being hurt, rejected, or abandoned, the fear that she once felt herself. A bad girl is like a tornado, a thunderstorm, and an earthquake all rolled into one, leaving a trail of destruction through a man's life. She's the most potent heartbreaker of all because by making a man feel like he's hot, she not only manipulates him to do her bidding, but she makes him fall in love with her even more.

The bad girl, emboldened by her past pain fueling her hardened heart, gives off an air of confidence and cockiness that cuts through a man's resistance. How she also manages to appear like a damsel in distress, bringing out a man's inner knight, is what gives her an air of mystery, elusiveness, and enchantment. She is a paradox of dainty damsel and demanding diva. She's fragile, yet fearless. She's irresistible.

A bad girl is able to carry this off because she has underlying ulterior motives – whatever it is she's after. She can risk looking like the fool because she knows that she will never give her heart whole-heartedly to any man. She's out for something. So although her seeming self-assurance is really a 'faux' confidence or pseudo-cockiness because it's hiding a heap of pain, only she knows this. And, meanwhile, she's making good use of her power over men.

Unlike a good girl, who just wants starry-eyed love, a bad girl is looking to fulfill her specific desire or need. She has a different mindset. It's a jungle out there, and like the contestants on "Survivor," the bad girl hones her strategies to win. No mushy heart for her. This allows the bad girl to go after men with a goal-directed boldness and charisma that is almost 'man-like' in its brazenness. Stirring up a potent mixture of feelings in her prey – amazement and admiration, as well as a need to rescue – the bad girl pursues her hidden agenda.

Bad girls are radically different from good girls, who chase men simply because they have a crush on them. Good girls become clingy and desperate to 'make' men love them – and nothing pushes men away faster. Another paradox is that, although good girls seem easy to get and not enough of a challenge for men, bad girls seem even easier and, in fact, come on to men. The secret is that, while bad girls are flirting outrageously, sleeping with men on the first date, and pursuing them, they have an air of danger that good girls don't. Men know – consciously or unconsciously – that they are risking something by allowing a bad girl to put them under her spell. But since she pursues them with such gusto, these men allow themselves to believe that she is truly madly in love with them. And just like the Royal Canadian Mounted Police, 'the bad girl always gets her man!'

What does a bad girl want?

The great question that has never been answered, and which I have not yet been able to answer, despite my thirty years of research into the feminine soul, is "What does a woman want?"

— Sigmund Freud

Just as puzzling to women is, "What does a man want?" The reason the answer to these questions has been so elusive is because both men and women are paradoxes – they want to 'have' and to 'be' contradictory things at the same time.

For the most part, a good girl wants to love and be loved, to walk into the sunset holding hands with her prince charming, and to live happily ever after together – just like all the fairy tale endings promised her. Sadly, most good girls still wind up with frogs who break their hearts, but that's another story.

Bad girls have given up on fairy tale endings and have more cynical desires. If a bad girl can't get men to give her love, she's determined to extract something else from them. Most men say they want honesty and devotion in a woman, but swoon over a bad girl who is dishonest and self-absorbed because the bad girl pretends to be madly in love with them when she is simply after something she can get. Depending upon what type of bad girl she is, that 'something' can include money, drugs, sex, protection, an affair, a man to hang in there without a commitment, a husband, someone else's husband, a lifeline, a toy-boy, a yes-man, or revenge. The one thing she doesn't want is to be vulnerable. You will discover more about what each type of bad girl wants, why she wants it, why men fall for her, and how each type of bad girl goes about twisting men around her little finger to get it. But first…

If you're a woman, are you a bad girl?

The Bad Girl Test

Ladies: For each test item that describes you, circle the "BG" for "bad girl" next to it. At the end of the test, count up all your "bad girl" responses and see how "bad" you are.

You have a predisposition to becoming a bad girl if you:

Were angry towards your father growing up. BG

Wished your father could have given you more. BG

Thought your father should have given you more. BG

Approach men with a chip on your shoulder. BG

Were hurt by men – father, brother, men you dated. BG

Have been hurt by a bad boy and are looking for
a good boy to lick your wounds. BG

Were sexually abused as a child. BG

Were physically abused as a child. BG

Felt neglected growing up. BG

Have been dumped by men whom you still loved. BG

Were jealous of the love and attention
your father gave your mother. BG

Saw your father treat your mother badly
and want to get back at men for this. BG

Saw your mother treat your father badly. BG

Saw your mother manipulate your father to get what she wants. BG

Hear your biological clock ticking loudly. BG

Feel scared or angry about not being able
to attain the lifestyle you envy. BG

Feel entitled to a life of luxury. BG

Are addicted to alcohol or drugs (street or prescription). BG

Use your sexuality to get what you want. BG

Use withholding sex as a weapon to manipulate men. BG

Are married but want another man, too. BG

Are afraid of making a commitment to a man to get married. BG

Are desperate to have a husband and a white picket fence. BG

Are not careful about birth control, hoping pregnancy
will snag a man. BG

Enjoy the thrill of stealing some other woman's husband. BG

Feign helplessness to get a man to rescue you. BG

Go after men who are at least 10 years younger. BG

Emasculate men to control them. BG

Take revenge if you get dumped. BG

Stalk a man to get him to come back to you or to hurt him. BG

Want to be like a man, able to have sex without falling in love. BG

See men as a buffet table and want to devour everything. BG

Feel that you have to manipulate a man into loving
you because you are not loveable enough for yourself. BG

If you scored…

1 – 5: You're a Wanna-Be Bad Girl.

6 – 10: You're a Bad Girl.

11 – 20: You're a Very Bad Girl.

21 or more: You're a Man-Eater!

Why are men attracted to bad girls?

More about bad girls and their secrets will be revealed in ensuing chapters, but now let's turn to the men who become their prey. What goes on in their psyche to make otherwise intelligent, high-achieving, charming, attractive, warm, and generally upstanding guys fall for these wicked women? The answers can be found by exploring the parts of a man's psyche that relate to his feelings, his experiences and attitudes towards sex and relationships, his other current behaviors and situations, his childhood, and his parents. The three most important factors that make a man vulnerable to a bad girl are feelings of inadequacy and emasculation, a father who was emotionally or physically absent, and a mother who made him feel unloveable or fearful of an overpowering woman. Let's take a deeper look into this man's psyche.

Feelings (yes, men have feelings, too)

The man who is most vulnerable to a bad girl is one who – consciously or unconsciously – is afraid he's not good enough to 'get' and hold onto the woman of his dreams because he doesn't have 'enough' money, power, good looks, intelligence, job status, charm, or a big enough penis. Bad girls have problems, needs, and desires. The more a man can make a bad girl dependent upon him for something that he does have or he is willing to accept – like her alcoholism, or her ball-busting, or her having a husband – the less likely she will be to leave him. Of course, acquiescing to her bad girl demands brings about problems for the man.

Struggling under the pressure of the economy, terrorism, natural disasters, and other world problems, many a modern man feel emasculated. He is confused and exhausted, trying not only to answer the age-old question, "What does a woman want?" but to give it to her. Since a bad girl pursues him, he doesn't have to do much to attract her and there is less risk of rejection. He can feel safe because she makes it so clear that she's interested. Men's egos are more fragile than women realize. The bad girl's brazen attitude allows her to walk that fine line between showing enough interest and being too available.

Other feelings make men vulnerable to bad girls, too. For example, a man who feels guilty over some real or imagined hurt, illness, or problem he caused his mother growing up, is likely to want to make it up to a woman or want her to punish him for having been bad. A man who is feeling bored or depressed is easily captivated by a free-spirited bad girl who brings fun back into his nights and makes him feel alive. A man who is still wrestling with his inner nerd becomes the 'prom king' or 'captain of the football team' when he's able to satisfy a bad girl's needs.

Sex and Relationships (it's not just about 'getting it')

A man's experience and attitude towards sex and relationships also determines whether he will be easy prey. Most bad girls are hot in bed and make the man feel like the world's best lover. Whenever a man says, "I'm madly in love with her, but I can't tell you why," it is likely that the woman is exploiting some unconscious psychological vulnerability and he is too intoxicated by the sex or too caught up in the drama to figure out which button she's pushing, or to care. His ego gets in the way. He wants to believe he's irresistible to such a hot chick, so he convinces himself that she's not after 'something' – just him. Bad girls tell a man what he wants to hear, give him lots of attention and admiration, and make him feel like he's a big man.

The most vulnerable man doesn't want a good girl because she's either too clingy, too real, or too powerful – and she makes him feel as if he's not good enough for her. With a bad girl he doesn't have to commit to the extent he would if she were a good girl because, at some level, the man knows that the bad girl is holding back a part of herself.

Vulnerable men want to rebel against their parents by bringing home a woman he knows they won't like. He may want to shock them or prove to them that he is man enough to get such a blatantly sexual babe. Or if a man is embarrassed to ask his friends and family for their opinions or advice about the woman he's dating, it is often a sign that he doesn't want to hear the truth about her, though at some level he knows it himself. Other people can be more objective and can warn the smitten man about all the red flags she's waving.

Current Behaviors and Situations (what's really going on)

One of the tried and true tricks of a bad girl is using alcohol (and occasionally even drugs) to get a guy into bed in the shortest amount of time, or to generally impair his judgment throughout their relationship so that he doesn't realize he's getting into deep trouble until it's too late. Plus, the more addictive a man's personality, the more likely he is to become addicted to a bad girl the first time he tries her.

A man's attitude towards risk-taking contributes to the likelihood of his becoming enthralled with a bad girl. For example, if he's looking for adventure and he's already tried (or is afraid to try) bungee jumping, motorcycle racing, or skydiving, he might erroneously think that a bad girl is a safer sport. A lot of men want the challenge of taming a bad girl – like breaking a horse – because it makes them feel like a cowboy in a 10-gallon hat.

One of the easiest targets for a bad girl is a man who is a workaholic or has other time-consuming commitments. He doesn't have the time or energy left to look for a good girl and is easy prey for a woman who does all the work for him, especially if she knows when to make herself scarce so that he can get on with whatever he needs to do. This seems like a perfect set-up until the man lifts his head up from his computer or his tools and realizes what a mess she's made of his life while he wasn't paying attention.

Childhood (where it all begins)

Of course a man's childhood, especially his relationship with his parents (as you'll soon see) is key to determining how vulnerable he will be to a bad girl. For example, if his boyhood home was chaotic it may send him on an unconscious search for the chaos that a bad girl would bring because, even though it's unpleasant, it's familiar. Occasionally a vulnerable man has had a "Leave It to Beaver" childhood that stifled and bored him. Also, men still long to be the heroes of their boyhood stories – knights, princes, adventurers, and superheroes – and bad girls allow them to act out their fantasies.

Parents (our first loves)

The number one predictor of how likely a man is to fall for and be trampled on by a bad girl is the type of parents he had and his relationship to them growing up.

The most consistent factor in the background of men who are easy prey is an unavailable father. These men have fathers who were not physically present because of divorce, workaholism, work-related travel, abandonment, or death. Or their fathers were emotionally unavailable because of depression, addiction, affairs, or just not wanting to be involved and leaving the childrearing to Mom. Many complain that their dads didn't go to their games, share any of their boyhood passions, or even give them hugs.

These unavailable fathers also didn't give their sons advice about women – how to spot a bad girl, how bad girls hook them, the dangers of confusing lust for love, the dangers of thinking with your penis, or the necessity of using birth control. They didn't explain the difference between women you date or have sex with and women you marry. Nor did they explain the importance of choosing a wife for inner qualities, like her capacity to love, over whether or not she's a 'hottie'. Bombshells may look more enticing, but a woman who loves a man for himself and is not just after his money or whatever else he can give her will make him happier in the long run. An unavailable father is not only a poor role model, he conveys the message to his son that he is not man enough or worthy enough to attract a good girl.

The little boy's relationship with his mother is trickier and at least as crucial in determining his relationship to women when he grows up. If a mother is too close and smothering or too distant and harsh, either extreme can make a man easy prey for a bad girl.

Many a man who has been crushed by a bad girl readily admits that he was, or still is, a "mama's boy." When a mother fawns over her son to the extreme of smothering him or making him too dependent upon her for goodies or approval, she creates a man who falls into the role of obeying or putting up with a bad girl because he has been playing this role all his life. He's used to being the devoted and dutiful son, so when he grows up, he simply transfers his affections to a bad girl who seems to fawn over him like his mom. Too late, he learns that bad girls have ulterior motives.

On the other extreme is the man who lost his mother in childhood because she abandoned him, divorced his father, or died, or because she took her love away. A mother may withhold love when her son was unwanted or she's unhappy and blames him for her unhappiness, or she's preoccupied by work, an affair, or some other distraction, and may even become abusive to him. Since a little boy's first love is his mom, this heartbreak is the most powerful and devastating of his life. It makes him feel unloveable and, when he grows up, it makes him afraid to be the pursuer. So he's vulnerable to a bad girl who comes on to him and seems like a sure thing.

A mother also inadvertently influences her son to be easy prey by exposing him to her own problems. If a mom is ill, or an alcoholic, or poor, or has an abusive husband, for example, her little boy is likely to harbor fantasies of wanting to rescue her. Since he's too little to accomplish this, he is unconsciously drawn to trying to rescue a bad girl when he grows up.

Men who have been preyed upon by bad girls possess certain characteristics that make them vulnerable to falling under their spell. Sometimes just one of these characteristics is enough to make a man a 'sitting duck', but the more of these features a man possesses, the more vulnerable he is.

If you're a man, are you a sitting duck?

The Sitting Duck Test

Men: For each test item that describes you, circle the "Q" for "quack" next to it. At the end of the test, count up all your "quacks" and see how much at-risk you are for being preyed upon by a bad girl.

FEELINGS

You feel lonely. Q

You feel horny. Q

You feel depressed. Q

You feel bored. Q

You feel isolated. Q

You feel abandoned. Q

You have low self-esteem or a poor self-image. Q

You wish that people would pay more attention to you. Q

You feel unattractive. Q

You feel emasculated. Q

You feel shy or insecure. Q

You are attracted to drama. Q

You put on a façade of invincibility but feel like a nerd inside. Q

You have an unfulfilled yearning to be accepted into a cool in-crowd. Q

You have a fear of abandonment. Q

You are very trusting. Q

You feel competitive with other men and want them to think
you're a bigger stud because you have a hot chick on your arm. Q

You feel guilty (although you may not know why)
and like you deserve to be punished. Q

You feel inadequate as a man. Q

You feel unloveable. Q

You have attained material comforts, but feel lacking
in inner richness. Q

SEX AND RELATIONSHIPS

You have never had a relationship that lasted more than a few dates. Q

Your first love left a hole in your heart. Q

You have just been dumped and you're still hurting
from this break-up. Q

You are still in love with your ex-girlfriend or ex-wife. Q

You have had a string of failed relationships. Q

You are secretly afraid you're not good enough to hold
onto a woman of your dreams. Q

You are looking for love, but willing to accept sex as a substitute. Q

You get distracted by sex and pretend to yourself
that it's as good as love. Q

Your girlfriend just left town for a vacation,
a work assignment, or a family matter. Q

Your girlfriend recently moved out of your town or city. Q

You haven't had sex for a while. Q

You have a girlfriend or wife but she doesn't treat you
the way you want to be treated and doesn't make you feel
special or like a big man. Q

There is stress or a problem in your current relationship
that you would like to escape from. Q

You have a desire to rescue women. Q

You have felt that you were madly in love with a woman,
but can't explain why. Q

You have a mad crush on an unattainable movie star or
celebrity and are attracted to women who look like her. Q

You are attracted to women who look like an ex-girlfriend
or ex-wife who you still long for. Q

You attract women too easily and would like a challenge. Q

You are disillusioned by women and ready to give up
ever finding a good woman. Q

You have had a dry spell and long to be back in the game. Q

You have performance anxiety or real sexual
performance issues. Q

You have no time to date because you're too busy
with work or other commitments. Q

You are longing for a warm family and hoping to share
your woman's family. Q

You need reassurance that you're not the monster your
ex-girlfriend or ex-wife told you that you were. Q

You are embarrassed to ask friends or family for their opinions or advice about women you date. Q

You want to rebel against your parents by choosing a woman they won't like – even if it hurts you. Q

You don't want children. Q

You are in the middle of a separation or divorce. Q

You are a virgin. Q

CURRENT BEHAVIORS/SITUATION

You sometimes smoke pot. Q

You sometimes use other drugs (street or prescription). Q

You sometimes drink alcohol. Q

You sometimes go to bars. Q

You have an addiction to drugs or alcohol. Q

You recently moved to a new town or city. Q

You recently started a new school or job. Q

You are of short stature. Q

You are very poor or very rich. Q

You are very young or very old. Q

You lost your job or other source of income recently. Q

You are a ladder-climber looking for more money or higher status and would be happy to have a girlfriend give you a leg up. Q

You like to flirt with danger and live on the edge. Q

You get turned away from the hottest nightspots and want a cool-looking chick to help you get your foot in the door. Q

You are intrigued by the media's glamorization of bad girls. Q

Illness, injury or surgery is making it difficult for you to take care of yourself. Q

You have ended up in the hospital and were asked for the names of your next of kin. Q

You are an artist or writer or other creative type who needs
a benefactor or patron. Q

It is your birthday month. Q

You are having a mid-life crisis. Q

You are distracted by pressing situations in your life,
such as financial issues, family matters or property repairs. Q

You don't lie or manipulate, so you don't know
what to look out for. Q

CHILDHOOD

You were adopted. Q

You were sexually, physically, or emotionally abused. Q

Your parents didn't give you enough love and attention. Q

You grew up in a chaotic household. Q

Your childhood home was too boring or inhibiting of you. Q

As a child you liked to escape into stories
of adventure or superheroes. Q

You were raised to be a good boy and not ask questions. Q

There were family secrets that everyone knew not to talk about. Q

You were competitive with and jealous of your sister. Q

You were poor or from the wrong side of the tracks. Q

You were picked last or next to last for sports teams. Q

PARENTS

Your parents divorced. Q

Your father was not around during your childhood
or was not emotionally available. Q

You were a 'mama's boy'. Q

Your mother made you feel unloveable. Q

Your mother abandoned you. Q

Your mother or father became seriously ill during your childhood or recently. Q

Your mother or father died during your childhood or recently. Q

When you were growing up you wished you could rescue your mother from a situation that was making her unhappy or ill. Q

Your parent remarried during your childhood or recently. Q

If you scored…

1 – 5: You are in mild danger, but not out of the woods.

6 – 10: You are in moderate danger; extra caution advised.

11 – 20 : You are in serious danger; psychotherapy advised.

21 or more   You are in very grave danger! Do not venture out to the dating front until you have had at least six months of psychotherapy!

As you read about the dozen dangerous damsels in the following chapters, you will see how good men with these traits have been turned into 'sitting ducks'. And you will find out how bad girls go about preying upon them.

This book is not about creating an army of bad girls to torture and traumatize good guys. It's about helping men recognize the red flags so that they won't fall victim to bad girls, and about helping women discover the secrets to a guy's heart so that they won't feel so lost in the dating jungle. Women will ultimately discover that the answer is not to become very, very bad, because relationships based on a web of deceit won't end well for anyone. Still, if more women learn the secrets to a man's heart, it will send more couples, arm in arm, down lovers' lane and perhaps even into the sunset….

Chapter 2
THE GOLD-DIGGER

What does a Gold-Digger want?

A Gold-Digger wants a sugar daddy to pamper her with money, jewelry, designer duds, a sports car, exotic vacations, nips and tucks, dinners at fancy restaurants, and all the other trappings of an upscale lifestyle.

Why? To compensate for the poverty she feels inside – not just a literal lack of means, but emotional and spiritual bankruptcy. Whether or not a Gold-Digger grew up on the wrong side of the tracks, she grew up on the wrong side of her daddy. She feels angry and entitled to take from a man what her father couldn't or wouldn't give her. The money and gifts lavished upon her are worth far more than their weight in gold; they are reassurances that she is loveable, after all. In The Gold-Digger's dysfunctional family, love and affection were not the local currency, so to her... money talks.

The Gold-Digger has been raised to believe in Cinderella. She has only to leave her rags and scrubbing brushes at home, then dress up and pretend to be a princess just long enough to capture the lustful eye of a prince. Indeed, her godmother's admonition, to flee the ball at the stroke of midnight before her flaws are revealed is a time-worn bad girl secret: fascinate them, then mysteriously disappear, leaving them wanting more.

Despite the progress that women have made towards having successful careers of their own, The Gold-Digger is still alive and well on the dating front. From the streets of the hood to the clubs of Hollywood, these bad girls keep their shovels ready. In fact, some Gold-Diggers make a career out of it. They're called the "Bigger, Better Deal" girls, and they flit from one man to another until they meet one who seems like he can offer a bigger, better deal than the one she's with.

It takes a lot of work to be a Gold-Digger. She needs to look as though she fits the lifestyle to which she would like to become accustomed. This takes devotion to hair, make-up, working out, and shopping. The only scouring this Cinderella does is on the Internet – looking for parties, salaries, art galleries… and anything else that will give her the edge in her search for Mr. Deep Pockets.

You've heard the slogans describing this type of bad girl: "Like a hooker… only smarter" and "No Rolex… no sex." Some do use sex as their primary tool to drill for gold, while others manipulate simply by playing on a man's insecurities, loneliness, and desperation. And others, like the Pussycat in Edward Lear's poem, sweet-talk their man and then brazenly propose:

The Owl and the Pussycat went to sea
In a beautiful pea-green boat.
They took some honey, and plenty of money,
Wrapped up in a five-pound note.
The Owl looked up to the stars above,
And sang to a small guitar,

'O lovely Pussy! O Pussy, my love,
What a beautiful Pussy you are....'
Pussy said to the Owl, 'You elegant fowl,
How charmingly sweet you sing!
O let us be married! Too long we have tarried.
But what shall we do for a ring?'

Why do men fall for Gold-Diggers?

As you will soon see, the men who are most vulnerable to this type of bad girl are those who don't feel loveable for themselves and secretly fear they need to 'buy' a woman over whom they can feel power and control. These men may be CEOs, music moguls, investment bankers, surgeons, star athletes, trust-fund babies, retired millionaires, or simply career-oriented workaholics. Most have no time to search for or meet women, so The Gold-Digger makes it easy by prospecting for them.

Men who fall for this type of bad girl work hardest at convincing themselves that she is not lusting after their gold, but rather after them. But deep down they wonder whether she's noticed their receding hairline or advancing paunch and worry whether they have enough cash to keep her.

These men grew up having a weak or unsuccessful father and strong mother. They are driven towards Gold-Diggers because they are still trying to please or prove themselves to their mother. And they want to win a woman's love by being the successful man their father never was.

Such men are playing out the story of "Jack and The Beanstalk."

Jack and his mother are down to their last cow when he sells it for some magic beans that, fortunately, sprout into a beanstalk reaching up to a wealthy ogre's castle. Jack climbs up and steals a bag of gold coins, returns for a hen that lays golden eggs, and then a golden harp, until he inadvertently wakes the sleeping giant who bellows after him, "Fee-fi-fo-fum!" Jack rushes towards home, chops down the stalk, and barely escapes. Indeed, a man who falls for this type of bad girl is unconsciously running from a different angry ogre, a father who is jealous of his son's greater success. Little boys learn that it's not until Jack brings his mom the gold that she bestows her love on him again.

And when little boys graduate from fairytales to pop culture, like Madonna's hit song "Material Girl," the message is repeated:

Some boys kiss me, some boys hug me, I think they're okay
If they don't give me proper credit, I just walk away.
They can beg and they can plead, but they can't see the light
'Cause the boy with the cold, hard cash is always Mr. Right.
'Cause we are living in a material world
And I am a material girl.

Real Stories from Men on the Dating Front

The Wannabe Merry Widow
Dating a bad girl can break your heart… literally, as Ben found out.

As I was in the recovery room of Valley Hospital, my triple by-pass a few hours behind me, Debbie, the lady I had considered marrying, leaned over and insisted that I go to her house for recuperation. A single man, my wife dead for four years, I nodded feebly and with appreciation. As I was being tucked in that first evening at her place, she leaned over and said, "Put me in your will now. Please."

When Ben met Debbie at a classical music singles event in Philadelphia, he was still grieving for his dead wife, feeling lonely and yearning for feminine softness.

She liked classical music and he had a subscription to the Philharmonic. It seemed like a match made in heaven, and it almost landed him there. While Debbie was arousing his dormant sexual passions, Ben's upscale address and story of having recently sold his lucrative business aroused her passion for gold. Over the next few months, Ben made the two-hour trip to visit her on weekends, and she played his instrument like a virtuoso.

Debbie claimed she was a descendant of Charlemagne. I love history, so I kept thinking about this. There are no kings in my ancestry. I have only pickpockets!

Then he invited her to his home for the weekend to meet his grown sons. Lying in bed together, Ben suddenly complained of excruciating chest pain. Debbie called 911. He was rushed to the hospital and then into open-heart surgery, where he had a near-death experience.

I was under an enormous amount of stress probably because

I was making a bad decision to be with Debbie and living with it. After the surgery I was in terrible pain and I felt extremely weak. In the hospital Debbie said, "You've got to recuperate at my place." I was very grateful and simply nodded because I couldn't speak. My sons helped me get to her house. She set up a bedroom for me. One day as I was lying there trying to get my strength back, she came over and whispered, "Please put me in your will." I wondered if she knew something I didn't know. We're not even married. She kept mentioning it and each time it made me want to do it less. I couldn't leave because I couldn't walk or take care of myself.

While I was there recuperating, I came upon the first red flag by happenstance. Debbie had been married to an older man, apparently for his money, and I discovered that his son was suing her over some property. Then I found out, as the bills were coming in, that she had charged things on my credit card. More and more purchases were showing up and I knew they weren't mine. When I questioned her she was vague about it. My ego had gotten in the way, but I finally realized it was not me she was after. My foremost thought was to drive away and call it quits, but I couldn't move. And I appreciated that she called 911. I thought she saved my life, so I felt guilty ending the relationship.

Eventually I said, "Give me those bills. I'll pay them and then I'm done!" She replied bitterly, "After all that I've done for you, you're going to leave me? I saved your life!" I finally let on that I knew she was after my money, then I cut my losses and fled. I remember smiling when I drove up the turnpike, getting farther and farther away from her.

But even this wasn't far enough. After they broke up, Ben took his healing heart to Africa, trekking and canoeing to Timbuktu. He's sworn off intense relationships and now contents himself with walking his dog with a female companion who points out the various species of birds along their path.

Ben attributes his uncharacteristic surrender to bad girl Debbie, in part, to his nostalgic longing for his mother after his wife's death. Both women were brunettes who loved music and had a touch of Scarlett O'Hara in them.

Cinderella Buys Her Glass Slippers at Bloomingdales

Growing up in the Midwest, Jessica fantasized about becoming Cinderella, and she moved to Manhattan to find her prince. When her friend had a fix-up party, she put on her finery and glass slippers and went after the richest man in the room. Stephen was in his late thirties and had never married because his career was driving his life.

When I met Jessica I was ready to settle down. She put on a great act. She wasn't the stereotype of a gold-digger, that is, a woman who says, "I only date guys who drive a BMW or take me to certain restaurants." I had a great salary and position at an ad agency. My parents had several homes – all in cool places. Jessica decided I was her meal ticket. Her family was working class and they had real financial and emotional problems, but I only discovered this when it was too late.

Jessica was very beautiful and intelligent with a great sense of humor. She had a terrific job working for a foundation that was socially oriented so I thought she cared about others. When we dated there were many telltale signs of her gold-digger agenda, but

I overlooked them. Of course, she wanted me to pay for absolutely everything. When I sent flowers to her office, she'd say I was embarrassing her and when I went on a trip and sent postcards every day, she complained that the neighbors saw them.

Jessica apparently wanted to keep her relationship with Stephen secret, undoubtedly because she had a bigger financial fish on the line that she was trying to reel in. Stephen chose to believe that her embarrassment was only because she came from a dysfunctional family where she was not used to positive attention and affection. Then after a few months of dating, Jessica pulled a Cinderella act and disappeared.

I thought we were broken up because she wasn't returning my calls. Two weeks later she called and, like nothing was wrong, said, "Hi, oh I was just too busy to call." Then she told me her lease was up and claimed that since she wasn't getting along with her landlord, he didn't want to lease to her again. Her obvious solution: to move in with me.

After she moved into Stephen's castle, Jessica told him she was having problems with her boss and wanted to quit her job. She got angry when he wouldn't go along with this, but hung in there until he married her a year later. Soon she became pregnant.

About two months into her pregnancy, Jessica announced that she couldn't take the subway anymore because she was pregnant and, therefore, couldn't go to work. Yet she could take it to go to the gym and meet her girlfriends for lunch. She joined a prenatal *exercise class. The women there were well off. She was envious of these women who didn't work. They tried to outdo each other with their kids' birthday parties. For our son's first birthday, we rented out a hall and had it catered. It cost $2,000.*

After we had our first child, she felt entitled to my parents' money. My parents were well off, but I became successful on my own and did not want to ask them for anything. But when we bought the co-op she wanted, I had to ask my parents for a loan. Later, she threw a fit when I wanted to pay the loan back. When we had two kids and she still wasn't working, she asked me to call my parents for money. They gave us $1,000 each month. I don't know where the money went. I still feel ashamed.

Jessica came into the relationship with a lot of debt. The money went as fast as I earned it. She needed a maid, nannies, a psychiatrist, a holistic healer, a trainer, private school for the boys, and whatever else was part of the lifestyle she felt entitled to. "I don't do laundry," she insisted. So I did the laundry, the cooking, and the bathing of the kids. My friends thought I was insane. But otherwise she'd get teary-eyed, become moody, and break things. And a loving husband wants his wife to have what she wants.

Soon it wasn't enough for Jessica to be a princess in Manhattan. She needed to move back to the Midwest to flaunt her good fortune before her family. There, she cajoled Prince Stephen into setting up castle all over again. She needed the biggest house in the best part of town, fancy cars, maids, nannies, and all the rest. But since fairytale princes never run out of money, Jessica hadn't thought about how Stephen would be able to pay for this lifestyle once he left his Madison Avenue advertising firm.

I let her keep the books and pay the bills. I trusted her one hundred percent. Only later did I find out that it was like the fox guarding the hen house. We ran through all our money in months. I started asking questions. She said she didn't know where the bills or receipts were. One time she said they were in her car. When I said, "Let's go look," she announced, "I want a divorce!"

After we divorced I found out that she had secret credit cards and had locked bank statements, checks, and receipts in her car trunk. She'd even stolen the money I'd put away for our kids' college fund. Whenever I'd say, "No," she'd gotten what she wanted anyway. She'd drained me of money. And once divorced, she falsified her income and expenses to keep child support high, but dressed the kids in rags while she bought $160 rain boots.

What was her secret? It's like "Survivor." The people who win are good at manipulating, lying, breaking their word. She knew how to keep me off-balance by trying to get me to focus on my problems instead of hers. "Don't look here, look over there." When I married her I was not myself. Before meeting Jessica, the woman I'd wanted to marry had turned me down. And the other women I dated were physically attractive, but I couldn't put up with their low self-esteem. Jessica seemed very self-assured. She knew what she wanted.

What Jessica knew was that she didn't want the same life as her mother, who wound up having to support her dad, who injured himself falling into a sink hole when Jessica was young. He then became extremely obese and decided not to return to work. Jessica's father, an emotionally unavailable man, did not seem to care about the impact his self-indulgence was having on the family.

It caused Jessica to grow up feeling angry and entitled to take what her father couldn't or wouldn't give her from the man she married.

Stephen's attraction to Jessica's seeming self-assuredness came from his admiration of his strong-willed mother, whom he dearly loves and to whom his family owes their wealth. She developed a thriving business, while his father, though a loving man, was not a financial success. After the car shop he was given was broken into and the shopkeeper across the street was murdered, he quit and went to work for Stephen's mother. This sent Stephen on his quest to please his mother and win her love by being the successful man his father never was.

Although he did amass a princely fortune, he feels that his life, once prosperous and filled with promise, has been spent. These days he takes it very slow and checks a woman's credit score before thinking of scoring with her.

Affairs of the Heart and Hard Cash

When Heather came on to Russell, he told himself to resist her. Not only was she nineteen years his junior, 23 to his 42, she was also his employee. As the CEO of a booming company, he knew all about sexual harassment laws and was not about to fall into that trap. But Heather wouldn't take no for an answer. She kept giving hints that she was available and attracted to him.

"So what are you doing this weekend?" she asked, as I was walking out the door. "I'm going to catch up on work," I answered. "Well, I'm going to be with my family because I don't have a boyfriend." Hint. Hint. Or she'd flatter me with, "You came up with this concept by yourself? It's so original, brilliant." Or she'd

say, "You're in such great shape. I'm really attracted to older men because guys my own age don't interest me."

One night I was in my office. I couldn't concentrate. Should I pick up the phone and call her? I just did it. I felt safe doing it because she had made it so clear she'd be interested! Like buying stock after doing research. I met her after work. We had a drink and talked for three hours. I was mesmerized. She had such a non-gold-digger personality. I was attracted to her wholesomeness. She was a woman-child. Horses were her passion. We started going out late at night after I finished work. I'd have a 3,000-calorie meal and we'd be up until 4:00 A.M. doing horizontal gymnastics. I was not sleeping or eating properly.

Bad girls can be dangerous to a man's health, as Russell discovered months after their first liaison.

I was in a tennis tournament. The racket started to feel like it weighed 30 pounds. I lost. I showered and came back to the office where one of the secretaries said, "You don't look too good. Let's go to the hospital." Hours later an intern told me I had a heart attack. I'd never been in a hospital before. It was my first brush with mortality. It freaked me out. You're in ICU and the guys to the right and left of you are taken away in black bags. I had to stay home for six weeks. Heather quit her job and moved in. She was by my side day and night, reading books about heart- healthy diets and cleaning out my cupboards to get rid of foods that were not in these books. She was a tower of strength. That's when I fell in love with her. She took care of everything!

Heather took care of everything, all right, including going off birth control pills. She knew that while Russell was musing about his mortality, the time was right to give him an heir. Not only would he be more likely to go along with this plan, though he had made a point of asking if she was on the pill before they'd begun their gymnastics, but she would have a better chance of getting pregnant than of getting a ring this early in the relationship and time could be running out.

She got pregnant about one month after my heart attack. It was a shock. I said, "I thought you were on birth control." She said, "I know you wanted a family, so I went off the pill." I did tell Heather I wanted to have more children since my first wife had gotten custody of my son, but I did not say I wanted them with her. Before she said she was pregnant, I hadn't even thought of marrying her!

The first sign that Heather was a gold-digger came after she told me she was pregnant. A lawyer friend advised me to have her sign a pre-nup. I told her I wanted her to sign it before telling her parents we were going to get married. Though I was upset that she got pregnant, getting married seemed like the right thing to do, and I was in love with her. At first she said she'd sign to show me she was not after my money. But then she changed her mind, supposedly because her lawyer told her not to sign it. I was very insulted and said I wouldn't marry her – and didn't until eight years later.

About one year after that first drink with Heather, Russell

found himself living on a horse farm outside of the city, with a live-in girlfriend, a baby, and 19 horses. The first years were bliss and he forgot about the unsigned pre-nup. Russell set Heather up in business, buying and selling horses. She was in horse heaven, while he was paying for everything.

One day Heather said she needed more money for the horses. I told her to sell some of the horses to get money. She said it was winter – not a good time to sell – and ended the discussion with, "Screw you, I'll get it somewhere else!" Then I started looking at the bank statements from my personal account. I always took out $250 at a time. I started seeing $300, $196, and other odd amounts. She knew where I kept my ATM card and figured out the password from our other passwords. She stole $10,000 in two months. I was crushed. It was as if she wasn't faithful. She said, "It's your fault. I asked you for the money. What did you want me to do, let the horses starve?"

But this was a lot of hay, far more than the horses ate. Next came the real dividing line. It was time for their daughter to go to kindergarten, and Heather wanted to send her to a private school. They had been living a low-key lifestyle out in the country, but this brought Heather into a milieu of incredible wealth – wives of hockey players, social pillars of the community, and social climbing.

It wasn't just their daughter who started school. Heather got her schooling from the other women: Entitlement 101. Of course, she had had a head-start in gold-digging and moved easily to the front of the class. Heather started spending more time at social events alone, while Russell was working or home with their daughter. They drifted apart.

When I met her she was a farm girl. She had never gotten her hair or nails done, or shopped for expensive clothes. But after meeting the mothers at the school, Heather was into all of the trendy stuff. And she constantly went to psychics; she had a fascination with them.

One guy who had a son in our daughter's class was into racehorses. Soon Heather said she was not into buying and selling anymore; she was into training racehorses with this father. She spent more and more time with him, training horses by day and going to the races at night. I wasn't happy with this, but I was like a little child closing my eyes and ears. I thought she might be having an affair, but I had no proof. Whenever I complained about her spending money or anything else, she'd say, "You're no fun anymore."

Russell thought of leaving, but he didn't want to lose custody of another child he deeply loved, an unspoken tidbit Heather used to her advantage. And as their daughter was getting to the age of asking questions, Heather told Russell that their daughter would be very disappointed if she discovered her parents weren't married.

I got married for my daughter's sake and I thought maybe Heather would change. About a year after we were married, I was going through the medicine cabinet and I saw a box of Maxipads. Something told me to look inside. I went through it and found a card that said, "Life without you is not fun. Looking forward to when we're together all the time." I didn't know who it was from. And I found notes, her scribblings from psychics. I finally caught on. She was going to psychics to plan her exit: Who am I going to meet? Who am I going to marry? How many children will I have?

"Don't piss her off," my lawyer warned me. "Try to look at it as a business transaction with no emotion. You're doing it for your daughter." I came home midday and put on my best poker face. Heather was having tea with a racing form. I said, "I want to talk to you." She said, "I don't think we should be married anymore." She pulled out an organized note. "I want this… this… that…. And if you don't agree, I'll go to a downtown lawyer." I said, "Okay, fine." She was shocked. "You're not mad at me?" I said, "I want an amicable relationship, so I'll hold my nose and agree."

It turned out that it was racehorse man's brother who wrote the note I found. He was also married. She had been having an affair with the racehorse man, his brother, and at least one more guy! When she stole the money, my gut told me she would be capable of having an affair, but I didn't want to believe it.

What Russell didn't know before he fell in love with Heather was that behind her fresh-faced seeming innocence was a strong matriarch who'd taught her how to go from farm girl to bad girl, and that it was just as easy to love a rich man as a poor one. Her father, a civil servant struggling to support five kids, always favored Heather's oldest sister. She was the apple of his eye because, ever since she was a star pupil in grade school, she continued to move up in the world through higher education. Heather wanted to prove to her dad that, despite her limited high school education, she would move up in the world, too. Russell's family background was similar.

My father was a lackadaisical salesman, so we always had money issues. We were lower middle class and barely holding onto it by a string. My relationship with my dad was similar to Heather's relationship to hers. My older brother was the apple of my father's eye because he was gifted academically and lived out my dad's dream to be a doctor. My parents slept in different bedrooms. Growing up, my mom used me as a confidant to get me to explain her side to my dad and why the marriage wasn't working. She felt she wanted a man and he wasn't one. It was very hurtful and I didn't want to hear it. He was like a baby. He was not a knight. I decided I was damn well going to be a success because I had a tremendous fear that I would turn out like my dad.

Walter Mitty Meets The Gold-Diggers

When Fenton turned 40 and found himself still sitting in a tiny cubicle crunching numbers for an accounting firm, he decided it was time for a drastic change.

My fatal flaw was to reach an age milestone that made me feel reckless and desperate. On the West Coast size matters… the size of your portfolio. And mine wasn't winning me a wife. I felt life passing me by.

So he contacted an organization that introduces Russian women to American men. They sent him tapes of 50 Russian hopefuls who they claimed to have screened just for him and encouraged him to play Russian roulette. Fenton chose a girl who appealed to him because she was beautiful, tall, and thin, and he began getting to know her through letters and long-distance phone calls.

When I visited Moscow to meet her, something happened that made me realize it wasn't going to work. We were at dinner. I went to take her hand. She recoiled. I recognized that, though she wanted to come to America, she was not attracted to me. So the office manager quickly found another girl for me to meet. Katiya was average looking, but less formal and seemed happy and vivacious. We spent three or four evenings together. I knew I had to get engaged on this visit or else go home empty-handed.

After committing to an engagement of sorts, Fenton corresponded and talked with Katiya for the next six months. But when she came to the West Coast to get married, she had changed. Gone was the happy and vivacious blushing bride he had courted in Moscow. Instead she was a nagging, whining, complaining, hypochondriac, with rather severe mood swings. Katiya presumed that once she got here, Fenton wouldn't send her back, so she could stop being on her best behavior.

On top of this, she was frigid. When she came here we started sleeping together. After a few times, she decided she didn't want to do it anymore. I was given three months to decide if I was actually going to go through with the marriage. I had her bags packed twice to send her back, but I married her anyway because I felt too guilty to send her back to her parents, who I'd met in Russia.

Most Russian brides come for a green card and leave the man soon after they get here. But Katiya had gone to medical school in Moscow and had another agenda in mind. She wanted me to support her until she was accepted into a residency program and could finish her training to become a doctor.

We had sex about once a month when she'd accede to my begging, and our son was born a couple of years later. Around the time she moved on to begin her residency, I found the strength to divorce her. Since her long hours and cramped quarters would have made it impossible for her to be a single mom, I moved on and happily took my son with me. Katiya signed a note for the money I spent on her and promised to pay me back, but I don't think she ever will.

Fenton's fortunes increased, having now worked his way up as a CPA in a firm in his new locale and ultimately buying the firm and investing in real estate. Unfortunately, though he was still looking for change, his vulnerability to Gold-Diggers stayed the same. This time, searching for a stepmother for his son, he turned to Internet dating and found Pamela, the perfect, sweet stay-at-home mom... or so it seemed. He was a bit put-off on their first date when she appeared to be paying more attention to her cell phone than to him, but he shrugged it off and asked her out again.

Shortly after our first date, Pamela explained that she had to be 400 miles away four days a week to care for her Alzheimer's-ridden 92-year-old grandmother. Then she came up with other excuses, so I couldn't see her every weekend. I was busy with my work and investments, so I didn't get irritated that she wasn't more available. Besides, she was pretty, intelligent, and had three children, so my son fit right in. She was always asking me how business was going. She said she needed to know that I was doing well enough to support her. I proposed. She accepted. But it was all an illusion.

Fenton couldn't believe his luck. Money was flowing in and he was married to the girl of his dreams, or so he thought. But his reverie was interrupted when, seemingly out of the blue, Pam demanded that Fenton put her name on all of his assets. Even though there had been the worrisome shopping sprees where she would spend $3,000 in one day at Neiman Marcus and Jimmy Choo, nothing like this had ever happened before.

I told her, "No, not after a few months of a part-time marriage. Maybe after a few years of a full-time marriage." I felt disappointed and betrayed. I kicked Pam out and filed for an annulment based on fraud. But when we were separated I started thinking. Maybe I misunderstood her. So I suggested that we go to marriage counseling. Pam couldn't tell the counselor she married me to fleece me, so she waived her demands that I put her name on my assets and we got back together.

While they were married, unbeknownst to Fenton, Pam had registered "BCBS" as a fictitious business name. Then she told him she needed $7,000 for Blue Cross Blue Shield health insurance for herself and her children. She told him to write the check to "BCBS." Weeks later she wanted another check, ostensibly for another health insurance payment. This time he wrote it to "Blue Cross Blue Shield" instead. He mailed the check on a Friday. On Saturday Pam told him they wouldn't accept it, and she wanted a replacement check payable to "BCBS." On Monday Fenton drove to the address where he had mailed the checks, which Pam had said was her insurance agent's office.

It turned out to be a trailer with a "For Sale" sign and Pam's cell number on it. The manager said she'd lived there for years. I drove home and gave her two minutes to explain "BCBS." She started to say, "It's Blue Cross...." I cut her off and told her I'd been to her trailer. She took my car and high-tailed it out, my mother's diamond ring still firmly on her finger. There was no misunderstanding this time; I'd married a con artist. I changed the locks and filed for divorce.

My lawyer subpoenaed her cell phone records. There was a12-inch stack. I found 10 calls every day to and from the same number. I thought it was her new boyfriend. Then I saw it was the same 10 calls every day, month after month, the whole time I knew her – even three calls on our wedding day and three on our wedding night after I fell asleep. I put the number into a Google search. It came up for a guy selling a Porsche. "If interested call Daddy Cash." Then there was a number she called five times a day. It was an AT&T voicemail box. I wondered why she would have another mailbox when she had a cell phone with voicemail. I started dialing and couldn't believe my ears. There were calls to hotels and several girls every day, calls to and from hundreds of different men, one or two times in a day, and then not again. With each identified number, the sickening picture became clearer. I had married a prostitute and madam!

Fenton had to know more. He had his computer hard-drive

analyzed and found countless emailed love letters to her pimp, Daddy Cash. "We are soul mates 'til death do us part. The others keep me busy during the week, but I'm always thinking of you," Pam wrote. And splashed across the many dating websites he checked, there was Pam's profile. Her relationship status was always listed as "single," despite the fact that they were married at the time. For what she was "looking for in a man," the profile purred, "Help me test the laws of physics."

She knew how to play men and give them what they want. Men have a great fantasy of how it would be with a hooker, but it's all about the money. Pamela never looked at me when we were having sex. She wanted to get it over with. Afterwards she just turned over. She never wanted to pillow talk or cuddle. I was just another trick, but she wanted me to pay at the end – not up front. I said, "You never told me you love me." She said, "I told you once."

As the divorce proceeded, Fenton found out more about Pamela's double life: her two ex-husbands, who she was still scamming for alimony and child support, and her pattern of marrying or moving in with the richest guys she could find at the moment and keeping them on the side, while devoting herself to her pimp and prostitution.

She moved into these guys' homes after she knew them for about a week. Guys are guys. They want sex available all the time, so they'd invite her to come and move in. She'd stay with them until they kicked her out because she couldn't hide her anger against men. She may have been molested. Her father was very sexual. Pamela used to complain, "My father and mother – all they do is have sex."

Pam also complained that her father was cheap and didn't give her what she wanted when she was growing up, though she invented stories about her parents being multi-millionaires.

Pamela claimed she was the heiress to the Singer Sewing Machine fortune. She said her dad hires people to work for him, so I was expecting to meet a charismatic businessman. But he was a jerk, constantly spouting stuff that was irrelevant. Their house had hurricane damage, so they rented a place in a not-so-great neighborhood. I did wonder why they rented there if they were so rich. And they were driving an older model car. But I dismissed it as they didn't want to show off. I could've asked her about these things, but I believed her. I was vulnerable and naïve.

When Fenton's parents met Pamela, his father didn't say much. His stepmother, not wanting to make him feel bad, but picking up on something, commented that Pam was wearing quite a revealing dress for a stay-at-home mom.

Fenton grew up as the middle son, competing with his older and younger brothers to get whatever love was available from his mom, the matriarch of the family, while his father was uninvolved.

He was a failure as a father. He was working a lot. He didn't come to see me in school plays or sports. My mom came to our baseball and football games. I don't know where my dad was. I was Woody Allen, growing up in a dysfunctional home.

When Fenton's mother, the only woman he'd been close to, died years ago, he felt adrift. Alone in his West Coast cubicle crunching numbers, he'd fantasized about meeting the wife of his dreams. But just like the meek Walter Mitty, whose fantasies of personal triumphs were interrupted by harsh realities, Fenton had allowed his hopeful romanticism to carry him into the arms of two Gold-Diggers.

Famous Gold-Diggers

Anna Nicole Smith – It was not just the billions that Anna Nicole was after when she flashed her breasts at elderly Texas oil tycoon J. Howard Marshall. Abandoned by her father when she was a little girl, Anna hoped he would give her the love and luxuries she didn't get from Daddy.

Oksana Grigorieva – Russian pop singer Oksana has a sketchy past and moved in quickly on Mel Gibson, becoming pregnant with his child and wresting him away from his wife, Robyn, and their children. In a big hurry to cash in on his rubles, she drove him over the edge when he finally realized she didn't love him.

Heather Mills – Paul McCartney found out the hard way that "Money Can't Buy Me Love." After Heather made him believe that they would make beautiful music together forever, she left Paul singing "All You Need Is Love," while she ran off with his money.

Lorelei Lee – In the movie "Gentlemen Prefer Blondes," gold-digging Lorelei sings, "A kiss on the hand may be quite continental, but diamonds are a girl's best friend."

Candy Spelling – It was not enough for Candy to live in the lap of luxury while her husband, Aaron, was alive. Now she's feuding with daughter Tori about his $500 million inheritance. Candy blames Tori for hastening Aaron's death by her estrangement, and Tori blames Candy for having an affair while Aaron was dying.

Marla Maples – "Best sex I've ever had!" screamed the headlines. How could Donald Trump not marry her after this publicity extolling his virility?

Katie Lee Joel – Billy Joel is the "Piano Man," but Katie played him for all he's worth, or at least as much as she could get, while she was cooking up more than comfort food with a younger man.

Charlene Marshall – Dubbed "Miss Piggy" for her greedy ways after marrying Anthony Marshall, Charlene masterminded the plot to steal the fortune of his mother, Brooke Astor.

Olga Khokholva – This Russian ballerina captured Picasso's heart when he was going through a "blue" period and vulnerable to her charms. She tried to change the Bohemian artist into a socialite, seeing him as her ticket to Parisian high society.

Rachelle Spector – Despite the fact that Phil Spector was 41 years her senior and charged with murdering Lana Clarkson, Rachelle, a waitress, married him. She denies being a Gold-Digger and claims to be pining for him since he's been in jail.

Chapter 3
THE ADDICT

What does an Addict want?

A bad girl Addict not only wants her substance of choice – alcohol, street drugs, or prescription drugs – but also a man who will be her enabler.

Why? To help her escape from her emotional pain and sadness, and to help her fill the void that she has inside. Women who grow up to be bad girl Addicts have not been given enough love and attention from the time they were infants and may have also been mistreated. This lack of nurturance has left them with a deep, dark hole inside, which they then try desperately to fill up with substances such as alcohol and street or prescription drugs. Their parent may have died when they were little or have been an addict themselves who neglected them. Or their childhood dreams may have been nipped in the bud, leaving them lost and sad, still searching for a sense of fulfillment. Instead, they find self-destruction.

"The Red Shoes," a story by Hans Christian Andersen, allegorically describes how the self-destructive life of The Addict bad girl can spin out of control. In the story, a poor little motherless girl becomes envious of a princess who wears beautiful red shoes.

Obsessed with nothing but owning a pair for herself, the little girl defies the kind old lady who took her in by sneakily obtaining and flaunting red shoes, longing for people to pay attention to her. "Dear me, what pretty dancing shoes!" exclaims a passerby.

Suddenly the little girl could not help it, she was compelled to dance a few steps; and when she had once begun, her legs continued to dance. It seemed as if the shoes had power over her.... At last the kind old lady and her coachman were able to take off her shoes and, once they got home, put them in the cupboard.

Even when the kind old lady fell deathly ill, the little girl couldn't resist going to the ball where she began to dance.

But when she wanted to go to the right, the shoes danced to the left, and when she wanted to dance up the room, the shoes danced down the room, down the stairs through the street, and out through the gates of the town. She was compelled to dance far out into the dark wood. She was frightened and wanted to throw the red shoes away; but this time they stuck fast and wouldn't budge.... Suddenly she heard a menacing voice, "Dance you shall in your red shoes, 'til you are pale and cold, 'til your skin shrivels up and you are a skeleton!"... Compelled to go on dancing through the dark night, the shoes bore her away over thorns and stumps 'til she was all torn and bleeding as she reached the executioner's cottage. When she confessed all her wrongdoings, the executioner struck off her feet with the red shoes still attached. And they stared in amazement as the shoes danced away with the little feet across the field into the deep forest.

Alcohol and drugs can provide a temporary escape from the

harsh realities of life into a more euphoric place, but, just like the red shoes, they take their toll on The Addict along the way. This is when an Addict bad girl realizes that she would be much better able to perpetuate and take pleasure in her addiction if she had a man to enable her. Not only would he help her to replenish her stock, he would love her and accompany her along the lonely path into the dark woods of addiction.

Since most Addict bad girls feel they have been wronged by men – a father who left her, a teacher who molested her, a lover who abused her – it seems only fitting that another man should make it up to her by remaining devoted to her and her addiction no matter how horribly she treats them.

Bad girl Addicts can have other substances of choice, such as shopping, gambling, or work. The shopaholic or gambling bad girl would best fit into the Gold-Digger category, since they need gold to maintain their addictions. The workaholic, who uses work to avoid closeness with a man, would best fit into the Commitment-Phobe category. But whether she is addicted to alcohol, drugs, shopping, gambling, or work, she is always spinning out of control and dragging her man along with her as he trips over himself trying to keep up.

Why do men fall for Addicts?

Men who are involved in relationships with Addicts are enablers. They consciously or unconsciously encourage the woman to continue her addiction so that she will be dependent upon them, either for the means to obtain the substance or to provide food, clothing, shelter, and medical attention, as well as companionship. These men also provide excuses for The Addict and help her to cover up her addiction to her family, friends, and coworkers. They may also find themselves taking over her responsibilities, from walking the dog to taking her children to school. These men do whatever it takes to smooth the way for The Addict, all the while proclaiming that they wish she would stop using.

Then why does a man continue to rescue his bad girl from the consequences of her addiction? He's afraid that if the woman is able to clear her hazy head, she will realize that she doesn't want to be with him and he is terrified that she will leave him. He's already had problems holding onto the love of the first woman in his life, his mother. These enabling men grew up with mothers who were cold and disapproving or overly needy. Often it was a struggle not to let the anger they felt towards mom overwhelm them and to try to feel loved and wanted by her. Some also had fathers who were disappointed in them.

And some men, in love or lust with Addicts, are looking to escape, themselves. Their responsibilities seem onerous and her free-spirited lifestyle calls to them like the Pied Piper. How tempting to join her in irresponsible bliss, to go back to a time when one could just drop everything and travel to a new place, or get lost in a new experience without worrying about mortgages and job security. This is so tempting, in fact, that, before they know it, they are having a few too many drinks or trying a line of cocaine along with their bad girl. Just as the 13th century minstrel, costumed in flamboyant colors, played his pipe and seduced the rats and then the children to follow him, The Addict bad girl, with her seductive laughter and promising potions, can irresistibly lure her unsuspecting lover out of his living room and into the river to drown.

Real Stories from Men on the Dating Front

Homecoming Queen Leads Valedictorian Astray

Even valedictorians are led astray by bad girls, as Robert eventually had to admit when Jacqueline destroyed his illusions and his life with her unstoppable penchant for alcohol and street drugs. Robert's small farm town existence consisted of milking cows, gathering eggs, and going to school. It hardly prepared him for the sudden arrival of Jacquie, a 16-year-old wild child, whose father hoped that farm life would tame her, or at least get her out of his hair. She'd been getting into trouble sneaking out to meet boys and getting high.

I was very attracted to her. She was the 'big city girl'. She had different music from the big city and she seemed more worldly. But she was dating jocks, and I wasn't a jock. She had parties, but I was never invited. She gave me a ride home one time. I was editor of the school yearbook and newspaper, so she asked me to write her senior paper. She was homecoming queen. I wasn't homecoming king. I went to my senior prom alone. She did give me four poses of her senior photos... I still have the photos.

After high school Jacquie moved far away to live with her stepmother in another big city, and Robert went to college. Ten years later when Jacquie returned to the farm, ostensibly to visit her grandmother, she paid a visit to Robert to check out what had become of him. When he saw her his heart beat just as quickly as it had done in high school.

She was wearing a stellar outfit when she walked into my office, had a cool job as a clothing rep, and still seemed like the big city girl. She looked so beautiful, confident and independent, and was so well-spoken. I was taking investors to Hawaii to try to raise venture capital. I sent her an email asking if she'd like to go with me. She said, "Yes." In Hawaii, we started a relationship. What attracted me? One night when everyone went to the beach bars, she said, "Let's do shots." She was dancing on the tables, adorable and full of life, and she streaked to the beach. We had sex and a great time.

Jacquie came to visit him the following weekend. And after two visits she decided to move back to the farm. They got married 28 days later, ironically the same number of days as drug and alcohol rehab.

We eloped to Vegas. At the wedding reception, we found out from my uncle that my father had dated her mother and that was romantic. Everyone thought it was serendipity that we found each other and so sweet. Before we got married, I knew she'd been a party girl in high school and that there was lots of alcohol at these parties. And I knew she'd continued partying when she moved away. Jacquie hung out with a cool club crowd who had access to drugs. She'd taken cocaine, special K, and Ecstasy, on top of the booze. I went through college and grad school without one beer because I was on a Fulbright scholarship and I didn't want to screw up my life.

But all that changed when he married Jacqueline. She got him to join her on drug and alcohol-fueled 'parties for two'. And after a while she started complaining about how there wasn't enough fun in their small farm town.

Jacquie kept saying things like, "This town sucks!" and "You're only a small town boy!" I wanted to prove I could be just as successful in the city, so we moved to a metropolis in the Northwest. We rented a condo. Jacquie started working in a clothing store. Things were going well until Ava – a bad girl and a bad influence – walked into Jacquie's store. I had a high-pressure job that involved a lot of travel, so she and Ava got to be good friends. Jacquie started staying over at Ava's and doing lots of drugs. Then she would come home, cry, and apologize. It got really bad, but I kept trying to rescue her and hoping we could make it work.

In time Jacqueline became pregnant and Robert stopped his occasional dabbling in drugs as soon as he found out.

Jacquie swears she stopped using alcohol and drugs during her pregnancy. But the morning after our son was born, they told us he had lots of congenital problems. And he was developmentally delayed. I was traveling a lot during her pregnancy, so I will never know if she really stopped or not. There was a lot of regret and weird emotions from Jacquie after he was born. She quickly resumed cocaine, Ecstasy, and alcohol, getting high even more often to escape from her guilt and from our son. She was downtown five days a week with Ava getting loaded and shopping and staying over at Ava's again. One time she came home distraught with a sprained ankle after jumping off Ava's balcony into a hot tub. I told her she needed to be a mom. But she was the one who needed a mom or a babysitter 24/7.

One night Jacquie and Ava coaxed Robert into snorting a line of cocaine and having a threesome.

Ava performed oral sex on me and wanted to have intercourse. I couldn't do it with her. It came out that, not only was Jacquie doing lots of drugs at Ava's intimate parties, she was having sex with lots of men... and with Ava. It was a mind grenade. I felt insecure, cheated on, disgusted, and sick. It was beyond what I had allowed myself to imagine went on at Ava's. We went to counseling, but when I confronted Jacqueline to find out the sordid details, the session broke down quickly. At home we got into a final fight. We both said horrible things to each other and then filed for divorce.

But Robert was as addicted to Jacquie as Jacquie was to drugs and alcohol. They stayed together a while longer, sleeping in the same bed. Jacquie didn't want the divorce. She hugged him, cried, and kept apologizing. They tried marriage counseling again. Robert finally realized she wouldn't change, and he moved out.

I had a constant erection around Jacquie. I'd see her in the kitchen and get an erection. I read the Kamasutra. We could have *sex five or six times a day. But after the divorce, I couldn't get an erection for months. I'm still having problems.*

Before Jacquie I dated a girl for a few years who I almost married. We had fun skiing together. But she always made me feel like a lousy lover because she intimidated me sexually. She wanted to do things out of porn movies – like barking and commanding me to do things. She'd say, "I want you to come in my face." I thought it was degrading. She was never gentle. I could lay in bed with Jacquie and just hold her and be content.

When Robert and Jacquie met recently to do an exchange of their now toddler-age son, she told him that she wished they could do cocaine together and talk. Sadly, she's still trying to fill the empty hole left by her mother's death when she was three years old. Her father married wives number two and three while she was growing up, but they were not nurturing, and she never got along with them. Instead, Jacquie retreated into loneliness, alcohol, drugs, and boys until her father dumped her off at the farm, making her feel even more rejected and unloved. It's no wonder she fondly remembered Robert's high school crush on her.

When I started high school, my mom told me, "Don't go out with girls because they just want to take the farm. If you get one pregnant, you'll be stuck here!" Jocks would get cheerleaders pregnant and then they'd marry them. I never had a girlfriend during high school. I just fantasized about Jacquie. My uncle was married two or three times. Each time he got divorced, the women took money out of the farm. My mother was the one who tried to get Jacquie and I together because she knew Jacquie would never want to live on a farm. One time after a fight, I was so angry at Jacquie that I called mom and said, "This is the girl you told me was so good to marry and now look!"

My dad met my mom in a city near our farm and brought her back when they got married. When I was growing up, they'd argue in the kitchen all the time. "Why do I live on a farm?" my mom would gripe. "I'm not just here to take care of the boys and do dirty laundry out in the middle of nowhere!" My mom felt trapped against her will. I never understood what was wrong with the farm. What were we doing wrong to make her unhappy? It was the same with Jacquie. She felt trapped, too, even when we moved to the city.

Robert's dad made him feel as though he was doing something wrong and making him unhappy, too, because he wasn't a jock.

I was on the basketball team for four years in high school, but I hardly ever got to play. My dad had been a star ballplayer at the same school. He went to every game. My brother was a sophomore on the varsity team when I was a senior and even he got to play more. I really disappointed my dad because I only rode the bench.

Robert had a family history of addiction, which undoubtedly contributed to his vulnerability to The Addict bad girl.

My mom smoked her entire life, but I've never seen it. She'd say, "Dad and I need to go to the video store," or make some other excuse so that she could get out of the house to smoke. Two of my aunts are textbook alcoholics, out of a Charles Bukowski novel. My dad drinks and he was forever hiding his chewing of Copenhagen snuff.

Above all, Robert was smitten with Jacquie and enabled her to continue using alcohol and drugs because of his fear that she would leave him if he didn't. Despite his subsequent accomplishments and the fact that high school was years ago, he still feels like the small town farm boy who was never reason enough to keep his mom down on the farm or to make his dad proud that he was a jock.

Jacquie is a free-spirit. We know it can't work out, but we reserve a little bit of our hearts to hope that someday it still might work.

Dating The Addict bad girl can get to be a habit that's hard to kick, as Robert has learned. He has gotten himself into another free-spirited 'hot mess', a bartender at a club he happened into one night.

I met this girl, Zoe, and fell head over heels. I gave her my card on a Friday night and she called me that Saturday and asked me out. She's in a band. We ended up spending Saturday through Wednesday nights together. I'm still seeing her. She loves to drink. She tends bar until 2:00 A.M. So she'll come over at 3:00 A.M. and say, "Let's make cocktails and dance!" I discovered that I hadn't completely gotten over my sexual problems that began when Jacquie and I were no longer together. With Zoe I would be hard until we took our clothes off. Then I couldn't maintain an erection. Still, when we got up last Thursday morning and I told her I had to fly to Vancouver, she said, "Give me the key and I'll let myself out." I gave it to her. When I came back a few days later, I found the note she'd left me: "Darling, I love you so much. You make me smile. Let's run away to Borneo!" And she sends texts saying, "This is real, this is love." I don't know if it's real, but it's really awesome! She says just what I want to hear!

'Hot mess' is the term I use for a girl like Zoe who is so much fun to be around. I have an intense job with a lot of employees and travel. These girls give you a sense of freedom and fun. They're nonchalant about tomorrow. I worry about tomorrow. These hot messes want to backpack around Europe. You fall for them because it harkens back to the freedom you had in college.

Men like Robert are envious of 'hot messes' because they secretly wish that they, too, could have a carefree waif-like lifestyle and be taken care of, instead of having to be responsible all the time.

They're fun to adore from afar. You tell yourself you can't have a relationship with them because it will end in disaster. But you jump in. My heart goes pitter-patter if a day goes by and I haven't seen Zoe. Consciously, I know it won't work, but I adore free-spirits. You think you don't have to take care of them much because they don't want much – but it's not really true. 'Hot messes' want a lot of attention. They're very sweet and adorable, but damn if they don't need a support system for their drama.

Getting High in High School Can Be Dangerous

The year that Brian dated Martha, they were in high school and her father was sexually abusing her. She started using cocaine to try to escape the horrors at home.

She told me she loved me after two weeks. I knew this should have been a red flag, but I was a guy who was desperate to be in love. As Martha was coming unhinged, I became very depressed, couldn't eat, and lost weight. My health was bad. I thought I was going to be everything she needed. I thought I could be her 'knight in shining armor', her safe person. She became increasingly addicted and I couldn't save her. I didn't know what to do with her.

Meanwhile, Martha's ex-boyfriend, who was also on drugs, didn't want anyone else to date her if he couldn't have her. He threatened Brian on several occasions. One night after Brian mouthed-off to him, the ex and his friends tried to kill him.

They followed Martha and me as we were driving home from the movies. Their two cars pinned us between them – one in front, and one in back. Her ex got out and came over to the driver's side, where I was. He said, "Am I going to have to drag you through the window?" Just then another car pulled up behind us. It was like a miracle because no one usually drives this back road so late at night.

Angrily, the ex-boyfriend and his friends left and vowed to find Brian later. But it wasn't these threats that finally made him break up with her. It was his inability to rescue her from her drugs and her dad.

It ended very badly. When we broke up, she went further into drugs. She'd call me every once in a while telling me she wanted to kill herself. I always felt bad, wondering if I made her worse.

Indeed, Brian's guilty ruminations drove him into missionary school.

Chaos Has Its Charm

Thomas is an adult child of an alcoholic. And though he didn't inherit his father's predilection for alcohol, he did find himself attracted to women who would create the same chaotic environment as his dad had when Tom was growing up.

I was used to being around an alcoholic, with their mood swings and anger issues. Dad was a British charmer. The ladies loved him.

His mother stayed married to his father for 35 years until he died of alcoholism.

My mother was the classic enabler. She put up with my dad's drinking and bad behavior. He was the breadwinner, so she didn't enable him financially, but she enabled him emotionally. After my dad died, my mom asked, "Did you want me to divorce him? Then you'd be a child from a broken home instead of an alcoholic home." I told her I wanted her to draw a line in the sand, so either Dad would get sober or not be in our home.

When Christine poured on the charm, like Tom's father did,

and exhibited other familiar behaviors, he was drawn to her. He didn't realize that he was unconsciously acting out a scenario from childhood, when he wished he could rescue his mother from his father's alcoholic behavior or his father from himself. And he didn't consciously acknowledge that Christine was an alcoholic until years after he married her.

I missed the first red flag, when she went berserk during one drinking episode. She controlled her drinking for months. Then every few months when she'd drink at parties, she would verbally abuse me. I told her that if this behavior continued, we were going to have to get divorced. Later on in the marriage when she knew I was beginning to suspect how much she was drinking, she'd visit her girlfriends and drink and drive home.

Thomas did divorce Christine, only to go out of the frying pan into the fire, and the arms of another charmer. He got involved slowly with Deirdre, as he was separating from Christine. One day he happened to mention that Christine acted badly when she drank too much, and this innocent remark tipped Deirdre off that she'd better hide her drinking. There were problems from the beginning.

Deirdre got drunk one time, but I thought it was no big deal because she was eating cake with rum in it. She didn't get drunk again for months, so I fell head over heels for her. Then she started acting weird and nasty, and I didn't know why. I was a wine connoisseur, so I took her to tastings. I paid particular attention to how she drank her wine. I noticed that she never gulped it, just sipped. It turned out that she was only able to do this because she

drank beforehand – vodka in her milk and Baileys in her coffee.
Little did I know, she was sharing liquor and dope with her teenage
kids to get them to be co-conspirators.

Tom acknowledges that he was an enabler, though he still
denies that this was due to any of his own psychological issues
and attributes it simply to Deirdre's charms. Indeed, he wasn't the
first one to find her charming.

She was a high-priced call girl in Vegas before she met me.
She told me this early on. She was open about everything except
her drinking. She knew exactly what she needed to hide. In public
she looked like she was on top of the world. Meanwhile, I was
crazed because I couldn't understand her seemingly inexplicable
behavior and I loved her. Finally I told her we were going to
go to Alcoholics Anonymous and Al-Anon meetings. We went to
seven meetings in seven nights. She stopped going. I continued
because I wanted to protect myself from more failed romances.
Deirdre realized I was going to stop enabling her, so she left. I was
heartbroken. I became suicidal. I managed to survive the ordeal,
but vowed, "Never again."

Heroin, HIV, and a History of Crime, Oh My

When little George lost his Pooh Bear on a family vacation,
his parents wouldn't go back for it, despite their knowing how
attached he was to Pooh. George became determined never to lose
anything else, or let anything get out of his control.

It was completely traumatic. I haven't recovered. We were at a little hotel near a lake in New Hampshire and I forgot Pooh there. I got a substitute, but it was never quite the same. I cried when I realized I lost it. My parents understood it was a big deal, but they didn't go back for it.

When George grew up, he kept bumping into Anna rock climbing. They finally made plans to get together to climb a cliff... interestingly enough, in New Hampshire. Unconsciously, he hoped that she might help him return to the place where he had felt comfort and unconditional love from Pooh. But George got more than he bargained for.

I was excited about going there with her. I thought it was a date. But Anna showed up at my house with her boyfriend and a buddy. I was disappointed and petulant the whole weekend. I never knew she had a boyfriend before then. He was an addict. She wasn't using at that time, and she eventually dumped him. When we met again in the spring, she was single. We went from our first date to living together in 48 hours. It was a very intense attraction for both of us. Before we consummated our relationship, during these first 48 hours, Anna told me she was HIV positive. At the time, it didn't faze me. After the fact, I was trying to figure out what I was getting into, but I was already high on the relationship.

George and Anna became inseparable and bought a house together within weeks, where her back-story continued unfolding. When Anna was 18 and desperate to leave home, she married an older man who was shooting dope. Before long, since addiction ran in her family, he got her to shoot dope along with him. Since he was very abusive, she escaped from this home, as well, but not before contracting HIV from a dirty needle. She got clean for a while.

Then Anna moved to New York City and became part of the artsy-music-hip scene, shooting dope and living in a hotel in Chelsea. She became a criminal. Her partners were running a multi-million dollar prescription drug ring. They forged prescriptions and knew what doctors to go to. They were arrested and during their trial the prosecutor pushed a shopping cart into the courtroom and pills started rolling everywhere. Just Anna's partners went to jail – not her – because they didn't roll over and tell the police about her. She would always scream at the TV set when we watched "Law & Order" because criminals would sell out their partners so they could get a lighter sentence.

When George and Anna took that first rock climbing trip, she'd been clean for two years.

At the beginning she told me she had been a drug addict for 17 years. To this day I still don't think she told me the whole truth. She never used drugs during our relationship, but she had a drug addict's mindset. She had a lot of insecurities and anxieties. Whenever she was in her car, she always had a weapon – a knife, a baton, something – within reach. Because she'd been violent, she was always expecting to encounter violence. She was the enforcer in the gang world. Like in the movies, she was the crazed blonde enforcer – that was her. I don't know if she ever killed anyone, but she was very violent.

Over time George discovered that Anna shot-up more than dope.

One incident she told me about was when she fired-off several rounds trying to shoot someone as they were running down 24th Street.

George was no stranger to the wild and crazy lifestyle of drugs, sex, and rock and roll before he met Anna. He started using drugs and alcohol when he was 13 years old and continued on and off.

There were years when I smoked dope every day. I've used hallucinogens a couple of hundred times. I drank. It didn't interfere with my work. After I finished work I would smoke a joint, drink 5 fingers of scotch, watch TV, and go to bed. When I was younger, I could party – drugs and sex – all night and still work. Now I need my beauty sleep. When I got together with Anna, at first I was still partying, but I knew I was going to stop. She was the catalyst. I haven't done anything in years, ever since I've been with her.

When they moved in together, George traded in his addictions to alcohol and drugs for an addiction to sex.

Anna was adventuresome in bed, fabulous. We both liked sex a lot. That first year we had sex one to three times a day, every day. It was a period of being totally high emotionally, like it is when you're with someone for the first time – but this was every time.

After she'd told him she was HIV positive, he tried to find out how contagious it was. They used rubber condoms, practiced safe sex, and he got tested twice a year.

I got what I wanted from the universe – Anna was beautiful, smart, and talented. But I didn't know to ask for a woman who was emotionally healthy. The relationship was a roller-coaster, with real highs and lows. I was in therapy most of the time we were together. I went from having no feelings to being more in touch with them. The therapist told me it was like I stuck garbage in the back of the room, and eventually it started to stink. As I was cleaning out the garbage, it made me less willing to put up with Anna's insanity.

It was a fitting analogy since George's mother had obsessive-compulsive disorder and was a hoarder. She was also addicted to shopping.

My mom has been nuts my whole life. She didn't talk to me for two years, when I was seven to nine, except maybe to say, "Here's your dinner," and that would be all she said to me that night. Anna's insanity was my way of working out the pain my mother's insanity caused me. When my mother dies, I'll be alone.

Despite his anger towards his mom for the cold, chaotic, and confusing childhood she provided, his fear of losing her caused him to be attracted to Anna, who, with her history of crime and addiction, and her HIV positive status, seemed least likely to leave him.

Anna's mother was addicted to prescription drugs, so she was not emotionally available when Anna was growing up, leaving a void where love and attention were supposed to be. Anna's father also contributed to this void, ultimately sending her in search of substances to fill up the empty hole inside.

Anna and her dad were very close until she was about 13 years old. Something happened. She went to jump into daddy's lap and she was squirming around. He probably got a hard-on and this flipped the switch. He threw her out of his lap and this permanently changed their relationship because he felt frightened and upset. He died when she was 18 years old.

After eight years of the 'high' wearing off, Anna and George ended their relationship. Fortunately, George was still HIV negative.

From Crack to Cockroaches

For the five years before Alan started dating Felicity, he had a crush on her. He didn't dare ask her out because he was only a shy boy finishing high school and she was a little older and already in the working world doing sales. When they were in their twenties, she answered his prayers.

She came onto me first. She said, "Let's get together," or something like that. I didn't ever ask women out. I felt unattractive. If a woman wanted to be with me, that's all I needed to know and I would be with her. Felicity had a fantastic body and a pretty face, which is a winning combination for me, especially because she was dynamic and confident.

This was the most exciting relationship Alan had ever had. Though he was adventurous, he wasn't sophisticated. Felicity brought him into her circle of more sophisticated friends and her world of clubs, higher-end restaurants, and travel. She paid for almost everything, even the apartment they lived in together, which he felt was another big bonus.

It was wine, women, and song! I knew Felicity was a casual drug user – a little pot and drinking. Then she developed an interest in trying heroin. The street corner doctors told her there's a way to use it where you can control it and not get addicted. I told her to go ahead, not that I was giving her permission exactly.

When Alan told Felicity to "go ahead" with the heroin, he was unconsciously hoping to make her dependent upon him so that she wouldn't leave. But he didn't anticipate the turmoil that followed.

She descended into becoming a full-blown addict and progressed to crack, too. It took a physical and emotional toll on our relationship, watching her go down to double-digit weight and hustle everyone. It seems like pure madness to be with an addict. But the sex was fantastic. Felicity was the kind of woman who guys call "psycho-sluts" or "crazy-sluts." Every crazy woman I've ever been with has always been sexually bold, and this perk has made it difficult to walk away from them.

Once drugs kicked in, the relationship didn't exist on its own merit. It was all about drug use: getting her clean and my mistrust.

I was begging and pleading with her to get clean. In her pursuit of drugs, I think Felicity was having sex with other men. I had no hard proof of it, so I was able to stay in denial, though my mistrust grew. I didn't want to confront her because if I rocked the boat too much, I was afraid I'd end up alone.

She'd fall asleep in her food when we were out. Felicity was killing herself. It became gut wrenching. I didn't know what was worse, seeing it or imagining it when she was away from me. She was a train wreck waiting to happen and I wanted to be there to pull her out of the wreckage.

Felicity kept promising Alan she would get clean. The more she broke her promises, the less he trusted her. It wasn't just the drugs that bothered him. She was always comparing him to other men and putting him down. Alan's life had come to revolve totally around Felicity. He barely kept his job, lost his friends, and began drinking more and more as their relationship went downhill.

The drinking was to sedate myself to go to sleep. It was how I coped with this horrific relationship.

Felicity's drug use finally got her fired, so she couldn't afford their apartment anymore. She moved back in with her parents, and Alan got his own small place.

I was living in a roach-infested basement apartment. I had to sleep with the lights on so the cockroaches wouldn't crawl on me. Felicity spent time with me there, but it wasn't an environment where I could invite her to live with me. I had to face the fact that the relationship had brought me down to this.

But when Felicity got clean, got her job back, and got another place, Alan eagerly moved back in, only to discover that whether she was on or off drugs, she still put him down and treated him badly.

I was clinging to her for dear life. She's the one who decided to end it. Out of the blue, after four years, Felicity said, "I can't do this anymore!" I never got an explanation. I went to pieces. I got angry and upset and spent a lot of time crying. I didn't move out right away. It took me a while to find a place.

Alan kept stalling, hoping she would change her mind and they would stay together. But Felicity wanted to end it 'cold turkey'. Alan had to ask himself why he'd clung to this bad girl Addict.

I realized how much my relationship with my mom affected my relationships with women. I attempted to date women who were the opposite of my mother. I looked for sexually bold women, those who guys would call promiscuous because my mom was chaste, a religiously-oriented woman who was a virgin at 31 when she married my dad. But in another aspect they were exactly like my mom because they all disapproved of me.

Dancing As Fast As I Can

Sophia's dreams of being a ballerina were dashed when she had to hotfoot it out of her abusive home and found herself pregnant at 16, and then pregnant again soon after. When Vincent met her at his friend's nightclub, she was splitting her time between being a drink waitress there and a stripper somewhere else. Vincent was an artist with a colorful past. He grew up on the wrong side of the tracks, literally.

When I was a kid, the number one emotion I felt was gut-wrenching fear. I got roughed up in my neighborhood and there was no escaping from the constant chaos because when I got home my parents were always fighting. My dad grew grapevines. One time they got into a horrible fight and my mom went out and chopped down his grapevines! There were only two safe places in my tough Texas neighborhood: the art museum and the library. So I became good at art and sold my first painting at 15.

One night when it was slow at the club, Sophia sat down and started talking to Vincent.

I was a sucker for hot chicks, especially blondes. I found out Sophia had been a ballet dancer. Had she given up the dream? Dancers don't give up the dream until their legs fall off. She said she was still taking classes and that she "danced" at Rocky's Bar. Strippers were go-go girls – wannabe dancers. I didn't know by this point she'd had two children and was struggling to survive. When someone is as good-looking as Sophia, you're willing to take the chance she's the one dancer who's not a manipulating psychopath.

Vincent finally got up the nerve to ask her out. He took her to lunch and a movie, brought her back to her house, and kissed her goodnight, restraining himself from asking for more. After the first date they saw each other almost every night.

She was used to guys picking her up at 2:00 A.M. after work, and Vincent was happy to wrap his life around hers.

On the second date she did this elaborate astrological star chart and decided that we were perfect for each other. I certainly was not going to argue with that. On our third date she had another surprise. Even though I grew up with drug addicts and thugs, I'd stayed away from drugs and hardly drank. But when this babe pulled out a bong and started blowing marijuana smoke down my lungs, I gave up my drug-free body in order to play with hers.

A few weeks later when Vincent picked her up after work and put his arm around her, he had another surprise.

She freaked out, then she was all over me, and then she passed out in the car. It was weird. I started seeing pills around. I didn't like it, but by then I was getting emotionally attached.

One night Sophia told Vincent she'd gotten a lawyer to try to get her kids back. She admitted she was hoping that by having a stable relationship with him, it would help to show she was on the right track. When he asked her why she'd lost her kids, she said she'd had a drug problem, but had gotten it under control.

I wanted to believe it. She never used 'needley stuff' in front of me.

However, Vincent soon uncovered many more dark secrets. Not only was he finding uppers and downers in strange places, but Sophia's increasingly erratic behavior was up, down, and all over the place. He also discovered that she had sold herself to pay for drugs.

I knew that I should run, but when she was sane she was really a loving person. She would make half-hearted attempts at getting straight, but she always went back. It was driving me crazy because I really cared for her.

They continued being lovers. One night Sophia, who drove a motorcycle, had a wreck and broke her arm. Her girlfriend called Vincent to tell him about the accident. He brought flowers to the hospital. Sophia was thrilled. She depended on him more after this and they got closer. But then the painkillers took over. These kept her away from her non-prescription drugs, but before long, she became hooked on the painkillers. Vincent was confused about what behavior was coming from the prescription drugs and what was coming from the non-prescription drugs. All he knew was that her behavior was getting weirder. Months passed. Vincent had business out of town, so he told Sophia he'd see her in a week when he got back. As it happened, he returned sooner than expected. He went to her house and knocked on the door.

This guy looked through the peephole. He called to Sophia that there was a guy at the door. She yelled back, "Ask who he is." I told him who I was and he told her. She called out, "He's my baby. He's my baby. Let him in." The guy looked like an ex-con, hair to his shoulders, tattoos, like a biker prison-escapee. I went in and asked, "Who are you, dude? Where's my girlfriend?" "She's back there," he answered. I went into her bedroom. There was Sophia, semi-conscious, lying on the floor, with only her panties on and a needle stuck in her arm. A second drugged-up dude was there. This one was sitting on the bed, a tourniquet on his arm, shooting up. My head started spinning. "Who are these freaks?" I heard myself say. "My friends." "Want me to throw them out?" "No, they're my friends," Sophia repeated. She was slurring and out of it. Then she said, "Want some H?" and I said, "No, I don't do this shit and I thought you didn't do it either. Why don't you come to my place?" She yelled, "No. Get your fucking hands off me! Nobody told you to touch me. These are my friends. I can do what I damn please." I told her, "If this is what you want, I'm out of here." My first instinct was to throw these punks out and smash their heads in the concrete. I was hurt, put down, humiliated.

Vincent walked out, shocked and numb. He couldn't believe the disturbing, distorted scene of destruction he had just witnessed. It was like an abstract Picasso painting he'd first seen in his youth. The next day Sophia called him trying to coax him to come back.

She said, "I hope you're not mad at me. Don't be mad. I know these guys from way back when and you know I haven't been that way." I said, "I'm glad you're alive. I didn't know what to do. Call the cops or an ambulance. Forgive me. You need help. Neither I nor anyone else can have a relationship with you. You told me you quit the hard stuff, and if losing your kids wasn't enough to get you to quit, then I won't be."

Before Vincent walked in on this ugly scene, Sophia had confessed that, in the past, she had turned a trick – taken money for sex to pay for her drug habit – and that this contributed to why she lost her kids.

I'd known women who had done these things and turned their lives around. Sophia never said she was a prostitute. I grew up with some girls who became prostitutes. I know they can smile at you and pick your pocket at the same time. But I thought she was reforming and had a stake in it for her kids. She said she only did it a few times a few years ago. I wanted to believe her. But when it re-manifested itself, I realized it was not just in the past.

Why did I hang in there? I was a guy thinking with my little head. The sex was fabulous. She made me feel special and loved. When she had an orgasm she made me feel like a big man, like I was taking care of her. She put on costumes and wigs. She persuaded me to tell her what my fantasies were and made me feel comfortable whispering them. Then she put on a show and acted them out. Sophia could read my mind and did it exactly the way I fantasized.

Vincent, like many men, wanted a woman to be the good mother they never had. Good, nurturing mothers just know how to give their babies what they want without the baby having to say it. Vincent's mom had not been like this. She was cold, an emotional vacuum, who found the one blade of grass he had missed and made him mow the lawn all over again. His father had married her because, as a dark-skinned man of Mediterranean origin, he'd faced hurtful prejudice in the South, where they lived. Vincent's mom was an attractive blonde, so his dad had hoped that their children would have lighter skin and not have to suffer like he did.

The last Vincent heard, from the friend who owned the nightclub, was that Sophia had gone back to Oklahoma, where she had come from.

If I'd heard she was doing wonderfully, I might have been tempted to look her up.

Fortunately, Vincent never did look her up. But the passionate – and painful – memories still burn inside of him. While he was involved with Sophia, he was continuing to paint mushrooms and frogs. But after their torrid and traumatic ending, he turned to painting dancers, putting his smoldering emotions into his work and touching people's hearts to wide acclaim.

Famous Addicts

Brooke Mueller – Empty vodka bottles were found in Brooke's car halfway through her pregnancy, and she had to go into rehab. Charlie Sheen blames her drinking for the congenital heart problems of one of their twin sons, and this has spelled doom for their marriage.

Gwen Cummings – In the film "28 Days," Gwen (Sandra Bullock) is forced to break through her denial and admit she's an alcoholic. Though resistant at first to the 28-day rehab, she eventually gets with the program.

Courtney Love – Making headlines more frequently for her drug addictions and out-of-control behavior than her music, Courtney, an alternative rock musician, seems hell-bent on continuing to be self-destructive, despite having lost custody of her daughter.

Britney Spears – Britney's controversial career has come a long way from the "Mickey Mouse Club." Her psychological problems, exacerbated by alcohol and drugs, continue to plague her and keep her on a very fragile and tenuous path.

Amy Winehouse – In her song "Rehab," Amy croons, "They tried to make me go to rehab, but I said, 'no, no, no!'" However, her rebellious abuse of alcohol and drugs has caused her to overdose and threatens her stardom and her life.

Lindsay Lohan – Despite her stints in rehab, party girl Lindsay has continued to get into trouble with the law, diminishing a once-promising career. A lost little mean girl, she makes endless tabloid fodder for DUIs, hoarding, feuding, and other self-destructive behavior.

Witchy Woman – In the song "Witchy Woman," the Eagles sing the praises of The Addict: "She held me spellbound in the night… and she drove herself to madness with a silver spoon. Woo-hoo witchy woman, see how high she flies."

Patsy Stone – In "Absolutely Fabulous," a British sitcom, chain-smoking Patsy (played by Joanna Lumley) appears drunk or stoned most of the time. She is undoubtedly trying to escape memories of a bleak childhood with a jealous mother who neglected her.

Drew Barrymore – Thanks to her mother's fondness for partying with the rich and famous, Drew developed a fondness for substance abuse beginning when she was a pre-teen. However, she seems to have picked herself up and deserves kudos for being in recovery.

The Girl in "She Talks To Angels" – This song by The Black Crowes poignantly describes a girl hooked on heroin who escapes to her own reality where angels know her name. The lyrics, "She gives a smile when the pain comes. The pain's gonna make everything alright," refer to the pain of the needle.

Whitney Houston – Whitney admits to having been addicted to cocaine and marijuana – and to her bad boy Bobby Brown.

Judy Garland – In "The Wizard of Oz," Judy clicked her heels and said, "There's no place like home," but she had trouble feeling at home in the world after film execs plied her with drugs to control her weight and started her on a lifelong addiction. She married five times, attempted suicide, and died of an "accidental" drug overdose.

Chapter 4
THE SEX SIREN

What does a Sex Siren want?

A Sex Siren wants to be put on a pedestal where she can be idolized and worshipped for her sexual powers, and can use sex as a weapon to turn men into little lap dogs who do her bidding.

Why? To make up for the imbalance of power that The Sex Siren has suffered at the hands of men in her past. Most of these bad girls have learned to use sex as a survival strategy to get what they want, often because they were sexually abused as children. When a little girl is sexually abused, she grows up to become either a promiscuous Sex Siren, or the other extreme, a Sexual Withholder, as we'll see in the next chapter.

Marilyn Monroe, the most powerful Sex Siren of all, never knew her father and was discarded by her mentally unstable mother. Marilyn grew up in a succession of foster homes and other hastily assembled living arrangements, where she was sexually abused on at least one occasion, and more such abuse has been reported.

I knew I belonged to the public and to the world, not because I was talented or even beautiful, but because I had never belonged to anything or anyone else.

A wise girl kisses but doesn't love, listens but doesn't believe, and leaves before she is left.

Being a sex symbol is a heavy load to carry, especially when one is tired, hurt, and bewildered.

Marilyn Monroe

When a girl becomes a Sex Siren after being sexually abused, it's because it is a psychological defense to try to hide the pain of the abuse from herself and pretend that it never happened, or that it was not as hurtful as she knows it was deep down. To accomplish this pretense, she identifies with the aggressor, the man who abused her, and becomes sexually aggressive herself. Despite the seductive outer trappings of The Sex Siren, this type of bad girl is actually afraid of sexual intimacy for fear of getting hurt again. So, she settles for a string of shallow sexual liaisons and secretly prides herself on acting like a man when it comes to sex.

Sometimes called a bombshell or "femme fatale," French for "deadly woman," The Sex Siren seduces her man, ensnares him in invisible bonds of ardor and rapture, and carries him away to do or provide something for her or simply for the pleasure of showing that she is this powerful. Once he is entranced and entrapped, she lures her man to compromising, dangerous, and sometimes deadly circumstances. These once-rational men are driven to obsession and exhaustion as she uses her debilitating power to trifle with their affections.

The Sex Siren is narcissistic, a trait she has learned from a narcissistic or self-absorbed mother who has put her own whims and desires above those of her daughter and failed to protect her from dangerous men. The Sex Siren's father was not there for her, physically or emotionally, and she resents him for it. If not the abuser himself, he, too, failed to protect his daughter. She wishes she had had the power over her dad as a little girl to make him stay and love her. Since she didn't, she wants to punish her dad and all men.

Since sex is the quintessential allure of bad girls, the call of The Sex Siren is especially powerful. She likes to have a man under her spell who she can use as home base, while cheating on him with other men who will spoil her, treat her like a slut, or both. This adds to her mystique, since men are not only eager to bed her themselves, but to save her from all the other men who have "taken advantage" of her. The adage "be careful what you wish for" often rings in these men's ears, as they discover that their Sex Siren has a more voracious appetite than they anticipated.

Why do men fall for Sex Sirens?

In the epic poem "The Odyssey," written by the Greek poet Homer, Odysseus is warned about the Sirens, who live on an island in the middle of the sea. Their song is so beautiful and captivating that all men who hear it cannot resist attempting to get closer to them. Whether they steer their boats or jump in the water to head towards the sound of this seductive music, men end up crashing on the rocks that surround the Sirens' island. When Odysseus passed the island on his journey home, he resisted this fate by having his sailors plug their ears with beeswax and tie him to the ship's mast.

Hearing the Sirens' song, Odysseus begged his men to untie him, but they bound him tighter, as he had ordered them to do before he fell under the Sirens' spell.

Unfortunately, modern man is not as capable of resisting The Sex Siren as Odysseus, and many find themselves crashing and drowning in rocky relationships when her charming song enthralls them. In part, this is due to the early influence of their mom. Men who fall for Sex Sirens have mothers who are narcissistic or self-absorbed, like The Sex Siren and her mom. For these mothers it's all about them, not about nurturing their child. The fathers of men who fall for Sex Sirens often have strait-laced careers, such as in engineering or the military, and have been attracted to the flamboyance and frivolity of Sex Sirens because they are so much less inhibited than they allow themselves to be.

But the simplest and truest answer to why men fall for Sex Sirens is that they want to show other men in the locker room that they have the biggest penis. In their arrested development, they still feel that the man with the sexiest toys wins. He struts along, a Sex Siren on his arm, thinking that the sexier looking she is, the more he can fool other men into believing he's the biggest stud on the block. Ironically, just as these men try to prove they have the biggest phallus, Sex Sirens flaunt their breasts, trying to prove that bigger is better and offering men the false promise of nurturance.

Real Stories from Men on the Dating Front

Penthouse Pet of the Year

Kimberly's agent steered her across the room when he spotted

Nicholas poolside at the Hollywood party they were attending. Nick had just been written up in the Hollywood Reporter for having sold a screenplay after only two weeks in town. "Hot New Writer Hits Hollywood" the headline blared. Kimberly had read it, too. They both hoped he could do something for her, like get her a part in a movie. She'd already succeeded in becoming a Penthouse Pet of the Year and a Playboy centerfold, but what she really wanted to do was act. Nick called her a few days later and they began a relationship.

Kimberly was gorgeous in a flashy sort of way, and she stopped traffic. She didn't start out as centerfold material, but she knew how to flirt, the way she dressed and moved. Her parents were nudists, so they made her get over being nude when she was young. I always wondered if it was legitimate nudity or inappropriate behavior. Kimberly wasn't completely estranged from them, but I never felt like I'd be brought home to meet them.

She worked hard at reinventing herself, changing her name, hair color, and having her plastic surgeon on speed dial.

She had her boobs done three times – each time bigger. Now anything even bigger would be grotesque. I kidded her and told her she looked like tomato plants on stakes – with her breasts pulled up high.

But Kimberly was the most boring woman in bed. Her attitude was, "I'm Kimberly, a centerfold, turn me on." I had to envision her in the magazine to get turned on. She was just not into it. Later I met other men who said they had to do the same thing. They thought they were the only ones. She was turned off emotionally and made no vocalizations. I felt like saying, "Are you awake?" As pretty as she was, she couldn't give me an orgasm, or at least it took a lot of work.

Why did I keep going out with her? It gave me street cred to say I was dating a Penthouse Pet. I got the reaction I wanted from people. They would say, "Isn't that Miss March?" or "Isn't that Kimberly?" She went well with my Mercedes Benz.

Though men who answer to The Sex Siren's song do want to show her off and be the envy of other would-be suitors, their flippant remarks are really a defense against acknowledging how vulnerable they let themselves become to her and how much they were hurt when she dumped them. They're not as cavalier as they sound, but they don't feel it's manly to admit it. In fact, what kept Nick hooked were the glimpses of vulnerability he saw in Kimberly because this would mean she would be less likely to abandon him if she didn't feel as perfect as she looked on the outside.

Every once in a while I'd sense more depth than she'd show. Like with Marilyn Monroe, there was the movie persona and the hidden one. I'd realize Kimberly was a sad little girl. At Christmas I was going back East to visit my parents. Before I left I bought her a Christmas tree and gave her a Persian kitten. She was touched and thanked me for the whole next year. She was more appreciative than if I gave her a Lexus. I wanted to throw her in the shower and take off her makeup and big hair to make her more real. She knew she could do sex kitten, but didn't know if she could do vulnerable. Every time I allowed myself to feel something for her, she'd do or say something to smash my illusions.

Kimberly, too, had illusions. Hers were about how talented she was as an actress. Though she got some small parts in TV shows and B movies, mostly in shower or bedroom scenes, she was never taken seriously by casting directors.

With her voice, she tried to be like Marilyn Monroe and got the role of the ditsy blonde. Our relationship became more about "what can I do for you?" and "what can you do for me?" I tried telling her I was not able to do anything to get her into movies. As a writer I got propositioned once a day by some of the most beautiful women. I told them "I'm prepared to let you do what you want to do to me under the table, but I can't do anything for you. Sleep with Michael Douglas. He's the one who can get you into the movies!"

After a year Kimberly gave up hoping that Nick was her ticket to Hollywood stardom and dumped him to find another leading man who would take her from the casting couch to the silver screen.

About 10 years later, when I was running a modeling agency, Kimberly came to me for representation. I found her a great photographer and helped her to build a legitimate modeling portfolio. I paid for her pictures with the understanding that she'd pay me back. She never did. One day I got a notice in the mail announcing that she was suing me because I was demanding she pay for the photos. Next I got a call from "People's Court" asking me to agree to try my case on national TV. I went on-camera with the letter from the photographer, saying Kimberly owes me the money. I thought it was a slam-dunk. That month Playboy had done a spread called "Bimbos of Hollywood." Kimberly was in it. She brought the magazine to court and was circulating it to the audience, who was in awe of having a Playmate in their midst. Then she produced a letter from the photographer claiming the opposite – that she doesn't owe me any money. Both letters were signed and on his stationery. The judge was perplexed and he ruled in favor of neither one of us, which meant that I didn't get paid. I was so angry because it made me look bad. I tried to console myself by thinking that no one would ever see the show, but it kept being re-run and people would say, "Hey, I saw you on TV." Kimberly walked out like she'd won the Miss Universe pageant.

Kimberly never got married, though Centerfolds usually marry well, and quietly become legitimate. Now they're no longer Miss January, they're Mrs. L.A. Rams CEO, or Mrs. Plastic Surgeon, or the wife of some other big shot.

Ironically, while Kimberly was trying to get Nick to open doors for her in Hollywood, his biological mother, unbeknownst to him, was trying to open those same doors for herself. In fact, it was to pursue acting that she gave Nick up for adoption 10 minutes after he was born.

I didn't know if my birth mother was a hooker or the Queen of England. I was hoping for Whistler's mother. As an adult I finally tracked her down and she turned out not to be the sweet little old mom I was hoping for. She was a professional actress on Broadway and TV, and a real diva. She abandoned me to pursue her acting career. She told me my birth father had taken off, claiming that I was not his son. She didn't want to have to live in her car and raise me by herself. She thought that if she kept her baby, she'd wind up as a secretary and never become an actress. It was all about her.

My mom was strikingly pretty. She was like Bette Davis in the movie "Cabin in the Cotton," who brushed off her lover with, "I'd love to kiss you, but I just washed my hair." She was in Lee Strasberg's class with Richard Burton. My mom was in the cocktail set and went to fancy clubs. My stepfather, the man she married after my birth father, was an engineer who went along for the ride. He liked women who were flamboyant, although this made it hard to live with them. My birth father liked flamboyant women, too. Neither one of these men were flamboyant themselves. These men married women who were not like them, women who are the life of the party, who sing at the piano. It's like having the Cadillac you never drive. It's like Kimberly. You think, "How can I enhance my image?"

When Nick found his birth mother, she initially slammed the door on him. When she finally acknowledged being his mom, she never said she was sorry for having given him up, nor that she would keep him if she could do it over.

I asked her if she thought about me, like on my birthday. She said, "I forgot what day your birthday was!"

Real Life Seinfeld

Ross, who we will meet again in future chapters because he is addicted to various types of bad girls, is stuck in a sitcom and can't get out. Make that several sitcoms. As a young man he became shipwrecked on "Gilligan's Island" and is perpetually searching for bad girl Ginger, instead of good girl Mary Ann. He is also George from "Seinfeld."

In an episode of "Seinfeld," George uses a photo of Elaine's very attractive friend, Jillian, to get a date with an equally attractive girl who is out of his league. He manages this by pretending to her that Jillian is his deceased fiancée. Instantaneously his status is raised in the new girl's eyes, who realizes she must have been mistaken in her first impression of him as not being good enough to date. She agrees to go out with him and brings him to the "forbidden city," a nightclub where other attractive women and models hang out. George shows the same photo to the women at the nightclub and finds himself surrounded by women vying for his attention and wondering what he's got that would make such an attractive woman go out with him. When George accidentally burns the photo with his hair dryer, he clips a picture of a model out of a magazine, returns to the club and tries his same fiancée line with a new bevy of beauties. Unfortunately, one of them happens to be the model from his magazine clipping. His cover is blown and he gets kicked out of the "forbidden city."

Ross uses a similar cover to hide his insecurities by choosing women to date based upon the impression he wants to give others. Yang Li was one such woman. Eating lunch at a fast food Asian restaurant one day, Ross stopped mid-bite when he saw her behind the counter serving food.

Yang Li was breathtakingly beautiful. She had a nametag on, so I wrote her a note. She called me. She told me she was married, but that it had been an arranged marriage, and they were more like brother and sister. She and her husband were from wealthy families, with drivers, and had grown up together in China. Their fathers had been leaders in the Chinese Communist Party, and they decided that a union between their children would be fortuitous. I called her my "Chinese princess." We fell in love and saw each other on and off.

Though Yang Li didn't need to work, she did so because she was bored. But Ross wasn't content having a girlfriend who just served fast food. Like George of the "Seinfeld" episode, he needed to boast that he was dating a model.

I told her she should model. I took her to a top-modeling agency. They signed her and put her on a calendar.

Ross brought Yang Li to parties at his firm.

One colleague said, "Are you really sleeping with her?" I was proud, but I was really taken aback. He'd never been out with a woman who looked like that and obviously didn't believe that such a beautiful woman would go out with me either. I felt like I was in the "Seinfeld" episode where George pretended he was dating a model. When one woman recognized the photo, he was no longer part of that world.

I was not always faithful to Yang Li, but she was married. Her husband knew I was involved with her. Finally I couldn't take it anymore. I wanted her to be my wife. I bought a ring. I knew she loved me. I went down on my knee. I expected her to run into my

arms. Instead she took the ring and said, "Let me think about it."
She wore my ring on her right hand.

Ultimately Yang Li said, "No," but kept the ring. Eventually, Ross realized that Yang Li had been using her exotic beauty to play him like a lute. Many months later she knocked on Ross's door. She'd been having another affair and had gotten pregnant.

I opened the door and she asked to get married. I was dating the ballerina by then, so I said, "No."

Of course, the ballerina turned out to be another bad girl, The Damsel in Distress type, who broke Ross's heart into even more pieces. But that's for another chapter.

A West Side Story at West Point

How do you get The Sex Siren to stop having sex? Marry her. She'll at least stop having sex with you. This is what Brad discovered after marrying Bambi. But let's start at the beginning.

Brad was a 19-year-old cadet at West Point. He stuck out his thumb to hitch a ride and his life was changed forever when Bambi and her stepdad picked him up. The next day, with her parents' encouragement since they wanted her to marry a West Point graduate, Bambi called the Military Academy and asked for Brad. She said that she was glad they had given him a ride, and that she found him interesting and would like to meet again. Bambi was attending a nearby women's college. They exchanged phone calls and letters, and started dating.

Bambi was drop-dead gorgeous. She was an all-American

petite blonde, blue-eyed cheerleader and straight-A student. She was my fantasy. I thought she was an all-American princess. I went to West Point like Pee Wee Herman and came out like Jean Claude Van Damme. I was twisted steel and sex appeal. We looked so good together, like Ben Affleck and Jennifer Aniston. We could have been the couple on the top of a wedding cake.

But I was a West Point outcast because I came from a poor family and the parents of the kids at the Academy made a lot of money. My mother was a high school dropout and a waitress. We lived in the South Side of Chicago. My clothes and shoes came from Goodwill. I was even afraid to go home because I would get THC in my blood from the second-hand smoke when my family was toking on pot, and they could court martial me or kick me out. West Point was a dream come true. Bambi was an upper class chick. She lived in a five-bedroom house with a swimming pool and a Mercedes. It was like West Side Story. I went from cockroaches and mouse turds on the kitchen counter to J.R. Ewing's ranch. She was a rich bitch, but it turned out that some girls in the hood had better values.

West Point had strict rules and a grueling schedule, so their relationship consisted mostly of Saturday night dates at his school dances, where they served hamburgers and fries. It was all very wholesome – no alcohol, no drugs, and no sex. Brad never got a real glimpse of who she really was until they got married because Bambi's virginal exterior hid the bourgeoning Sex Siren inside.

She had a hypnotic trance on guys. She could just talk and make a guy hot in seconds. Then there was the 'inadvertent' touching. The first time Bambi brushed my crotch, I thought it was an accident. But after the second, third, and fourth times, I thought this woman wanted me. She'd tickle my crotch with an evil smile. It was very exciting, but very frustrating. Many times I went to bed with blue balls because she wouldn't sleep with me.

Brad spent the spring vacation before graduation at Bambi's family estate. He got a ring, asked her to marry him and she said, "Yes." That night, when Brad was sleeping on the couch in the living room, Bambi crept down the hall and seduced him.

She held out until I said the "M" word (marriage). It was her strategy to hook a husband who would be a provider, while she was out having a good time. She said that now that we were engaged, we could do it – so we did. It was good. At the time, I thought I was the only one, but I later realized Bambi was not a virgin. I was. I had only done heavy petting with girls before her. I finally got a home run with her, but she was looking for a grand slam – with three guys on bases. I hit the ball and they all came running home. Even after we were engaged, she continued having sex with other guys. I didn't know I was sharing her.

Bambi's mother said she would give their marriage her blessing if Brad gave her his word that he would get her through the rest of college.

You can get kicked out of West Point if you lie. You are taught not to give your word lightly – even if it means your death. You don't cheat or steal either. I learned to keep my word, to do my duty and to honor my country. It became my mission to get Bambi through college.

So Brad and Bambi got married, and he started his obligatory years of service in the army, becoming a Ranger, a black beret. But even though his duties sometimes took him behind dangerous enemy lines, the military war zone was nothing compared to the battles he faced at home.

I got off duty early one day and she wasn't home. I had heard rumors. When I confronted her, she claimed she was with a friend. At the Officers' Club I heard snickers and talk of a guy named Tim "nailing" my wife. Finally I confronted him. He was a lieutenant, like me. I said, "I want to talk with you." I could see him getting nervous. I said, "I want you to stop fucking my wife!" He said, "Well, okay." That night when I came home, she smelled good and dinner was on the table. We were feeling romantic. After we had sex I told her, "Tim admitted he's been screwing with you, so I want you to stop." "It was just one time! I'm only human. It was an accident!" she cried. "Okay, if it was only one time, let's move on," I muttered. I still held her on a pedestal and I thought I'd married a classy chick. I wanted our marriage to succeed.

But it wasn't just one time and it wasn't just one guy. It was Tim, John, Ken, and Ralph, and most likely others.

Guys looked at her like she stepped out of the pages of Playboy, a wet, hot, licking-her-lips centerfold. Whenever I was gone, she was at the Officers' Club, wearing her miniskirt and pushup bra, screwing other guys. And whenever I confronted her, at first it was denial: "I never had sex with him!" Then it was blame: "If you were home, or not tired, or if you paid attention to me, this wouldn't happen!" So everything she did in someone else's bedroom became my fault.

I didn't have DNA or a blue dress to prove she was cheating on me. No one was being straight with me. Eventually she confessed, "All those suspicions you had – they were true. I did screw Tim, John, Ken, and Ralph. We even screwed in your car and our marriage bed." It was my final kick in the nuts. These four men were other officers. The military has a code: you don't screw each other's wives because if you go to a war zone with hand grenades and other weapons, there's a high probability that someone's not coming back. And you can always say it was an Iraqi insurgent.

As the years went by, Brad was denied plum positions and promotions, not because of his military service, which was exemplary, but because of his reputation of being a cuckold. The army was very competitive, and his peers delighted in spreading these rumors to increase their own prospects.

One lieutenant colonel told me to my face that he didn't promote me from captain to major because "a guy like you, who can't control his wife, couldn't control 500 soldiers!"

Every time I confronted her with suspicions of affairs, she countered with, "You don't earn enough. You're not man enough! Tim screws me and makes me suck his dick after!" She'd read women's magazines about adulterous wives, while I was watching TV football. Sometimes she read out loud, "'The modern woman has a husband and a guy on the side.' What's wrong with that? Why don't we have an open marriage? We'll still stay married and you can pay bills," she proposed. I hated these magazines. She highlighted paragraphs and I read them. Words like "polyamorous" and "polygamy." I saw none of this coming before we got married.

After we were married it was great for a few months, but she shifted from Sex Siren to frigid for some time and from frigid to non-stop complaints. But she could turn on the sexuality when she wanted something.

When he continued to bring up accusations of adultery, she'd slap his face, punch him in the arm, and sometimes give him a bloody nose. She knew he couldn't touch her because it was a court martial offense.

She gave me an ultimatum, "I'll change my ways if you get out of the army and make more money."

But Brad couldn't quit. He would have to go to jail if he didn't fulfill his service obligation, and besides, he loved the army and wanted to make a career of it. It was true that the life of an army wife was quite different from the pampered one she'd had before. She went from her parents' "Ewing Ranch" to a crummy one-bedroom apartment, and from dining in fancy restaurants to preparing macaroni and cheese. She liked four-star restaurants, five-star hotels, and generals with any number of stars. Her fantasy of marrying a kid from the wrong side of the tracks and living out "West Side Story" had seemed romantic until the reality of having little money hit her. So she looked for men of higher rank than

Brad.

Bambi constantly complained, "You don't take care of me. It's your fault that I go with other guys. You take me for a hot dog. They take me for steaks. You take me to Target. They take me to Neiman Marcus."

Why did I stay? I was in love and in lust with her. She exuded sexuality. Her pheromones were on overdrive. It was the way she carried herself, the touch of her hand – she was hot! She was great in bed. She gave great head. For a young man, it was a fantasy. She'd sex me up and I'd stay. She'd sex me down and I'd stay. Every time I got mad at her she'd spread her legs, promise to love me and I'd stay.

Despite a desire to screw many guys, she had a real difficulty achieving orgasm. Many times I'd have to stimulate her for over an hour before orgasm. So maybe she was seeking 'the' guy who could make her come in 15 minutes. I do not think it was a technique issue, nor a size issue, but instead she had something missing within her that she was trying to fulfill through sexual gratification. Just being near her made me horny and I knew that she had that effect upon other guys. I just did not realize that she would be handing out her 'cookies' to all the soldiers!

Finally, after four years of marriage, Brad couldn't take the humiliation and betrayal anymore. He filed for a legal separation, but didn't turn in the divorce papers until the last semester of Bambi's senior year in college.

I fulfilled my commitment to her mom. I stayed married for six years to pay for Bambi's final years of college. She didn't invite me to her graduation. She left me destitute. I lived like a monk to pay for all the credit cards that she maxed-out, including money spent on gifts for her boyfriends. I was left with only jeans and tee-shirts, dirt poor once again.

When we were together, she was flirty, but not 'slutty'. During the divorce she told me how great the guys were who treated her badly. "They treated me like the slut I am and forced me to do things. They'd say, 'Get down on your knees you little bitch.'" We had passion in the bedroom, but I didn't treat her like a whore.

Before Brad and Bambi got married, her stepfather had tried to warn him.

"You're sure you want to get married?" he said. I said nothing. "She really has her moments. She's not a Venusian virgin on a pedestal." He probably didn't feel at liberty to say, "Your girlfriend's a slut." I told him if the highs – like sex, dinner, and playing racket-ball together – are higher, sometimes you have to expect the lows to be lower and they'll even out. I was a naïve 21 year old with a hard on. I've wondered how much he knew about her being a slut. Even though she was already 17 when I met her, she would always sit on his lap; they may have been screwing. Her mom divorced him soon after we got married, which made me wonder all the more about what might have been going on between Bambi and her stepdad.

Bambi's biological father had died. He was her mother's first husband. She then had three more husbands. She was very high-maintenance and may have taught Bambi her tricks, since they were 'BFF', more like sisters than mother and daughter.

Brad's mother dropped out of high school to marry his father, a bad boy who swept her off her feet, gave her four children, and cheated on her. Brad blamed his mom for divorcing his dad, who then abandoned them and left them in abject poverty when he was four years old. From then on he was a latchkey kid with only one meal a day – the school lunch.

At 17 I was 5'6" and weighed 115 pounds. I was 35 pounds underweight. My siblings and I looked like starving Ethiopian children.

Brad's mom went through a string of men, including four more husbands. They either cheated on her or beat her up or both. When Brad tried to protect her, they would hit him. She left for work at 6:00 A.M. and got home at midnight, but had nothing to show for it because the men took her money or she willingly supported them so they wouldn't leave her.

Her husbands seemed to be good guys with jobs when they were dating, but then they became couch potatoes and fell into smoking dope and drinking beer with mom. We kids were not eating because Mom and her boyfriend were at the local bar, so when I was at Bambi's house, I thought I was in heaven. When I was growing up, I'd have to choose between a coke and burger, if I even got that. Bambi's folks put 16 burgers on the grill when there were only six or seven people eating. Until then I didn't know that

"Ozzie and Harriet" was real, that real Americans live like that.

You didn't want to go past my mom's bedroom. You never knew who was in there. She had boyfriends in between husbands. She was a virgin princess when she got married, but then she started having sex to alleviate the pain. She went from good girl to bad girl.

Just like Bambi.

The only love Brad got from his mom, whose sauciness he likens to Roseanne Barr, was tough love, except once when she came to his high school and saved him from being suspended and arrested, months before he went to West Point on a scholarship.

I walked past gang-controlled Hallway E, where a teacher had been raped. A guy jumped me to take my wallet. It was all the money I had in the world. I'd worked hard for it after school, and I needed it for food and the bus. I beat the hell out of him. I was just defending myself. His gang members said I jumped him. My mom was waving a switchblade at the principal. "I'll cut you up! I'll cut you up if you suspend my kid!" It was the first time anyone stood up for me! I was scared to death. She might have been on PCP. Finally they realized one white kid wouldn't jump one black kid with five of his gang friends behind him.

Brad didn't have his dad around when he needed him at times like these. In fact, he had only seen him a few times since he was four. His dad was an Army helicopter pilot who did three tours in Vietnam.

In high school I joined ROTC because I wanted to show up my father, and I thought that if I was in the Army, I could track him down and get close to him. When I was in my senior year at West Point, he promised to visit me during Thanksgiving break. We were going to bond. He never showed up. I called. His wife gave me the news. He'd had a heart attack. Bambi came with me to his funeral.

I've asked myself time and time again, "Why did she choose me?" She could've had any guy at West Point. I guess I had the word "sucker" tattooed on my forehead! I was the kid who fell off the turnip truck. I didn't have a mom or dad who taught me about women or love.

Soap Opera Diva

Vincent had barely finished licking his wounds from his traumatic relationship with Sophia, his Addict bad girl, when he moved into a singles apartment complex in another Texas town. There was a central courtyard with a pool.

A chair was open next to a strikingly attractive Hispanic woman with long black hair. I didn't know she was big stuff because I never watched Mexican soap operas. I asked her out. We started dating. It didn't take long to figure out that Maria was a well-known Mexican soap opera actress because the Latin press was snapping photos of us wherever we went.

Mostly Vincent and Maria went to Latin nightclubs where the bands played conga drums and horns while they danced the night away. He found it exciting to be in a world where she was queen of the hill and they were treated royally.

She asked if I wanted to be in her soap opera. My Spanish was not that good, but she said they would give me the lines ahead of time. I had a minor role. I played a jewel thief who had robbed her of her diamonds. In the soap she had mixed emotions about me. She could have found out that I wasn't a jewel thief after all, that I was the good guy. She could have made me good or bad, depending upon whether she wanted to keep me around – in real life and the soap.

After several months the plot thickened in their real life relationship, as it became clear that Maria was more of a prima donna than Vincent had anticipated.

Maria got a swelled head and I was getting one from hanging out with her. I was like a chick hanging out with a rapper. At first I thought she was just having fun with me. Then I realized she was a confused person. She was in a soap opera in real life. She referred to herself in the third person: "Oh, Maria is thirsty. Go get her a drink." She had convinced herself she was the character – unless she was a method actor and I didn't know she was practicing.

Even in the bedroom Vincent couldn't get Maria to take off her mask.

It was all about the build up: slow kissing, sitting on my lap, all very dramatic and over the top. But once you got past that, it was great, but not over the top. She saw herself as a passionate woman who made men melt, but there was nothing special. And I never knew if her emotions were real.

She started to boss me around. I was the last person on earth to boss around because of my bossy mother. I had had my fill of that. I realized she didn't see me as more than someone to hang out with. She liked me, but she was so into herself that she couldn't care for anyone other than herself. Finally I said, "You're gorgeous, but I'm a human being. I would appreciate it if you would communicate with me, not like you're reading a script from a soap opera." In a theatrical tone, she said, "I'm so fabulous you should be thrilled to be in my shadow!" So I walked. She called me a few days later and told me, "I will allow you to apologize." I didn't. When she was ready to show emotion, it was showtime, but when I realized her whole life was a performance, it was too much.

When we broke up, I was killed off on the soap, murdered. And Maria went back to sorting through her fan mail and reading all the proposals.

Spanking or Spoiling: A Schoolgirl's Dilemma

Paul loved skydiving, made over 1,000 dives, and even became a skydiving instructor and jumpmaster. Yet he dove right into a relationship with Lisa without checking his equipment or heeding any of the danger signs warning him he was about to get his heart broken. Indeed, Paul was ill-equipped to contend with Lisa, since he was still mourning his wife and soul mate, who died a few years before. Lisa was on her own secret mission to inflict suffering on vulnerable men, as men had inflicted upon her when she was a vulnerable little girl.

Paul and Lisa worked for a regional airline in the Midwest,

she in reservations and he in information technology (IT). They had noticed each other at work. Paul thought she was beautiful, but too young for him. Lisa thought differently. She had noticed his still-boyish looks and his meteoric rise to a good position with their company. One morning she emailed him, telling him she had a computer problem and asking him to fix it. She had problems all right, but not with her computer. It turned out to be a ploy to meet him.

She demonstrated interest by the looks she gave me; a man can tell.

But he wasn't sure, so he baited her.

I emailed her that I was doing research into woolly mastodons and I gave her a link to a Scientific American article. She looked it up and read it. It was so improbable that she was actually intrigued by woolly mastodons that it seemed to prove she was intrigued by me.

A week of emails of intensifying interest followed in which Lisa asked Paul about who he was dating and what kind of women he liked. She said she knew he had a reputation at work, which wasn't true, because he never dated at work, but she was fishing. Paul wasn't dating anyone. He was lonely and wanted a way out of the oppressive grieving that was haunting him. He had sold his house, changed careers, and wanted to break out of his old life. One evening Lisa phoned him at home.

124

She said she wanted to come over. I said, "Why don't we meet at the sushi place down the street?" We had a great conversation. It was obvious we were going to go to bed, so I felt we might as well do it tonight. We went back to the house. We made love. She was amazingly practiced for her age. Women like this are few and far between. I was hooked!

We began a mad affair. Sexy emails. I was smitten. She fed into it. I kept telling myself this can't be happening. I had a lot of reservations going in, but the sexual compatibility, her intelligence and beauty – it was bang, I was lost. Lisa was the type of woman that turned heads everywhere she went. Her beauty had an amazing effect on men, turning them into fools and causing them to ignore whomever they might be with, another female perhaps, and just stare as she passed by. Many were the times I witnessed this effect. The majority of women pretty much hated her on sight.

And while Paul had begun emailing her about extinct woolly mastodons, Lisa started emailing him about some sexual fantasies that were very much alive in her mind.

You and I will ride the elevator all day long.... Once the doors shut, I pull up my skirt and slide my hand in my panties while you watch.... When people get on to ride, I stop and we act as if we don't know each other.... Door closes, I pull off my panties.... More people climb on and the elevator is packed.... You pinch me and I let out a faint scream.... Everyone turns around.... We smile wickedly.... Door closes.... We are alone.... I unzip your pants and get on my knees.... You are nice and stiff already.... I take you in a couple of times.... Elevator stops.... I stand in front of you.... You

*are fully aroused.... Door closes.... You pin me against the wall,
pull up my skirt and slide your dick in.... I let out a sigh.... You
fuck me a couple of times.... Elevator stops.... People get on.... I
lean over and kiss you.*

As their relationship progressed, Paul and Lisa started living
out her fantasies.

*She would dress up in her best schoolgirl look, or simply dress
to the 9's with her fuck-me pumps and such. We would visit the
upscale area of town and she would enter a banker/lawyer/broker
watering hole and sit at the bar. The wedding rings came off by the
bucket-full as these oh-so-accomplished males made haste to try
and pick her up. I would wait awhile and then come in and watch.
When I judged the time right, I would walk up and lean into the
gaggle and say something like, "Young lady, you look really fuck-
able. What say we check into the hotel over there and screw each
other's eyes out tonight?" Lisa would grin and bounce off the
barstool with something like, "I've been waiting to hear that all
day. Let's go." And we'd leave together while the jaws hit the floor.*

*Lisa was a sexual libertine and quite kinky. I find kink
interesting and even fun, but I am not a devotee of the sport. If a
partner requests something funky, then I will go there with them if
it does not involve dangerous or gross practices. Lisa liked to have
her bottom spanked and to role-play. We did the daddy/daughter
game.*

As Paul continued diving into the relationship headfirst, he
did not recognize the significance of an email that Lisa sent him,

which was actually a template forecasting how their relationship would end. On the surface it seemed simply as though she was sharing a story about her teenage years, which ironically made him feel closer to her, instead of sending him running for the hills.

Most of my stories are not safe to tell, really bad stuff that I did as a teenager.... There were three of us girls, cousins.... I was the wildest of the three.... When Laura was attracted to a guy... she would worship the ground he walked on. Perhaps she was always too eager and that scared them off.... She would get upset that she could never get the guy, so whenever I came to visit it was my job to seduce him.... She never wanted to get even the way most girls do, she wanted me to seduce him, have some fun, then drop him! I would call him. Of course, I was always prepared. I'm a sweet-talker, could always reel them in so easily.... We would talk, go out, mess around.... After the guy thought things were going well, then I would just stop, leaving him clueless.... It was fun, but I'm not sure where the revenge actually fell in.

As it turns out, Lisa had an unconscious need to get her own revenge on men.

I felt a general unhappiness in her about her life. I tried to talk about it. Then about six months into it, Lisa came over one afternoon and told me she was ending our relationship. She said, "I can't do this anymore. You don't know my history. There are things in my life that I haven't told you about. You're too good for me. I'll only hurt you in the end." She wanted to cut it off. She did some crying and she left a bit afterwards. The next morning at work, I received her "abuse" email. She wrote, "After you read this, you will have nothing to do with me."

In the email Lisa revealed that from the age of six or seven until twelve, she was sexually abused by three of her mother's uncles who were living at Lisa's home after having immigrated from Asia. She and her younger sister were left in their care because her parents worked. She said that a major goal of hers was to accept the abuse in order to protect her sister. She said that two of the men left her alone after a while, but one persisted. This man is the one who still lives nearby. She is forced to see him at family gatherings and when no one is looking he "...grins at me." She hates him and claimed that she would kill him if she had the chance. When she got older, she reported the abuse to her parents. All the uncles denied it and the parents sided with them. They accused Lisa of being the "bad one."

Instead of this revelation driving him away, Paul felt tremendous sorrow for Lisa and still loved her. There had been hints of something deeply troubling her and now he knew what it was. He attempted to persuade her to go for therapy, but she wouldn't hear of it, brushing aside the notion by telling him it happened a long time ago and she was fine. What her revelation did do, however, was put a new light on their sexual relations.

It gave me pause and didn't make me feel good. I could understand why she was seeking pain. I found myself watching our role-playing and realized it went really deep. For example, she played a game where I was the professor and she was the student. In the game, she knew I was interested in her sister. She

had sex with me because she didn't want her sister to be bothered.
It was a convoluted game. When I found out that the reason why
she participated in the sexual abuse she experienced in real life
as a child was because she was protecting her sister, I told her we
couldn't play this game anymore.

After the revelation, despite Paul's assurances that he still
loved her and wanted their relationship to grow, Lisa gradually
became increasingly uncomfortable because she felt he knew too
much. She wanted him to be close, but then she didn't. He was
too close. She never did seek help. She did, however, continue to
move away from their relationship and, within a couple of months,
Paul noticed that there was an older man who started coming into
their company headquarters.

One day I saw a big bouquet of flowers on Lisa's desk. She
said this other man was coming on to her. I thought nothing of it,
but the second time I saw a bouquet, she said, "He really wants
to go out with me. I think I will." I said, "We need to talk about
this. I thought we were in an exclusive relationship." When she
told me about the man, it was like she was sticking a knife in me
and twisting it. She wanted to see us both. I said, "If you want to
see other people, that's fine, but you need to be honest with me."
It wasn't really fine. I was reeling, upset, confused, annoyed, and
wanted to hold onto her. But I couldn't go on, knowing that she was
dating and being intimate with another man. Finally I confronted
her. She said he owned a major business in town and was a multi-
millionaire who was spoiling her. He was also married. He had

his fling, got scared, and dropped her. It didn't take her long to go out with someone else. I told her, "I love you," but she said I was too good for her. She wanted men to abuse her. She went out with five or six men in succession. Then the airline failed after 9/11, and everyone dispersed. Afterwards I tried to get in contact with her, but all the leads I had for her eventually blew away in the wind. I still think about her and am sad for what could have been.

Paul had not known love when he was a boy. Neither one of his parents knew how to nurture. He always felt distant and called them by their first names, rather than Mom and Dad. His dad was a sergeant major in the Army, which meant that they moved constantly. Paul went to 13 schools before he was graduated from high school.

I had to fight bullies in every new school. There was always a bully waiting in the wings, always somebody wanting to beat me up.

Lisa had had to fight bullies, too – her uncles who were sexual predators. Not only had Lisa's parents failed to protect her from sexual abuse, they refused to believe her and rejected her. Her dad was distant. Her mom had angry mood swings when she didn't think Lisa was doing enough for her, and sometimes she even beat Lisa and her sister.

They accused her of being the instigator, the seductress, so she kept living out this role with all the men she was with, unconsciously trying to get them to abuse her in some way, like her uncles had done. She resented her parents and thought, *if you believe I'm a seductress, then I'll be one.* She was seeking to recreate abusive conditions so she could triumph over them, but she was caught in her own self-sabotage. She had been made to feel that the abuse was her own fault and to feel guilty. Her uncles had not been punished, so she identified with the aggressor and became them. She did to others what was done to her – caused pain.

Paul finally came to understand the message of the warning email about her cousins that she had sent him early in their relationship – the one that started out with: "Most of my stories are not safe to tell, really bad stuff that I did as a teenager...."

I couldn't see it then, but, in a nutshell, that email was our relationship, a capsule of her pattern, like she was warning me so she didn't have to feel guilty when she left me. She had a knack for hooking me. I became obsessed. I'm not even sure if she had a cousin.

Famous Sex Sirens

Madonna – Following in the footsteps of Marilyn Monroe, Madonna has used her sex appeal to attain fame and fortune. She has taken it to new heights by being a bolder and more controversial bombshell in everything from music to modeling nude in coffee table books.

Samantha Jones – In the TV show "Sex and the City," Samantha (Kim Cattrall) has a voracious sexual appetite that masks her fear of real intimacy. Afraid of getting hurt by love, she settles for sex and acts like a man pursuing conquests.

Cleopatra – To solidify her grasp on the throne, Cleopatra used her classic beauty and sexual allure, and conquered some of the world's most powerful men, including Julius Caesar and Mark Antony.

Megan Fox – A starlet whose star has begun to enjoy a meteoric rise, Megan has been called "America's Sexiest Bad Girl" on the cover of *Rolling Stone*. If her boyfriend doesn't already have body art, she's been known to make him get a tattoo of her name or face.

Mata Hari – Femme fatale Mata Hari became popular as an exotic dancer. What she lacked in true beauty she made up for in exhibitionism and daring. Thought to be dangerous, she was executed by firing squad as an alleged spy in World War I.

Vivian Ward - In the movie "Pretty Woman," Vivian (Julia Roberts) is a prostitute who Edward (Richard Gere) hires for her sex appeal and escort services. The story has a fairytale ending when he falls in love with her and rescues her from the streets.

Scarlett Johansson – The soft, smoldering appeal of Sex Siren Scarlett has been captured in an impressive list of films, juxtaposing her vulnerability with her sexual power.

Jean Harlow – Known as the "blonde bombshell" due to her platinum locks, Jean was a sex symbol and movie star of the 1930s. In her short life, she had almost as many scandals as hit films.

Dita von Teese – Her fondness for lingerie and retro-Hollywood glamour garb has drawn attention to her, as did her fetish modeling and burlesque routines. Marilyn Manson heard her siren song, but their marriage only lasted a year.

Barbie - When not going after 'Sugar Daddy Ken', one of

the latest incarnations of the Ken doll, Barbie would fit into this category of bad girl. In fact, as the icon of sexual beauty, she has surreptitiously been teaching countless little girls to become bad girls worldwide.

Paris Hilton – Though her efforts to be a star on the big screen have not succeeded, she has become famous for her starring role in "One Night in Paris," the sex tape that her then-boyfriend, Rick Salomon, has made millions on.

Miley Cyrus – This adorable child star has been transforming at an alarming speed into a Sex Siren wannabe. She shed her 'good girl' image and her clothes when she posed for *Vanity Fair* and followed up by provocatively pole-dancing at the Teen Choice Awards.

Chapter 5
THE SEXUAL WITHHOLDER

What does a Sexual Withholder want?

A Sexual Withholder wants to avoid having sex, or to only have sex under certain conditions that she imposes.

Why? To protect her fragile inner self, her wounded femininity. The Sexual Withholder takes the opposite approach to The Sex Siren, instead using the promise of sex to keep her man dangling, all the while hoping she will not have to surrender to it. Like The Sex Siren, this is often a reaction to having been sexually abused as a little girl, but where the abuse has caused her to go to the opposite extreme towards frigidity. After having had her innocence, her maidenhood, brutally ripped away and stolen by a man, she puts up walls to protect herself from all men.

There can be other reasons why a woman becomes a Sexual Withholder. Often these women are terrified of becoming pregnant because they don't love the man they're with and don't want to have a lifelong connection to him, don't want to have a baby out of wedlock, don't want to have a child get in the way of their life plans, or don't ever want to have children. If the woman was adopted, she may feel that staying chaste is a way to curry favor with her adoptive parents, or she may be afraid to get pregnant and

134

be in the same position as her biological mother, having to give her baby up for adoption.

Many Sexual Withholders become alarmed by the loss of control that orgasm entails and cannot let go or surrender themselves to the man or to the feeling of being out of control of their body. These women are often perfectionistic. Other Sexual Withholders are acting out their anger at men passive-aggressively, or are selfish and only want the man to pleasure them without having to reciprocate. They may have gynecological problems, such as dyspareunia (pain on sexual intercourse), causing them to want to avoid sex.

Some Sexual Withholders have had embarrassing, uncomfortable, or unpleasant prior sexual experiences and are hesitant to go there again. Others want to remain virgins until marriage because of religious reasons. And still others are lesbians who want men to be their 'merkins', the equivalent of a 'beard' for a gay man.

And then there are Sexual Withholders who simply do not want men to see them naked because they are ashamed of their bodies. They believe they are too fat, or too flat-chested, or have cellulite or stretch marks, or something else that they perceive as a flaw that will make them undesirable and turn the man off. Whatever the underlying issue is for The Sexual Withholder, she turns it around and, instead of being honest with her man and trying to work the problem out, she uses the withholding of sex as a manipulation and makes the man feel it's his problem that he wants to have sex with her.

The Sexual Withholder surrounds herself with a foreboding barrier, just as in "Sleeping Beauty," that only an illusory prince can traverse. When Sleeping Beauty sticks herself with a spinning needle unaware of the curse put on her by a vengeful fairy, she falls into a deep sleep. A forest of intertwined trees, bushes, and brambles with prickly thorns springs up around her, hiding her from view and protecting her virtue for one hundred years. Finally one stalwart prince overcomes the barrier to kiss and awaken her.

Why do men fall for Sexual Withholders?

The Sexual Withholder makes use of the psychological theory of intermittent reinforcement, rewarding a man's behavior only some of the time with sex. Anyone who has taken Psych 101 in school will remember that intermittent reinforcement of a behavior causes it to be the hardest to extinguish. So even though a man is stonewalled most of the time with this type of bad girl, he is captivated by the promise of a fairytale ending in which he is the prince who claims her as his own.

However, some men who are with Sexual Withholders are ambivalent about sex themselves. Consciously, they claim to want to have sex with her and to be frustrated by the lack of it. But unconsciously, they are fearful of sexual relations and have chosen a woman who is less likely to want to engage in them. In the collective unconscious of our society, there is a myth of the 'vagina dentata', the vagina with teeth. It symbolizes the danger of sexual intercourse, the concept that a woman could bite off or damage a man's genitals, making him feel like less of a man.

Just like The Sexual Withholder, these men may have had embarrassing, uncomfortable, or unpleasant prior sexual experiences and are hesitant to go there again. When they were little boys, they may have been sexually abused or exposed to the primal scene: seeing their parents having sex with each other or with another partner. Religious prohibitions against sex may have been instilled in them. Or, like The Sexual Withholder, they may be terrified of making a woman pregnant because they do not want to be responsible for a baby with her, or at this time in their life, or because they themselves were unplanned pregnancies and know the havoc this can wreak.

Women have used the withholding of sex to manipulate men from the beginning of time. The Greek comedy by Aristophanes "Lysistrata," portrays women withholding sex from their husbands in order to persuade them to end a war. There is much in the way of metaphor in this story. The women have seized control of the Acropolis, which contains the state's 'treasure', and defeat the men's efforts to get through the 'gate' surrounding it. In modern times there have been successful sex strikes in countries like Turkey, where women protested against inadequate water supply; in Italy, against dangerous fireworks; and in Colombia, against gangs. In Kenya political disputes moved into the nation's bedrooms when women held a sex strike to protest against renewed violence. One frustrated Kenyan man filed a lawsuit against the strike leaders, complaining of mental anguish, backaches, insomnia, and lack of concentration.

There is one caveat. Some men who complain of finding themselves with lots of Sexual Withholders need to first ask themselves if it's just that these women were not into them, as one such man confesses:

Ok, let me be honest here. Probably the majority of Sexual

Withholders I ran into were nice women who just did not go for me. I want to let that cat out of the bag and admit that my batting average was not necessarily that of Brad Pitt.

Real Stories from Men on the Dating Front

The Virgin Bride... Who Wasn't

Brandon and Rebecca have been married for 20 years.

Sex has not been high on my wife's priority list. We have averaged about three times a year for at least the last five years. Sad to say, I actually wrote it down on a calendar. My wife wouldn't miss it if we never made love again. She tells me she desires "non-sexual touch" and feels used by my desire to make love to her.

It wasn't always this way, or was it? Brandon and Rebecca met when they were in their mid-twenties and became partners on the swing-dancing circuit in California. Every week after dancing, they would have conversations that lasted late into the night, often discussing their other common interest, religion.

Rebecca was a virgin. Brandon wasn't.

She wouldn't kiss until we got married. At the beginning it wasn't a red flag because I thought it was cool having a woman who wants to not only save her virginity, but even the first kiss, for her husband.

But after a few months of swing-dancing, followed by talking until the sun came up on a romantic mountaintop or in front of the fireplace at Brandon's house, their sex life progressed to "heavy petting."

What should have been a red flag was that we engaged in heavy petting before marriage – but not kissing. I should have realized then that Rebecca seems to have confused and arbitrary views about her sexuality.

Before asking Rebecca to marry him, Brandon told her about his past.

I had a child out of wedlock with a woman I'd dated for almost three years. The relationship ended after she got pregnant and we realized we were too immature for a baby or marriage. The pregnancy drove a wedge between us. The child was put up for adoption. I don't regret not marrying this woman, but I regret not doing the right thing in the first place.

Rebecca was jolted by this news and withdrew emotionally from the relationship because Brandon had been with previous women, while she was saving herself. And she was worried that one day someone would knock on their door to say, "Hi, you're my dad." Still, when Brandon proposed, she said, "Yes," and they were married eight months after their first dance. Brandon prides himself on working very hard to make sex pleasurable for the woman and not being driven to satisfy his own needs. Yet his wedding night was not as he'd long envisioned.

We got to the hotel and started kissing and fondling. After I waited until what I thought was long enough, I started to proceed towards intercourse. Rebecca stopped me. She started crying. She said she was not ready yet. Although I had taken a lot of time to build up, she shut me down completely. After another hour of fondling and so on, we did consummate the marriage. This was another red flag.

During the early days of their marriage, Rebecca and Brandon had intercourse about twice a week and enjoyed having sex in different places – the floor, couch, and deck. But after a year, they started slowing down to once a week, and it went downhill from there. In the beginning she sometimes complained that it hurt each time they had intercourse, so he took it slow and was careful not to thrust too deep.

Then it went from pain to no reaction at all. There are only two days a month when she feels responsive. Otherwise, caressing her breast annoys her, and stroking her clitoris brings her no pleasure. Around 10 years ago, she gave up trying and started rejecting my advances. If I pushed, she would submit, but she would be a rag-doll. Her attitude would be "hurry up, get it over with, so I can get on with my day." I answered a question years ago that I have always regretted. She asked me, "How often would you want sex?" I said, "Every day." This has haunted me ever since.

As Rebecca's interest in sex diminished, her need for non-sexual touching increased. She complained that Brandon didn't give her enough of it, but also complained when he did.

If I touch or caress her, which in the past led to sex, she turns away or takes my hand away from her breast or fanny. She says she's afraid to respond if I'm touching or hugging her because she doesn't want it to lead to sex. And she doesn't want me to see her naked. She says she dresses in the closet because she's gained weight. On the rare occasions when we make love, it has to be in pitch darkness. If I try to initiate sex, she rolls over, complains of a headache, moves my hand away or pretends to be asleep.

Rebecca uses sex as a carrot to get Brandon to do what she wants.

She withholds sex to manipulate me. If I am a good boy and help with the children, do chores, make sure that I always put her feelings first, concede that my feelings don't count and that she is always right... then she will respond more warmly.

Brandon feels rejected and unloved, but he is committed to his marriage.

Our vows were for better or for worse, not just if I get sex every day.

Brandon learned about commitment to an imperfect marriage from his mother.

Growing up, I often wondered why my mom didn't divorce my dad. He was emotionally withholding towards her, unaffectionate, like Rebecca. I later realized my mom didn't divorce him because of her religious convictions. Divorce was not an option.

Yet Brandon's father strained his marital bond, especially as it related to Brandon himself, whose birth was an unwelcome surprise.

Dad had planned his life. I ruined his plans. He wanted to have two children and to retire at 50. My parents' third child was an inconvenience. Their fourth child – me – messed up his life completely. Now he couldn't retire. The house had to be big enough for six and he resented me for being there. During pregnancy my dad accused my mom of sleeping around and insisted that I was someone else's child. But when I was born, I was the spitting image of my dad. All he felt was animosity towards me – no love and no affection. He resented that I was around. He was very hard on me. I could never do anything right. He made me do all the chores perfectly. One of my chores was to empty the trash. If I missed a Q-tip, I was punished. I was either grounded, lost permission to ride my bike, couldn't do an extra-curricular activity, or got a spanking.

Just like his dad, Rebecca made Brandon feel that she wished he wasn't around and deprived him of affection. Rebecca's childhood, which she'd described as a disaster, was lacking in affection, as well.

Neither parent was looking out for her. She was estranged from her father, who was involved with everything else but Rebecca.

Her parents were separated. They were going to divorce, but her mother died from complications of a long illness before their divorce was final. Her mom was sick all the time and in and out of hospitals, while Rebecca was growing up. The last time her mom went into the hospital, Rebecca was on a weekend retreat. They called and told her, but she didn't come home because she didn't think it would be any different this time. But this time her mom died. Her family was angry and never forgave her.

As it turns out, Rebecca withheld more than sex before she and Brandon got married. There was a little family secret she never mentioned.

After we were married I found out that, as young teens, Rebecca and her brother explored one another, playing doctor and other petting games. In recent years I found out that they had also tried to have sexual intercourse. She pretends that she's not sure if they ultimately succeeded. She claims her brother couldn't get it in or something. But I have to wonder if, as time goes on, I'll find out even more....

The 'Merkin'

Before Vincent met his Addict, and then his Sex Siren, he was married. In addition to his traumatic and chaotic childhood, trying to steer clear of bullies in his rough neighborhood and parents fighting at home, his first marriage added to his fears. Vincent was 21 and Margaret was 18 when they tied the knot.

Emotionally I was an infant. Growing up I'd never seen a good relationship between my parents. Margaret was a looker. She looked like Cher. She was smart, fun, a real catch. We did almost everything you could do except intercourse.

Before Vincent married Margaret he knew he didn't like some things in her personality, but he told himself he just had cold feet. They entered marriage with high expectations.

I needed to get more self-confidence and I thought marrying a woman would do it. I was clumsy sexually. Margaret realized I wasn't the person she thought I was. I realized I was not ready to be married. I saw things beginning to happen that reminded me of my parents and it really hurt me. My father worked hard. My mother respected his bringing money home, but never respected him. I saw Margaret starting to show the same disrespect.

After six weeks of marriage, Margaret and Vincent stopped living together. After three months, they divorced.

We just had a mutual realization that we made a mistake and we didn't want to go through life in a sham marriage. We were embarrassed and hurt.

When Vincent started dating again, he found himself with Danielle, a Sexual Withholder. Unconsciously, he chose her after his humiliating first marriage to avoid having to confront his fears about sex. Yet he did not want to take a chance on a virgin who would demand that they wait until marriage.

I wanted to test the merchandise before my wedding night because I hadn't had intercourse with my first wife before I married her.

Vincent met Danielle when they were both teaching art at an inner city school. She was warm, intelligent, and an attractive redhead. The more he got to know her, the more he liked her. But there was only one problem.

She was determined to wait until marriage. I respected her and her feelings, but my penis overrode my desire to marry a virgin. It was a dilemma. I felt bad because I liked her, but I was still reeling from my divorce, where we weren't sexually compatible.

Danielle attributed her decision to remain a virgin to the fact that she was adopted. She wanted to make her adoptive parents proud and happy that they adopted her and thought that the best way to do this would be to remain chaste. She didn't want to disappoint them. She also did not want to risk becoming pregnant and having to give up her baby for adoption.

I thought it was really nice to respect her adoptive parents, but maybe she was making too much of it. Also, I worried that if she was this self-righteous, there would probably be other things that would make for difficulties in our relationship.

Indeed, it wasn't just that Danielle wanted to remain a virgin. She did not want to do anything beyond kissing and hugging.

It was extremely frustrating. She wouldn't touch me – no manual or oral sex – and I had no release at all. I tried everything from logic to begging. She was hoping I'd fall in love enough to tolerate no sex until marriage. Meanwhile, we did nothing beyond junior high school kissing. Times were changing. Soon you would need a microscope to find a virgin.

After several months Vincent broke up with Danielle. It was not what she wanted, yet she didn't waver and still refused to become more sexual.

Danielle had a female roommate who was ecstatic when I broke up with her. Years later I heard she was still living with the same girl. Then I realized that she had been taking care of her needs with this roommate. Back then it wasn't like Ellen and Portia – where women could get married, find a sperm donor or adopt. Most lesbians married men to keep up an image or to have children.

And many still do. Vincent was unaware that he was serving as Danielle's 'merkin', a straight man escorting a gay woman and appearing to be her boyfriend, in order to camouflage her secret Sapphic lifestyle.

The Reluctant Virgin and the College Co-eds

Tyler was a virgin when he finished high school and joined the Navy.

The guys talked about their sex life. I lied about having had sex, but they knew.

He was still a virgin when he left the Navy and went to college. In biochem class during sophomore year at State University, Tyler met Patricia and things started looking up. Chemistry was not just some formula scrawled on a blackboard, but a feeling that was starting to bubble up between them. Tyler sat behind her and couldn't help noticing that Patricia was an attractive girl who made good grades. One day she turned around to him and asked if he would like some help.

She befriended me and offered to teach me "better study habits." She called me "Stewart" because she said I looked like the actor Stewart Granger, a romantic leading man. He had gray sideburns and mine were beginning to get gray. It was not endearing, but I just answered to Stewart after that.

Tyler gladly accepted her offer. She took him to a secluded pond and began giving him mixed messages.

It was kind of picnic style, with a blanket. Patricia dressed very provocatively, revealingly, when we went there. She was very diligent and got right to it. She let me know right off that we were there to study, and no "foolishness." I had no thought of taking sexual advantage. I wanted to, but I was shy. I wouldn't make the first move. She was very dogmatic about nothing happening. No, sex was not on my mind, and she squelched that anyway. After about three outings, Patricia told me she had a "crick" in her neck and asked if I was a good masseuse. That's how I came to actually touch her. She enjoyed my massage. It got a little intimate.

Subsequent study sessions would always involve touching and mild intimacy. Then Patricia revealed more… her true purpose. It was to lure Tyler, a good-looking guy, into becoming arm candy for her. She was a sorority girl and wanted to impress her sorority sisters by having him as her date.

Patricia would allow me some 'liberties', but always stopped me, saying that I could go further only if I'd agree to take her to some of her social events. She wanted me to take her to candlelight ceremonies, dances, parties, concerts, and things like that. I told her I didn't like Greek stuff. None of that was my lifestyle, so in the beginning I declined. But then, tempting me with the promise of more intimacy, I finally agreed and gave in.

In the first year of their relationship, Tyler saw her every day in the lab and the library and they would eat lunch or dinner together. Patricia continued to enjoy Tyler's massages and to hold out the promise of more intimate sex if he continued to be her date. She even took him to dinner if he'd massage her. Tyler never let her pay, but he went with her. They were both bio majors and a lot of their classmates would frequent one particular restaurant.

The other students assumed we were dating. Burt Reynolds was in my class. He wasn't a bio major, but he ate with us sometimes. He was real crude and rough. He assumed I was "banging her." He criticized me when he found out that I wasn't, saying, "You're not with it." He thought I was backwards. One night when it was just the two of us, we were drinking beer and there were girls standing around at the bar or dancing. He said, "Go over and try to get one of those girls." He called me "pussy" and said, "You don't know how to do it." He went down to where the girls were and walked away with one of them. It turned out that she had poison ivy and he got it all over him – and I mean all over.

I was very attracted to Patricia. She'd let me touch her breasts. I wanted to go further. The massages got more intimate. After the first year, we got to petting. I wanted her to be my girlfriend, but I was too shy to ask. She wanted me to touch her more as time went on. One time she wanted me to go further and I was too afraid. She let me know we could go all the way if I took her to more sorority events. I tolerated them to keep having a sexual relationship with her and I thought there might be a chance of going further sexually if I went with her. I was so shy I would never initiate sex.

Patricia didn't have any other boyfriends.

She used me because she didn't think she could get a good date. She didn't want to go deeper into the relationship. I couldn't pin her. She was just showing me off to other girls.

In their junior year Tyler started going out with Abigail, but kept seeing Patricia, too, who didn't seem to mind.

At first I didn't know why Patricia didn't show jealousy. Abigail was very different. When she kissed, it was like kissing a tree. Patricia knew Abigail. One night Patricia kissed me like a tree and said, "Does this remind you of anyone?" She asked if I was having sex with Abigail. I wasn't.

One night Patricia and Tyler were in the lab preserving shrimp and marine animals in ethanol, when she decided to try a different kind of experiment.

She started drinking the ethanol. It was very strong. Patricia got more amorous and took off some of her clothes. I was afraid someone would come in. She was loud, plastered. I told her it was not a good place for this kind of behavior. She said, "Take me to my apartment."

Tyler wasn't sure if she just wanted him to take her home or wanted to have sex when they got there, but he was too nervous to find out once they arrived on her doorstep.

She was a tease. I felt nothing would ever happen, but part of it was my fault. I bungled it. She gave me an opportunity and I didn't take it. She used me to satisfy her needs: dates, massages, petting. I don't know if she liked it or just tolerated it. But she was selfish. She didn't care about satisfying my needs. I just accepted that she was a tease, although I really wanted to be more intimate. I was hooked by the promise, that maybe I'd get lucky.

After the lab experiment fizzled, when Patricia snatched the ethanol for herself to no avail, she and Tyler continued seeing each other in classes and meeting for lunch, but stopped spending as much time together. In their senior year Patricia went out with her zoology professor. Apparently she wanted to show him off, just as she had done with Tyler, since when the class went on a hayride, she and her professor were lying in the hay under a blanket in plain view. The one time Tyler met her parents, they seemed to think the two of them were still in a relationship.

Her mom said, "You're Tyler. We've heard so much about you. We're glad you're not like her professor. You'd better not do anything bad like that."

It had been a scandal. Patricia had dumped her professor and he retaliated by giving her an F in the class, making it so that she almost couldn't graduate. As it was, she wound up not being able to march with the rest of her class at graduation.

Her parents were very, very protective. Her father was a milk toast, just there. In the end Patricia never allowed me to "go all the way." She just kept saying that "someday" she would.

If Tyler really wanted to be more intimate, as he claimed, choosing Abigail as his next girlfriend was a poor decision. She was a freshman music major at the same university, and Tyler liked her because she was quieter, more intellectual, and better-read than Patricia. He was also attracted to her thin body type, dark hair, and pretty face.

Most of all I liked how Abigail looked me in the eye and paid a lot of attention to me. She was my type: very shy, musical, fun to be around, but I could tell she had problems. She was socially withdrawn and didn't fit in with other people. She seemed to be sexless, expressing no desire to have any physical contact. However, when I became more aloof or didn't show her any attention, Abigail would flirt and entice me to be physically involved with her, mostly at the massage level. On rare occasions she'd want to kiss and do some light petting. She lured me many, many times with the possibility of being more intimate. She'd say, "Who knows what might happen?" But she called our relationship "friends," not dating.

Abigail was temperamental, hot and cold, just like Patricia, always holding out the promise of more intimacy, but never delivering. And just like Patricia, Abigail manipulated Tyler into doing things for her – from giving her a massage to going to the university clinic and pretending to have psychological symptoms.

She liked my massages. Sometimes she would take her clothes off when she wanted me to massage her, which led to intimate petting. Then she would say, "This isn't going to happen again. I need it now, but I'm not going to do it again." It was always me giving to her. Once I asked Abigail to massage my back to see if she'd do it. She griped, but she did it. Otherwise she didn't touch or do anything to me. When it got erotic she enjoyed it, though this was not often. It was quid pro quo, but not much quo.

She'd lure me by saying, "I'm really depressed." I'd say, "What do you want me to do?" She'd say, "Rub my back" or "Take me out." She even had me go to the school doctor and say that I was depressed to get meds for her. He gave me a prescription for Miltown (a sedative), and unexpectedly insisted on giving me a shot of something. Whatever it was, it was really strong. I went back to her car and passed out. Abigail left me in the car. The next thing I knew, it was a day later. I was really annoyed that she'd just left me in the car.

Other times, Abigail seemed to taunt him for not making a move on her or dare him to have sex.

She made fun of me. One time she said, "OK, let's do it now." I said, "We can't just do it." Another time she said, "You were lucky I didn't come into your bedroom and jump all over you. I really was horny." Then there was the time we were at her house and she brought a girlfriend over. Abigail said, "Why don't you two have sex and I'll watch?" The other girl said she'd do it. I said, "No."

Abigail was emotionless about everything. Even when her father died, during the first year she and Tyler were "friends," she showed no emotion, despite saying that they had been close. She was always mean to her mother.

Tyler never got to "go all the way" with Abigail. Just like with Patricia, there were false starts and stops. These Sexual Withholders were able to use sex to manipulate him because he had a secret of his own. Afraid of going further, Tyler had chosen women with sexual inhibitions so that he didn't have to confront his own fears.

Ironically, when Tyler was in kindergarten, he was taught by girls from the same State University he later attended, who were interning to be teachers. Their instruction included teaching the kindergarten children how to swim.

The little boys dressed with the little girls. I knew they were looking at my penis and giggling about it. I couldn't swim. The interns told me they would teach me to swim by playing the "sliding board" game. They had me hold onto their boobs and then had me slide down their body. I got erections. The interns said, "You can't tell anyone or we won't play anymore." I never told. I felt guilty about it. This planted the seed: sex was forbidden.

Just like Patricia and Abigail would do later, these State University girls teased Tyler, getting their own sexual pleasure by using his body to "massage" them. In kindergarten, Tyler learned a lesson that would last him the rest of his life: that sex was a guilty pleasure. He remained a virgin until he was 29, when a woman, determined to have her way with him, knocked on his door, ostensibly to borrow a cup of sugar, and took her clothes off before he could stop her. Now Tyler is a professor at a university where students continue to taunt him by propositioning him.

You know how they dress. They're attractive, but it's a dead end.

Taboo Secrets

When Ryan was a little boy growing up in the South, he was curious about sex, especially after he stumbled upon his naked parents having sex one day. This exposure to the primal scene confused him, as it does most little children, causing them to wonder whether their parents are fighting or making love, and whether sex is dangerous. It also made him ambivalent about sex so that when he grew up, he chose a Sexual Withholder for a wife.

In Ryan's senior year of high school, his best friend told him that Theresa had a crush on him. Except for Jan, a girl he had once asked to the movies in eighth grade, Theresa was the only girl who had made her attraction to him known. She was the first and only real girlfriend he had ever had.

I was attracted to her because of her long dark hair that went all the way down her back, and the fact that she liked me.

Before meeting Theresa, Ryan had stumbled upon another taboo sex scene that was difficult for his young mind to comprehend. This one involved his aunt.

I once saw my Aunt Bertha partially clothed when I was seven. Grandpa was helping her with a dress and shut the door quickly when they saw me. She was very cute at 17, with long, coal-black hair down to her waist.

Since then, like a moth to a flame, Ryan has unconsciously been drawn to bad girls with long, coal-black waist-length hair. Theresa was the first of several… but let's not get ahead of the story.

At the end of his freshman year of college, Ryan found himself going through another one of his bouts of depression. His stepmother suggested that he'd feel better if he were married. So, at 19, he and Theresa were wed. They were both virgins.

When we had sex for the first time, I was very disappointed. Then after we were married for three years, Theresa's mother made her cut her beautiful dark hair, telling her that she was "too old" to have such long hair.

These were harbingers of worse things to come. The first unmistakable red flag came when Ryan was in grad school and working at a radio station.

I had to get up at 4:00 A.M., so I went to sleep early. Theresa wouldn't come to bed with me. She was a high school computer science teacher who used her work as her excuse. It was more important for her to grade papers and do lesson plans. I was begging her to come to bed. She'd say, "I've got to get this done." Theresa never explained why she didn't want to have sex, but it was clear she didn't enjoy it. So it was very hard for me to make sexual overtures to her. It took 10 years for us to have our first child because it took forever to get her pregnant.

Theresa let Ryan chase her until she caught him. That is to say, she used the withholding of sex to try to get him to do what she wanted.

If I was nice, if I talked to her family, and was easy and fun to be around, I would have a better chance of her granting me sexual favors. But after her constant rejection, I rarely could be this way. I was sullen and jealous of her family because I was not close with mine.

Theresa came from a conservative religious background. She was closer with her father than her passive-aggressive mother, who had painfully low self-esteem. Her father was a minister.

She married me because she saw her dad in me. When we met I was planning on becoming a minister. I had preached my first sermon at 17. My grandma was so proud of me and certain I would be "the next Billy Graham."

As Ryan found out many years later when they were in marriage counseling, Theresa's family was 'closer' than he had suspected. Though she still refused to discuss how to improve their sex life, a childhood secret explained her aversion to sex.

It came out that Theresa was molested by Uncle Raymond, her father's brother, when she was eight years old. She was on the front porch of her grandparents' house and he was sitting next to her. He put his hand between her legs. She never told anyone because it would have devastated her dad.

Ryan was also keeping a deep dark secret that he had never told anyone: he killed his mother. Or at least that's how he felt.

I was very close to my mom and I was devastated when she died. I was only 14 and in ninth grade. It all started because I was the young runt hanging out with a group of older guys. One night they chopped down a tree. I was the lookout. One of the older guys was arrested for burglary. He made a plea-bargain and told on the rest of us. I was charged with vandalism. I told my dad. He said, "This is gonna kill your mother!" My parents had to pay a large fine. It was one week before Christmas and there went all the money for presents.

My mother was 34 years old. She had high blood pressure with spells that incapacitated her for hours. A few days after my parents found out about my "criminal" behavior and had to pay the fine, my mom picked me up after school. While she was driving, she said, "As long as I live, I'm never gonna help you out again with something like this!" She suddenly felt ill and, instead of driving home, drove to the doctor's office. This was the last time I saw my mom. They took her to the hospital. It turned out she had an aneurysm that burst while she was driving. My dad blamed me. Later that day he came home from the hospital after she died. I was in the kitchen making dinner for my younger brothers. I'll never forget the look on his face when he said, "You know what brought this on, don't you?"

Ryan's guilt over his mother's death has continued to haunt him. He feels undeserving of good girls and more comfortable with the punishment that bad girls mete out to him. As we will see in the next chapter, he soon became prey to Married Women on the Prowl.

Famous Sexual Withholders

Betty Boop – Although Betty was the first animated sex symbol, wearing provocative clothes and batting her eyelashes, her virtue was never compromised. The storyline often reflected challenges to her purity, as she begged would-be rogues, "Don't take my boop-oop-a-doop away!"

Janet Jackson's "Let's Wait Awhile" – The woman in this song tells her man, "There's something I think that you should know. It's not that I shouldn't really love you. Let's take it slow…. Let's wait awhile longer."

Sandy Olsson – In the movie "Grease," Sandy (Olivia Newton-John) refuses to give in to Danny, even though he is forced to reject her because her goody-two-shoes image makes him look bad in front of his cool friends.

Christina Aguilera's "Genie in a Bottle" – The woman in this song warns her man, "You're licking your lips and blowing kisses my way, but that don't mean I'm gonna give it away…. Hormones racing at the speed of light, but that don't mean it's gonna be tonight."

Nicole Kidman – Nicole has sometimes been called "The Ice Queen" by the media for her frozen appearance and demeanor. This has fueled speculation about her relationships.

Avril Lavigne's "Don't Tell Me" – The woman in this song puts her man on notice with, "Guys are so hard to trust…. Get out of my head. Get off of my bed…. Did I not tell you that I'm not like that girl, the one who throws it all away?"

Brooke Shields – Brooke's earliest roles sizzled on screen,

including playing a prostitute in "Pretty Baby." These early experiences of being a sex object undoubtedly contributed to her fear of real-life sex and her determination to remain a virgin. More recently, she relates this to poor body image and claims to regret it.

Anna Wintour – As *Vogue's* editor-in-chief, Anna is famous for her chilly demeanor and has been called the "Ice Queen of Fashion." The Miranda Priestly character, played by Meryl Streep in "The Devil Wears Prada," was 'fashioned' after her. Like Nicole Kidman, this has fueled speculation about her relationships.

Catherine Tramell - In the movie "Basic Instinct," Catherine (Sharon Stone) is a bisexual woman who, despite her predilection for not wearing underwear and famously flashing detectives, is a cold-blooded killer who determines if and when she and her man will have sex.

Chapter 6
THE MARRIED WOMAN ON THE PROWL

What does a Married Woman on the Prowl want?

A Married Woman on the Prowl wants to have her cake and eat it, too. She wants the passion and romance of a forbidden relationship, and the security of a husband waiting for her at home.

Why? To quell her disturbing feelings of dissatisfaction with her husband, her sex life, or her life as a whole. The Married Woman is a rebellious risk-taker who finds herself in an altogether too humdrum situation. She's bored, lonely, and - feeling quite sure that something is missing - goes on the prowl looking for 'it'. She may have suddenly discovered there are attributes that her husband lacks, which she now wishes he had – greater intellect, higher status, a buffer body, more time to focus on her, better handyman skills, an interest or hobby in common with her, the ability to talk about his feelings, and so on.

Of course, the most compelling missing attribute that sends The Married Woman prowling is her husband's deficiencies in the bedroom: his disinterest in sex or his inability to satisfy all of her sexual needs. Our stress-filled modern world is causing an increasing number of men to want to avoid the stress of having to perform in bed, or even to suffer from erectile dysfunction. The prospect of suffocating in a sexless marriage is unbearable for The Married Woman type of bad girl, especially if she is forced to wonder whether she is no longer desirable. She feels justified 'cheating' on him because she feels 'cheated' by her husband and angry at him for not providing everything she needs.

The Married Woman on the Prowl wants to know that another man is in lust or love with her and obsessed with the fantasy of stealing her from her husband so that they can run away together. This 'other man' may well be someone from her past, a star-crossed lover who she now wishes she had chosen instead of her husband – a sort of 'buyer's remorse'. If this 'other man' cheated on her in the past, she may want to settle the score by dallying with him now, but ultimately rejecting him and going back to her husband.

A Married Woman may have no intention of leaving her husband, at least when she begins prowling. She may not want a divorce or may feel that this is not the right time to ask for one, usually because of young children or financial considerations. Or a Married Woman may feel trapped and is, consciously or unconsciously, looking for her affair to be uncovered so that her husband will take the bull by the horns and file for divorce. These Married Women may be looking for another man to latch onto, though it is often out of convenience until she gets her divorced life in order.

A Married Woman who wants to feel single again and unencumbered by family responsibilities may find it satisfying enough to have dalliances where she can fantasize that she is single and then go home to her family. Others may actually want to divorce and feel single all the time. If a Married Woman married young, she may well be inspired to prowl to reassure herself that, if she were on the market today, she could still get a man.

The Married Woman on the Prowl accomplishes her goal of finding a man to trifle with in the same way that the wolf found his prey in Aesop's fable, "The Wolf in Sheep's Clothing":

A hungry wolf found great difficulty in getting at the sheep he could merely stare at, as they frolicked on the hillside, because a vigilant shepherd stood watch over them. But one day, the wolf found the skin of a sheep that had been flayed and thrown aside. The wolf realized that if he covered himself with the fleece, he could pretend to be a sheep and not raise any suspicions. So, as the sun was setting, the wolf put it on over its own pelt and strolled over to the hillside, roaming among the sheep. Deceiving the flock, the wolf led off the lambs, one at a time, making hearty and satisfying meals of them.

As a She-Wolf, The Married Woman lures a man in because she seems to only want an innocent relationship, when all the while she's licking her lips waiting for him to drop his guard so that she can pounce. Just like the wolf, The Married Woman disguises her true motives and puts on a cloak of non-threatening sincerity. A bit put-off because she's married, the man nonetheless succumbs to the temptation of this forbidden love and gets caught up in the whirlwind of never-ending frustration meted out by this unavailable woman. And just like the lambs, he is led to the slaughter.

Why do men fall for Married Women on the Prowl?

A man who falls for a Married Woman on the Prowl convinces

himself that he will be safe with her, that is, not in danger of falling in love and getting hurt, because he has been forewarned that the she is unavailable. He's just intrigued by the secrecy and having fun, or so he tells himself.

Men who are most likely to fall into this trap are those who lost their mother when they were young, through death, divorce, or simply through their mom being emotionally unavailable. This painful abandonment has taught them never to get too attached to another woman. So a woman who is already attached seems, paradoxically, like the perfect choice. Her married status seems to hold the promise of acting as a protective barrier for such a man's heart. Yet, in spite of himself, as the relationship progresses he feels anger welling up towards The Married Woman when she isn't as available as he would like because the long-held anger he has towards his mom is now displaced onto her.

These men, who have been raised in homes headed by their father due to their mother's physical or emotional absence, have become more entrenched in an Oedipal rivalry with him. They are driven to act out their unresolved Oedipal issues by becoming involved in another triangle, as is the case with this type of bad girl. The man finds himself competing with the Married Woman's husband to try to win her, even though this may not have been his conscious intent when he started out.

Also attracted to The Married Woman on the Prowl are men who have been married themselves and have felt ill-used by wives who took them to the cleaners, while making them do the laundry. Such men are attracted to Married Women because they feel, sometimes erroneously, that they are less at risk for the same fate if the woman already has a husband to fulfill such needs. Though this seems like a logical rationalization, even these men are likely to find themselves pining for their bad girl.

Country music artist Mark McGuinn captures the plight of a man caught in the throes of unrequited love for a Married Woman in his hit song, "Mrs. Steven Rudy":

I get up on Sunday, about eight-fifteen
Just to get the paper that I never read
'Cause I know she'll be there barely in her robe
Sittin' on her front porch paintin' on her toes
Her husband's always on the road....
Sometimes Mrs. Rudy calls cryin' late at night
'Cause her and Mr. Ugly have had another fight
We talk awhile, and I hear her smile
When she says thank you, I tell her that she's welcome
Like any friend would do, I only wish she knew....
Imagination, infatuation
I'm what she deserves
I wonder if she thinks about me, the way I think about her....
Oh Mrs. Rudy
That wedding ring is as ugly to me
As your husband is to you
Mrs. Rudy
You don't know, you don't know what you do to me.

Real Stories from Men on the Dating Front

Dangerous Liaisons

After Ryan had been married to Theresa, The Sexual Withholder, for 11 sex-deprived years, he grew increasingly restless and depressed. His mother's death and the guilt he struggled with chronically brought on bouts of depression. He had noted that sex with Theresa was an anti-depressant of sorts, but over the years, what little sex there had been had diminished. This made him more susceptible to look for a 'mood-elevator' somewhere else. Indeed, cheating had the extra benefit of punishing Theresa for her lack of affection, for which she never apologized and just expected him to accept.

When Ryan was working as a professor at a small college, he attended a conference in a neighboring state. When he laid eyes upon Amy, her long black hair down to her waist and a 'come hither' look, he found her irresistible, despite – or because of – the wedding ring she was wearing.

She was all over me in a New York minute. Slender, cute as a bug, she initiated a lot of touching and holding hands during prayers at the conference. I was vulnerable and a scoundrel.

Nothing sexual happened then, but they arranged to meet a month later at a resort mid-way between where they each lived. Ryan told Theresa he was going fishing and in a sense that was true... fishing for trouble.

As an excuse for the first night, I told my wife I was tired from having been out on the lake all day and wanted to stay over. Amy brought her girlfriend as a cover-up for her husband. We got into bed and started having sex. The girlfriend was in the other bed awake. I happened to slip my hand under the pillow and touched something cold and hard. It was a .38 caliber revolver. "What's the gun for?" I asked. Amy said, "In case my husband comes in." I thought, "How stupid am I?" But it was wonderful. I had never had the experience of being able to have as much sex as I wanted. It was very, very exciting.

Before long Ryan stopped worrying about the gun. Amy and her girlfriend planned to stay a couple of nights because she knew he'd come back for more. Ryan left in the morning, but called Amy as soon as he got home.

I told her, "I'm coming back." For the second night, I explained to my wife that I was restless and wanted to go back to stay a little longer. The sex with Amy was just as wonderful this night.

In the morning Ryan felt he needed to go home. He and Amy tried to figure out how they would secretly communicate. After he left he couldn't stop thinking about her.

I gave in and called her at a time when I thought her husband wasn't home. I called to tell her that I was taking my students to an event near where she lived. I had purposely arranged this as an alibi. I wasn't prepared for what came next. Amy said, "You and I committed adultery, so I think we ought to talk about getting married." I had trouble finding words. "Ummm, ummm, we'll have to think about that and talk about it," was the best I could come up with. I think she was feeling guilty and looking for another husband. She complained that her husband just drank beer and watched football. I think I was a turn-on because I was a college professor.

Ryan took his students to the event as he'd promised. He and Amy saw each other there and chatted. They couldn't do more without people suspecting something.

I thought it would be like the movie "Same Time Next Year" with Alan Alda. I showed up at the same conference the next year, but Amy wasn't there. I felt both disappointed and relieved. I liked her, but it was so tiring to make up stories. I didn't want to get divorced. It was just for the sex.

The fling with Amy didn't break Ryan's heart. But with Brianna, the next Married Woman on the Prowl, it was a different story.

Of course, Brianna had long dark hair. She also had nice breasts, a nice figure, and a lot of talent. They were the same age, 34. But most importantly, Brianna was married to the dean of students at the college where Ryan taught. This made her husband an especially worthy Oedipal rival since he was in a position of authority over Ryan, and it made their affair especially dangerous. On top of this, her husband was a muscular Vietnam vet whose office was just across the courtyard from Ryan's, where they would have secret rendezvous.

I was very attracted to Brianna, so I cast her in a play I was producing for the college. Whenever we performed, I gave her a hug backstage, as if to convey "break a leg." She brushed my arm with her hair, gave me flirtatious looks, and was always suggesting that we meet to talk about the play. I was driving home from one of the performances late at night on a dark country road with Brianna in the front and two students in the back. I reached for her hand. She squeezed back. Yes, there was a risk of the students having seen us. But I couldn't help myself.

When they got back to campus, they walked down the hall to Ryan's office.

At the end of making out, I tried to get more sexual. She didn't want to do it there. She said, "Let's get together next week." I was wearing a dark blue winter coat. She was wearing a lot of makeup. I had to stop in a service station on the way home to scrub it off.

The next week they met in a nearby town. Brianna went shopping as a pretext. She got into Ryan's car and crouched down on the floorboards until they got to a motel.

I hadn't seen a woman's body that looked like hers since Amy. Theresa had put on weight after having our two children and was even less interested in sex because she didn't want to show her body.

They went 'shopping' a couple of times a month. Then they risked more by meeting at Ryan's house at noon and had sex in his marital bed.

Was it dangerous? Yes. There were neighbors around and Theresa could have come home. But I was so addicted that I was beside myself. I just wanted to play, to feel attractive to someone, and be attracted to someone.

Ryan was clearly attracted to danger. First there was the gun under Amy's pillow. Then the handholding with Brianna that led into ever more reckless appointments for sex and the looming potential for getting fired.

According to rumor I wasn't the first guy on the faculty to have had an affair with her. One of my predecessors disappeared in the middle of the year. No one knew what happened to him. He was probably fired by Brianna's husband. I never asked. I didn't want to know for certain because I'd get jealous. She didn't complain about her husband, except to say he was a stick in the mud and she liked to have fun. He provided well and they had a nice house.

Their affair progressed from liaisons once or twice a month to three or four times a week. When they were involved with the same play, they saw each other every night. Two years into the relationship, sitting in the car in front of the theatre, a lovesick Ryan brought up the "M" word.

I hadn't planned to say it, but suddenly the words popped out of my mouth. "I'm very much in love with you and I want to get married." Brianna was astounded. She got distant and had a shocked expression on her face. It was as if I'd asked a high school girl to go out with me and she'd said, "Ewww. I wish you hadn't brought that up, we were having so much fun." Finally Brianna said, "I'd be a lousy wife. I already am. Let's leave it this way." I was afraid I'd lose her to someone. I didn't trust her to be faithful if she did this to her husband. When I saw her reaction, I was puzzled. I apologized and said, "I'm kinda rambling." Afterwards we continued our relationship the way it was and didn't seem to miss a beat.

Brianna was a poet, as well as an actress, and would send Ryan love poems. He kept them locked in his attaché case. One day, when he went on an out-of-town trip for work, he left the attaché case in his home office. He returned two weeks later and found Theresa sitting in a rocking chair in their living room. Without saying a word, she got up and dropped Brianna's love letters and poems at Ryan's feet.

She said, "You probably didn't know that I remembered the combination." She'd given me the attaché 10 years ago and we'd set the combination for my birthday. Apparently, she'd been suspicious for a long time. I was stunned. "Are you having sex with Brianna?" she asked. I denied it. She badgered me for eight hours until I finally confessed.

Theresa left the house. When she returned an hour later, she told Ryan she had gone to Brianna's house and recounted what had happened. When Brianna came to the door, Theresa slapped her as hard as she could. The next day, Ryan found Brianna sitting in her car in the parking lot on campus. She rolled down the window as he approached. Though he was still madly in love with Brianna, Ryan told her it was over. He was worn out from Theresa's badgering and he was frightened of losing his job and his children. Brianna didn't want to end it. She hated to admit that she lost to Theresa, but she was afraid that Theresa would tell her husband. Ryan, devastated at losing Brianna, tried drowning his sorrows. He wound up in a psychiatric hospital, suffering from suicidal depression. He ended up losing his job and his children and barely escaped with his life.

Ryan's father was an abusive alcoholic who never hugged him, just belittled him and made him feel like less of a man.

I was in the Thespian Society. He called it the Lesbian Society.

His father was violent towards Ryan's mother and then his stepmother and made Ryan feel helpless and small for not being able to rescue them.

The first time I saw my dad beat my mom, I was in first grade. I was awakened by her screams and I could see their silhouettes on the wall as he beat her. I was scared. I couldn't do anything. The next morning she wore makeup to try to pretend nothing was wrong. When I was 16, I almost used the shotgun he gave me. It was the night I was going to the prom. He was beating my stepmom. I yelled at him to stop. I was going to shoot him in the leg. He was drunk. He said "No prom!" and passed out. My stepmother said it was okay to go to the prom, but I didn't go because I was too depressed.

Ryan wanted to steal his mother and stepmother away from his father because he loved them and hated his dad, but his dad was a formidable rival.

Married Woman Madness

Though Peter is only 26 years old, he has managed to date and bed 12-15 Married Women.

It just happens because married couples lose that spark or men are just too macho for their own good. So when a man like me comes along, who is sensitive, caring, loving, and thoughtful, they lust over me. Some simply want flattery. Others want to take it to the bedroom. Timing is everything.

Helen was the first Married Woman Peter dated and, once this Rubicon had been crossed, sent him down the road to ruin. They were neighbors: Peter in one apartment, Helen and her husband in another.

They lived the punk-emo lifestyle – with dark clothes, the works. She was dragged into it, but didn't like it. We had backyard barbecues and went over to each other's places. When I met her, my intention was not to date or have sex with her. We were just hanging out. After about seven months, we asked each other what this was, whether we were dating. We said no, these weren't dates, and blew it off. There was an attraction, but neither one of us acknowledged it.

Then about a month later, in mid-summer, Helen called Peter.

She told him she had had an argument with her husband and asked, "Can I come and relax over at your place?" She came over. All it took was a couple of glasses of wine and 10 minutes of conversation before they became intimately involved.

We trusted each other. She never told her husband. We saw each other more intimately. She never said, "Let's stop."

But three months later, Peter saw Helen and her husband carrying their belongings out to a moving van. He didn't dare ask them why they were moving.

Maybe she looked in the mirror and felt it was wrong and that they should move so she could detach. Or maybe her husband found out on his own.

Whatever it was, Helen never said good-bye to Peter, and despite his bravado, it really hurt.

There were no emotional attachments to Helen. I knew she was unattainable, so I made the decision not to get attached. I was a little shocked at her sudden departure, but I sugar-coated it, and told myself that it was fun and tried to let it go.

Just like Peter had learned he couldn't trust the first Married Woman in his life, his mom, Helen confirmed the lesson that women are not to be trusted. It was the end of his innocence, and the beginning of Married Woman madness.

Peter met Amanda at a bar, where they enjoyed each other's company more with each drink. It was 2:00 A.M. and her husband was out of town, so they decided to continue their fun by having an 'after-party' at her home. Amanda professed that this was the first time she'd ever done such a thing.

They all say that. She lived in a fabulous home in a prominent area with multi-million dollar houses. She had me park my car on the side street so that neighbors wouldn't see that she was bringing a guy home, and because my car did not fit in with the kind these rich people had. Amanda opened a bottle of wine from their wine cellar and we started having sex. It was extremely passionate. She said, "It's been so long since I've been intimate – about eight months." We had sex all night until the sun came up. We were taking a shower together. She got out and suddenly I heard, "Oh my gosh, you have to leave!" I was thinking, what did I do wrong? It was Saturday. Her husband wasn't supposed to come home yet, but he was coming up the driveway.

Peter could hear the gravel crunching as the car drove closer. Amanda quickly tossed him a towel, put his clothes in a grocery bag, and told him to hide under the bed.

I said, "What if he's tired when he gets home and goes to bed for hours? I'll be stuck under there." I was scared for my life. Does this guy have a gun? In a panic, I wrapped myself in a towel and jumped off the balcony.

Fortunately, Peter landed on soft grass. He ran around to the other side of the house where his car was parked and sped away.

When we were in the bar, Amanda told me that she didn't have any kids, so I'd feel more comfortable coming home with her. But I think she was lying, because when her husband got home, she tossed me a "Dora the Explorer" towel.

And then there was Cindy, a Married Woman whose husband played baseball for the Kansas City Royals. While he was on the road, she started managing the apartment complex where Peter's mom lived.

My mom always wanted me to come over and get her groceries. And she was a big QVC person, so I had to keep on going to the apartment complex office, where Cindy was, to pick up packages of stuff that my mom ordered.

After a couple of weeks, Peter started a conversation with Cindy, invited her out for drinks and went back to her apartment.

Cindy had a lot of battery-operated things. She was sort of freaky. I started going over to her apartment almost every night. Since she lived in the same complex as my mom, my mom saw me and was wondering why I was there so much. After about a month, Cindy said, "I don't want you to leave me." She told me she had developed feelings for me. I reminded her that she was married. I entertained the idea of moving in with her. After all, she was a really cool chick, and if she was good enough for a professional baseball player, then she would be good enough for me. But after a while, I saw that she was getting sort of psychotic. She began calling me every hour with, "Where are you? What are you doing?" I dropped the intimacy level from a 9 to a 2. I had to be an asshole to get her to stop being so clingy. I stopped returning her calls and stopped coming over. You gotta know that if this happens at the beginning of a relationship, something is wrong. Finally, she knocked on my mom's door when she saw my car parked there. I had to take her outside to give her 'the talk'. I said we couldn't be together anymore. About a week later, she moved.

Peter admits that he likes Married Women because they don't usually demand a commitment, and it's harder for them to complain if he continues to date around, since they are married. And he's hooked on the forbidden passion, the sexual thrill.

Peter's childhood was filled with chaos that has unconsciously propelled him to recreate similar chaos in his adult life. His mother was an alcoholic and emotionally unavailable when he needed nurturing.

It affected me a lot. I still don't want to see her or talk to her when she's in that condition. It always annoyed me and her alcoholism drove my father away. When my parents' marriage was deteriorating, I would hear them yelling in the middle of the night. I got good about tuning out negative things. They separated about six times when I was growing up. My dad moved out and I was left with Mom. They each had affairs. My parents got divorced when I was about 14 years old. The lawyer asked me who I wanted to live with. I said my dad because of my mom's drinking.

After high school, Peter moved back in with his mom. He was an only child and wanted to be a good son. He felt guilty leaving her alone and held out hope that she would be more nurturing than she'd been in the past. But after a year, he couldn't take it and left.

When my mother's drunk, I want to be as far away as possible, but she depends on me. She treats me like a mama's boy. I didn't feel comfortable bringing women back to my mother's apartment. She always wanted to be in my affairs, but it was private and personal. I'm the only man she has in her life now, so she wants a lot more attachment.

It's no wonder that Peter is afraid of attachments to women who would totally depend on him like his mother does. So having superficial relationships with a string of Married Women seems like a safer road, until they hurt him when he discovers that they never had genuine feelings for him, after all.

I knew I was their temporary fix, so I never got attached and never got hurt. I figure I'm just gonna use them the same way they use me.

Indeed, Peter has gotten "good about tuning out negative things," except when the pain of these shallow Married Woman relationships breaks through his denial.

Attention Deficits

When Ashley broke up with Charles as they each left for different colleges, he was devastated. They had had a stormy relationship in high school, but he hadn't seen her abandonment coming. Both on the rebound, they became engaged to other people during their freshman year in college, who they were not as in love with as they had been with each other. Ten years later when they reconnected, Ashley confessed that when she had called Charles in the middle of freshman year, it was with the intention of getting back together. But not knowing this, and feeling hurt and defensive, Charles had pretended that he was happily dating and doing just fine without her. These star-crossed lovers then married their fiancés.

Flash forward 10 years. A mutual friend told Ashley that she had just seen Charles at their 10-year high school reunion. Seemingly out of the blue, Charles got an email from Ashley, and so began a series of emails and phone calls; each becoming more flirtatious than the last until Ashley emailed him that her husband was beginning to get jealous that they had reconnected. So he acquiesced to her desire to stop all communication.

But Charles couldn't resist going to their 15-year high school reunion, and apparently neither could Ashley, which is how it came to be that he found himself driving a bunch of old high school friends to the reunion – including Ashley.

It was very surreal, like no time had passed, except that I was in my car on my cell, having a political insider conversation with a guy from work. It was like a dream where you're back in high school with all the knowledge you've gained since then. Ashley was in the front seat next to me, like old times. She was still beautiful with her great smile, still smart, sardonic, and very passionate about her beliefs.

Nothing happened that night, except flirtation. They started emailing again, and the flirtation factor increased. They figured out a time and place to meet each other, without waiting for another high school reunion.

I suggested we could go to dinner without anything improper happening. She wrote, "I don't think so. I think I'm falling back in love with you." I flew to her hometown. She came to my hotel. She walked in the room and we started kissing immediately. We had not had intercourse in high school, so we finally consummated the relationship. It was very passionate. She had to go back and relieve the babysitter, so she couldn't spend the night. We had no regrets. We joked about putting something in the alumni bulletin. At the beginning, neither one of us considered leaving our spouses. But I was head over heels. Ashley really idealized me. There was something very pure about how she felt about me and saw me. My wife is sometimes sexually indifferent to me. I've felt neglected in my marriage.

I bought Ashley calling cards so she could call me from her cell without my number showing up. We talked several times a day and, in between, sent very explicit emails back and forth. She didn't like me talking about my women friends and called one of them "Lady Voldemort." Ashley kept saying, "I want to know everything inside your head." I'm a very private and cautious person, so this was making me uncomfortable. She set the rules: "I'm never going to ask you to leave your wife, like I won't leave my husband – at least not while there are kids in our homes." I agreed. I didn't know where this was going – but I knew I liked the very explicit emails. The only ones I didn't like were when she talked about having sex with her jock husband. Like when she wrote, "Jim is horny, so I gave him a blow job." But I thought it would all be fine, considering that we were both married – I recognize the paradox there – and living in two different states.

Charles and Ashley arranged another rendezvous, this time for a whole weekend in Martha's Vineyard, under the pretext of work-related meetings. It was the most time that they had ever spent together, and they used it for very intense lovemaking, talking about what might have been if they had stayed together after high school, and venturing out for the occasional restaurant meal.

It was hard on me because I was paranoid about someone seeing us, and I didn't like having to call home and put on a charade. I was enjoying being with her, but I was very conflicted. Ashley picked up on it and said, "You're closing yourself off to me and I'm feeling emotionally exploited." I was thinking it's not supposed to be like this if it can't lead to anything. I was not in a position to leave my wife. I admitted to Ashley that my feelings for her had been rekindled. I was still in love with her, but I was struggling with having a secret relationship.

When they got home, Ashley sent Charles emails about sexual fantasies she expected them to live out, while he was trying to cope with the strain of a baby crying through the night, the absences necessitated by his wife's work, and the challenges of his own career. He took his family on vacation to try to make things better and became distracted from Ashley.

I did not give her the attention she wanted. Then I confused her birthday with someone else's. She exploded and yelled, "You're

182

taking advantage of me. All you wanted was the sex. I'm not going to talk to you anymore!" I didn't hear from her for a couple of months. Then she emailed again, demanding a full accounting of why I got into the relationship with her. Before I responded, she sent another email. I could tell her anger was escalating. She wrote, "How dare you! We carried on an intimate sexual relationship!" Meanwhile, I was trying to put my life back together. I wrote back, "It was never my intention to hurt you. I believed I was in love with you."

Ashley wanted to know if I ever thought of leaving my wife. I said, "Yes, but we'd agreed we wouldn't ask each other to leave our spouses." She never said she wanted to leave her husband. She wanted me to say it to validate her feelings and to show her that I also had the fantasy of running away together. I thought we'd see each other once or twice a year, but not upset the applecart. I never wanted to ask her if she wanted to leave her husband because I was afraid she'd say, "Yes."

Despite his lingering feelings for Ashley, Charles was determined to make sure his children grew up in a traditional intact family.

My mother died just before my fourth birthday, which, of course, has affected my relationships with women. It's why I want my children to grow up with a mother and father in the house. I never want to take a chance of losing them.

Charles can only recall flashes of scenes with his mom: fixing his lunch, taking him to school, sitting next to him on the bed. They were warm memories; very much in contrast to the cold woman his father married a couple of years after Charles's mom died.

My father never talked about my mother's death, even at the time she died. I knew she was dead, but I didn't understand what that meant.

Charles's stepmother reluctantly took over the maternal role and said a lot of hurtful things to him, like how she wished she wasn't his stepmom. She made Charles take care of the two sons she then had with his dad.

My stepmom focused a lot of attention on my brothers. She wouldn't give me rides home from school if I wanted to stay for extra-curricular activities, but she would do anything for them. My dad would tell me to do whatever she wants. He never took my side.

It was understood that neither Ashley nor Charles would tell their spouse about their secret romance, so Ashley's next email shocked him.

She wrote, "I told my husband, for reasons I can't explain, that we had a flirtatious romantic relationship. I can never talk to you again." It really pissed me off. I felt she totally took advantage of me.

This hit Charles hard because it was a sudden inexplicable abandonment, just like his mom's death. And he was very worried because Ashley's husband had always suspected that she had unresolved feelings for him left over from high school. In fact, Charles had good reason to worry about Jim becoming a threat.

On a social Internet site, someone started talking about skeletons in my closet. Then I got an email from Jim that said, "Ashley finally confessed to me about that weekend in Martha's Vineyard. You must be proud of yourself for having fucked another man's wife! She told me you were bad in bed, have a small dick, and you're fat. She described the experience as awful." It flipped me out!

Yet this didn't stop Charles from succumbing to temptation with another Married Woman, a few years later who was feeling neglected by her husband, and pursued him with a vengeance. Soon after they met, through their commitment to the same cause, Ellen connected with him on Facebook and reminded him that at the last event she had shoved balloons into the trunk of his car.

She sent flirtatious emails: Wouldn't I like to go away with her for the weekend to the beach? I said, "No, I have to be with my family."

Despite Charles's hints that he was off-limits because he was married, Ellen showed up at the hotel in town where she knew he was staying for meetings and went up to his suite. Charles had been drinking.

Ellen was very flirty, with long red hair and a great body. She had a sluttiness to her, like she'd be a party, someone who would like to cut loose. She started kissing me. I backed off. She sat on the floor, slipped her hands into her jeans and started playing with herself. Her masturbating for me was really hot. We kissed again and had sex in the bedroom. I tried to make my situation clear, to give her no false promises so there would be no accusation that I'd led her on, like with Ashley.

But this didn't discourage Ellen from being hot and heavy with her phone calls and emails at all hours of the day and night, asking him to meet her again. Looking back, Charles realizes that her constant demands for his attention should have been a red flag, but he was enjoying her preoccupation with him, especially since his 'attention deficits' had always been his weakness.

I didn't know that Ellen was married until after she'd seduced me, which was actually the image she wanted to project. She seemed to have much greater free time than someone who was married and had kids. I only found this out after pressing her on some details of a trip she was taking, about a week after we'd had sex. She said she absolutely did not want to leave her husband.

With that in mind, Charles met her for "nooners" while they were working on a project for their cause. Then it started to unravel.

I thought things might be more secure with Ellen because she was married with kids, but I didn't count on her own issues of instability. Out of the blue, she called me at home and announced that she was pregnant! She'd told me she was on the pill. When we first hooked up, we were drunk, and we had unprotected sex. I went into panic mode and had a sleepless night.

Ellen began monopolizing Charles with a seemingly endless stream of phone calls and private encounters, demanding that they keep discussing their options. She was evasive and vague about the details of her pregnancy.

She never really articulated what she wanted to do or what she wanted me to do about her pregnancy. She did, however, keep threatening to come clean to her husband. She seemed to be hinting at a physical threat from him, but my greatest fear was her husband telling my wife. Meanwhile, I kept trying not to freak out while I was with my family.

Charles buried himself in work. A few days later, Roy, a colleague, who was working on the same project, confided in him that Ellen had told him she was pregnant with *his* baby. Since Roy didn't trust her, he'd needed to find out for himself. He invited her over to his house, seemingly for another tryst, and turned off the toilets so they wouldn't flush. Roy told her they were broken, but actually, he'd concealed a pregnancy test in each of them. After Ellen urinated, he checked the test, saw that she wasn't pregnant, and confronted her. Charles couldn't believe his good fortune. He had dodged a bullet.

I was relieved beyond all get out! The phone rang. It was her. I told her, "I don't believe you're pregnant, and if you are, I'm not the father!" She became unhinged. I told her I never wanted to speak with her again. About a week later, Ellen called me – and Roy – to say she miscarried due to a high fever. It was her way of not admitting she was never pregnant. It was all a ploy to get attention! But it nearly destroyed my life. That maxim is not true – that Married Women are safe. I am completely scared straight!

Portrait of a Lady

Hank couldn't help but notice Michelle in the cafeteria of their East Coast corporate offices because she was one of the prettier girls there. He told himself he should talk to her, but at 29, and new to the company, he needed time to work up the courage. Then one day, she seemed to disappear. He chastised himself for not having approached her sooner. When she reappeared six months later, Hank had to say something. He did and they started dating.

I liked Michelle because she was fun, very eloquent, intelligent, motivated and high up in the organizational ranks, even though she was only a year older. That was very attractive to me. And she had great hair. It was always bouncy and voluminous.

We started seeing each other every day. We spent our lunch breaks together at my apartment. At night, we went out to dinner, went dancing, or stayed in and made dinner at my place. Sometimes Michelle would say, "I need to get home." Other times she spent the night. There was a lot of playing jokes on each other and laughing. She left little post-it love notes around my apartment. We developed a really cool relationship. She met my friends. They thought I had quite a catch, too. We started saying the "L word." I was beginning to think Michelle was the one.

Except for one three-day weekend when they went out of town together, Michelle and Hank didn't see each other on the weekends.

She was a promoter-model and was always busy with celebrity charity events, like the Jimmy V Gold Classic. It fit in with my image of her as a powerful executive. She showed me photos of her hugging with Michael Jordan, Michael J. Fox and other celebrities. She told me she couldn't bring a date to these events. Her unavailability was frustrating, but it increased the attraction because I thought when she wasn't with me, she must be doing even cooler things. I felt like such a lucky guy. I'm the one who gets to laugh and have sex with her.

Eight months into what seemed like an idyllic relationship, Hank decided to surprise her. He made the trek to Michelle's office in a building on the opposite side of company headquarters. He had never been there before, since they worked in different departments. But he had a gift for her. She had mentioned that she was out of her favorite perfume, Angel, so he bought her a new bottle.

I wanted to show her that I was paying attention. I wrote out a card that said, "Thinking of you. Love, Hank." I also stopped and got her what she normally liked for lunch on my way up to her office.

As Hank appeared in her doorway, Michelle was on the telephone. She looked up at him with those pretty eyes that always made him melt and said, "Oh, my God!"

She seemed happy to see me. I was looking around the room as she was finishing her call and I saw a framed picture of her in a wedding gown on her windowsill. I thought to myself, she must've been married at one time and divorced. After she hung up, she said, "You know, I've been meaning to tell you about this." I suddenly realized maybe she's not divorced. I said, "Are you married?" I was stunned. My whole perception of what was going on was suddenly rearranged. I had been in the dark the whole time we were dating. She admitted she was married. I blotted out what she said after this. I was so dazed that I walked out of her office still holding the gift and the card.

Hank couldn't believe what had happened. Michelle hadn't expected to be discovered and wouldn't have been had it not been for Hank's little surprise. The surprise was on him, however.

I had the rug pulled out from under me. It was not real after all. She had said it was real.

After Hank found out the truth, he was confused, hurt and still in love. They continued seeing each other for a few more weeks, but it was strange and could never be the same. He reproached himself for all the red flags he had missed.

We only met at my place, not hers. Even though Michelle lived farther away, I had offered to pick her up and suggested that we go to her place instead of mine all the time. She said she liked it better at my house. She wanted to spend time "in" with me. We'd watch movies or have my friends over to play games. Our circles simply did not overlap. When we did go out, she would always have some "special place" that she wanted to go to, and it was usually quite a distance away from everything. I never thought anything of it, really, except that to me, Michelle seemed even more worldly since she knew about these cool restaurants way outside of our local zone.

She only gave me her cell number, and many times she put it on silent ringer. I just thought she preferred the cell and never questioned why she turned off the ringer because I thought she was taking a nap, getting a massage, or was with celebrities at an event. I never thought to question whether Michelle was at home with a husband. Looking back, it seems strange, but at the time I didn't think anything of it. I was aware she had another life without me, but I thought she was doing glamorous stuff, not at home doing the laundry.

Though he dreaded doing it, Hank's morality and the pain of betrayal made him break off their relationship, but not before a really rocky ride and lots of late night phone calls. Michelle claimed it was complicated. She told him that her marriage had not been good for a number of years, and that she didn't want children with her husband. But she concluded with, "I can't just leave him," as though this should have been obvious. She half-heartedly apologized, but countered with, "You never asked if I was married."

I was like the female. During one of our late night calls, I said,

"I thought this was going somewhere." She said, "It was just an affair." I went, "Whoa, maybe for you, but no one told me." That's when I knew it was over. When Michelle called it an "affair" it totally diminished what I thought we had. It finally made me see she was only using me. Looking back, I think that part of her allure was her unavailability, except on her schedule, and her secrecy. It seems so obvious after the fact, but it never even crossed my mind that she had a secret 'other life'.

Hank's last words to Michelle were, "Don't call me until you're single," and so far, she has never called.

So what made Hank, an otherwise brilliant man, who went off to become CEO of his own company, susceptible to a bad girl and blind to her manipulative behavior? Why didn't he ask the questions that would have blown her mysterious cover?

I was taught that to be a good little boy you don't interrupt adults, don't speak until spoken to, and don't ask questions.

But there was a deeper reason. There was a secret that Hank had always been afraid to find out more about, one that haunted his childhood.

Hank's parents met when they were toddlers. They grew up next door to each other. Home movies show them sledding together. When they got to be pre-teens, they became girlfriend and boyfriend and seemed destined to live happily ever after. That is, until high school, when a girl named Peggy Sue entered the picture, won his dad's heart, and caused his dad to do the unfathomable – break his mom's heart. After high school, Hank's mom eventually won his dad back.

But whenever the song "Peggy Sue" was played on the radio, his dad got a glazed look on his face as he remembered the romantic moments they shared and still seemed to be yearning for her. Sometimes, when his dad was thinking of Peggy Sue, he obliviously began singing this song on his own, until Hank's mom would punch him in the arm or show some other sign of displeasure. Growing up, Hank would peek in his dad's yearbook to look at pictures of Peggy Sue. She was the mysterious 'elephant-in-the-room' of his childhood. It taught him not to ask too many questions because the answers could destroy one's innocence.

Indeed, Hank had even more reasons to feel that his father was not doing right by his mom, and that Hank would have treated her better. Until he was eight years old, his mom stayed at home.

Mom was very nurturing, always singing songs to me, cooking, and holding us kids all the time. I felt sorry for my friends who didn't have a mother like mine.

But when his dad, an outdoorsman who did not believe in working his way up from the bottom, had a mid-life crisis, he simply decided to give it up and retire. This meant that Hank suddenly lost his nurturing mom, who then had to become the breadwinner. This crystallized Hank's rivalry with his dad and sent him into rebellion.

Hank always loved his mom's long, shiny, bouncy hair that made him think of the Breck or Pantene commercials, where a fan blew the models' hair in glamorous ways. Michelle, too, had reminded him of one of these models… and his mom.

Back To School Daze

When Patrick was at university, he got a couple of 'incompletes' – not in his courses, but in his relationships. Long after graduation, he's still trying to complete them. However, now it's more difficult... since these ladies are married. The only relationship he did complete was with Susan, who was already married to one of his college professors when he met her.

When Susan, a grad student wearing a wedding ring, walked onto the set of the big musical Patrick was also cast in, he dropped his lines and picked up the electricity between them.

Susan had a vibrant presence. She was very smart and we had great conversations. We were at opposite ends of the political spectrum, so I enjoyed talking politics with her. I didn't have an ethic for or against being with a Married Woman. I was not terribly introspective at the time. I didn't worry about getting hurt. All I knew was that she was wildly attractive and interested in me.

Throughout the run of the play, Patrick and Susan socialized during rehearsals and ended up back in his student apartment, creating love scenes of their own. She never disclosed the nature of her discontent with her husband, so Patrick never learned what caused her to stray. Then Susan brought down the final curtain.

She ended it. She stopped showing up. She stopped responding to my calls. Then I got a letter from her husband: "Mr. Johnson... My wife has committed grave errors, of which you were a part.... You are morally bankrupt.... Never intrude your odious presence into our lives again." It was a stern letter. It made me think I wasn't the first, but that the "grave errors" were with me. I don't know how he found out. She may have told him because I sensed that she felt guilty. I felt sad. I missed her and her attention. Her husband couldn't have gotten me expelled or anything because it was not against university policy to have an affair. But it weighed on me and I was desperately hoping to avoid a confrontation. I guess Susan wasn't about to leave her husband for a college kid with no prospects.

Patrick eventually married and had children. He never cheated on his wife, but her relentless criticism led to his falling out of love with her and a distressing impression of being choked by his marital bonds.

When he separated, Patrick became consumed with memories and regrets about Pearl, another woman he'd loved at university, the most haunting of his 'incompletes'. He long thought of her as the love of his life and the one he let get away. They'd had a relationship for over a year.

Pearl was the great love of my college years. I wasn't ready to get married. I was an immature jerk. She ended it because she didn't trust me – with good reason. I hadn't been true to her. One stupid mistake can change your whole life.

I've had some commitment issues, even back in college. I would meet a woman, like Pearl, charm her and get her interested in me. Then I'd cheat. When she grew disillusioned, she'd leave me. Then I became distraught, protested and implored her to get back together. I didn't stalk her, but I went to remarkable extremes. When Pearl ended the relationship with me in college, I was sad.

About a year after it ended, I was traveling to a foreign country in search of my roots. Dreaming of Pearl, I woke up freezing and crying. I wrote her a letter saying that I would meet her at The Tea Shop, a place where we used to hang out, at a specified time, soon after I returned. She wrote me back saying, "I won't be there and I suggest you don't come either." I went because I hoped she would change her mind. She didn't. I would've married her then.

About twenty years after college graduation – one marriage, two children, and a successful career later – Patrick returned to his university town for a social event. Across the room, who did he see? None other than his star-crossed lover, Pearl. Not surprisingly, she was already married with children. They agreed to continue on to dinner to catch up.

I confessed my attraction to her, which had lasted all of these years, even throughout my marriage. She listened. We both got teary. Pearl told me I had made a major impact on her life; I had caused her to have lasting trust issues. She didn't talk about her husband. We reminisced about our history and what it had meant. Then we went our separate ways. I found another reason to return to our university town, and we arranged to get together again for dinner. It turned into a kissing match when we got into the car. It was clear that I still loved her.

Pearl and Patrick began to get together whenever they could sneak away, about three times a year, always in private hotel rooms where they re-consummated their relationship. For two years, it became increasingly intense emotionally and sexually.

I fell more and more in love with her. The same things that attracted me the first time attracted me again. I loved her intelligence, her soulfulness, her independent spirit, her beauty, her talent in the arts, and her interest in me. I felt an inexorable force drawing us together. It was frustrating when I couldn't be with her. Pearl agreed that what redeveloped between us was inevitable. She'd say her current life wasn't what she wanted. She wished it were different. She wanted this.

But Pearl would also say that she didn't see a future in it. She told me she had no intention of leaving her husband because she'd made a lifetime promise to him. And she felt guilty. She expected something bad to happen because of what we were doing. Then "family circumstances" came up. She may have thought that this was the punishment she anticipated. She wouldn't divulge the reason, but she let me know her family needed her more now.

Finally, she said what I had been dreading. "I don't want to make love anymore! The romantic piece is over!" I saw her a couple of times after that. We only kissed and didn't make love. Then it dwindled down to only emails and rare telephone calls. I was very sad. I thought I had a chance of winning her away, but it turned out to be hopeless. Pearl broke my heart.

During this time, when we'd reconnected, I asked her why she didn't come to The Tea Shop that day, back in college. She said she'd decided she was done with me because I'd broken her heart.

But Pearl had not been done with him. She'd made him fall in love with her all over again, so she could break *his* heart.

Indeed, Patrick sabotaged his relationship with Pearl in college because he was fearful of the love he felt for her. It wasn't safe to marry her then because he was afraid she'd ultimately reject and abandon him, like his mom had done. So he waited until Pearl was married and it was safer to get close because deep down he knew that her husband was there as a rival and a barrier. In the end, he could pretend to himself that Pearl didn't leave her husband, not because she didn't love Patrick more, and not because she was just trying to settle their old score, but because she was simply honoring her marriage vows.

Neither one of Patrick's parents ever cheated. His mom stayed stuck in an unfulfilling relationship with his dad. After 30 years of marriage, she divorced him. She was a career woman who was sure she would have gone further, and perhaps even become a famous painter some day, if she hadn't had domestic demands put upon her. So, frustrated and full of rage, she simply walked out, leaving her husband and 14-year-old Patrick behind. Once a month, sad Patrick took the four-hour train ride to see her, even though "she didn't ever ask for me." And so we come to understand the strength of Patrick's need to feel wanted by a woman and his fear of getting too close. As we'll see in the next chapter, he has now graduated from Married Women to Commitment-Phobes.

Famous Married Women on the Prowl

Meg Ryan – When Meg met Russell Crowe on the set of their thriller "Proof of Life," she found him more thrilling than her husband, Dennis Quaid, whom she promptly forgot about until she divorced him after 10 years of marriage.

Francesca Johnson – In the movie "The Bridges of Madison County," Francesca (Meryl Streep) is a Midwestern housewife, whose brief rendezvous with a passing photographer while her family is at the fair lifts her out of the dust and brings back her passion for life.

Madame Bovary – In Gustave Flaubert's novel, Emma is a boring doctor's wife who tries to escape the emptiness of her provincial life by engaging in adulterous affairs. When they, too, prove painfully disappointing, she commits suicide.

Mistress of Martin Luther King, Jr. – According to an historian, Martin Luther King, Jr. admitted to his wife Coretta that he'd carried on a five-year romance with a married woman.

Emily Horne – This serial bigamist married four men by the age of 23 and confessed on her honeymoon to her fifth husband that she was still married. Emily's troubled childhood sent her on a search for security in marriage, hooking men with sex and lies: claiming to have been pregnant, raped and dying from cancer.

Anne Heche – Anne was still married to Coley Laffoon when she met James Tupper on the set of the TV show "Men in Trees." She divorced her husband for James and went on to have a son with him.

Annie MacLean – In the movie "The Horse Whisperer," Annie (Kristin Scott-Thomas) and her husband have fallen out of love. When she brings her daughter and her horse to be healed by The Horse Whisperer, Annie lets him heal her heart, too, but abandons him to return to her family.

Lady Chatterley – In this classic novel by D.H. Lawrence, Lady Chatterley feels oppressed by her loveless marriage to Clifford. Her frustration leads her into a passionate love affair with Oliver, the gamekeeper of the estate, who is ultimately fired.

Anna Karenina – In Tolstoy's classic novel, Anna is shunned by society and loses her children because she chose a torrid love affair with Vronsky over life with her husband. This ends badly in Anna's drug abuse and suicide, and Vronsky's disillusionment and decision to volunteer for a war from which he doesn't expect to return.

Mrs. Jones – In the song "Me and Mrs. Jones" by Billy Paul, her lover laments, "We both know that it's wrong, but it's much too strong to let it go…. It hurts so much inside. Now she'll go her way and I'll go mine."

Constance – In the movie "Unfaithful," Constance (Diane Lane) has a seemingly random meeting with a stranger that turns into a romantic affair. Her husband finds out and right after he kills the stranger, hears her leave a voicemail message saying that she wants to end the affair.

Audrey Williams – Audrey, the first wife of country music singer, Hank Williams, was unfaithful to him. He wrote his hit song "Your Cheatin' Heart" thinking of her, and warning her that "Your cheatin' heart will tell on you" and "will make you weep" with guilt and remorse.

Julia Biggs – Julia (Whitney Houston), in the movie "The Preacher's Wife," feels neglected by her husband, whose attentions are fixed on his church and its problems. When his prayers bring an angel (Denzel Washington) to help, Julia starts having some devilish ideas.

She Wolf – Shakira's lyrics warn men of the dangers of a Married Woman: "A domesticated girl that's all you ask of me… I've been devoting myself to you… Not getting enough… incentives to keep me at it… so I'm gonna go somewhere cozy to get me a lover…. S.O.S. she's in disguise. There's a she-wolf in disguise, coming out, coming out, coming out."

Chapter 7
THE COMMITMENT-PHOBE

What does a Commitment-Phobe want?

A Commitment-Phobe wants to avoid getting too close to a man, so that she can keep her options open and be free to change her mind about him or anything else in her life.

Why? To prevent herself from surrendering her heart to a man, for fear that she'll make a mistake and choose someone who runs away with it. We're all familiar with women's complaints that men won't commit, but we rarely hear about The Commitment-Phobe who is a woman. Indeed, many women hide behind their tales of woe about relationships that don't end in marriage when, in fact, they are deathly frightened of making that commitment themselves. Carrie Bradshaw, of "Sex and the City," is a prime example. Always running after Mr. Big – until she gets close to catching him – she treated the faithful and forlorn Aidan Shaw quite shabbily because he was too available. There were no deal-breaking obstacles to overcome with Aidan, as there constantly are with Mr. Big. These obstacles keep the relationship on an exciting precipice, while things with Aidan were too comfy and too close. Carrie, like many Commitment-Phobes, gave her heart away to her father as a little girl, and he took it and ran.

Fear is the overriding emotion of The Commitment-Phobe. She is afraid of a man seeing her flaws up close and personal and then realizing that he doesn't want her. She is frightened of making the wrong choice in a man since she believes that she will just get to pick once. In order to know which man will take her to the happily ever after ending, she feels she needs to test the merchandise longer. Whereas men usually let their penis decide who he's going to commit to, a woman pauses to ask herself, not just how cute he is, but whether he'll be a good provider and good father. The Commitment- Phobe not only pauses but stops dead in her tracks.

In "Goldilocks and the Three Bears," Goldilocks wanders into the bears' cottage and feels entitled to sample the porridge, the chairs and the beds until she finds the one that is "just right" – not too hot or cold, too big or small, or too hard or soft. When the bears find her asleep in the bed, she awakens, screams and runs away, so that she doesn't have to confront her choices.

Many Commitment-Phobes have cold feet because they are still devastated by one or more prior relationships that seemed to be heading towards marriage, until the man suddenly and inexplicably backed out. They don't want to walk down that path again after suffering the hurt and humiliation of announcing that this was the one, only to be left with a stack of *Modern Bride* magazines, gifts from an engagement party or – even worse – left standing at the altar. Of course, The Commitment-Phobe's biggest fear of all comes from her first broken relationship, the one with her dad. Unconsciously, she's terrified that if she gets too close to a man, he will break her heart like her father did, when he left her standing at the windowsill wondering where he went off to – another woman? The bottle? Death? The unknown? All that matters to The Commitment-Phobe is that he carelessly snatched her heart and took it with him.

Pamela Lyndon Travers, the author of the *Mary Poppins* children's books, insisted that Walt Disney not allow there to be a romance of any sort between Mary, a loving but prim and proper nanny, and Bert, the Matchman, when Disney produced his movie based upon her books. Although aware of Bert's affectionate feelings towards her, Mary remains non-committal. Indeed, whenever he gets too close, she simply opens her parrot umbrella and flies off into the blue sky with no promises of ever returning. Pamela Travers put herself into the character of Mary Poppins. Pamela's father died when she was seven. She then had to contend with a suicidal mother. So she learned not to get too close to anyone she loved, for fear that they would suddenly take off into the clouds.

Oh, it's a jolly holiday with you, Bert
Gentlemen like you are few
Though you're just a diamond in the rough, Bert
Underneath your blood is blue!
You'd never think of pressing your advantage
Forbearance is the hallmark of your creed
A lady needn't fear when you are near
Your sweet gentility is crystal clear!
Oh, it's a jolly holiday with you, Bert
A jolly, jolly holiday with you!

It's no wonder then that The Commitment-Phobe is alarmed at the thought of handing over decision-making power to a man. She doesn't want to have to compromise, especially with a man who doesn't meet all the criteria on her checklist. And she trembles at the prospect of giving up control of the power to say, "No, I won't marry you," because then her men might stop treating her well. She has seen what happened to her mother after she said, "I do," and does not want to be compelled to make the same sacrifices. Some Commitment-Phobes have trouble with other decisions, too, and can't commit to one school, one career, or even one pair of shoes.

Snow White seems to have this problem. And where is Snow White's father when she needs him? He's not there to protect her from her evil stepmother who orders the huntsman to take Snow White out into the forest and kill her. It's no wonder that she's willing to cook, clean and sew for the Seven Dwarfs. She's content to live with them, singing to the birds and forest animals, as long as the Dwarfs don't press her to make a decision as to whether she prefers Doc, Grumpy, Happy, Sleepy, Bashful, Sneezy or Dopey. Indeed, she keeps them all hanging and fawning over her to curry her favor.

Then, too, there's The Commitment-Phobe who is 'just not that into him', and keeps her man hanging so that he'll be around when she needs a date. Or keep him as a Plan B in case her ex, who she's hoping will come back, doesn't, or in case it doesn't work out with another guy she secretly has a crush on. She likes being in this no-man's land so she can luxuriate in the safety of a man who loves her more, while she's not as in love with him.

Why do men fall for Commitment-Phobes?

Men who fall for Commitment-Phobes are generally commitment-phobic themselves, and, like the woman, use their partner's fear of commitment as a way to avoid facing their own. But with The Commitment-Phobe bad girl, though the men may temporarily like the space she gives them, after a while it gets frustrating, especially after they have invested their time, money and love in her.

Men who fall for Commitment-Phobes are afraid of getting too close to a woman because she may disappoint, reject or leave him, like their mother did when they were growing up. Their unconscious fears are similar to those of men who fall for The Married Woman. But, whereas these men use the husband of The Married Woman as a protective barrier against commitment, the men who fall for a Commitment-Phobe use her own fear of commitment as a barrier to getting closer.

Real Stories from the Dating Front

To Be or Not To Be?

"Mary Poppins" had been Patrick's favorite story when he was a little boy. In fact, one of the few warm memories he had of his mom was her taking him to see the movie.

When we left Patrick, he was nursing his broken heart at the end of his relationship with his lost college sweetheart, The Married Woman. After some time, Patrick told himself that he needed to take another chance on love. This time he would look for a woman who wasn't married. He met Julie at a meeting of the professional society to which they both belonged. When he found out that she was single and seemed to have no ties, he congratulated himself on making a better choice. A couple of mutual friends warned him, however, that Julie was afraid of commitment and had left a trail of men in her wake. But did he heed their warning? No. Instead, it went straight to his unconscious mind and drove him into her arms.

Our mutual friends thought no one had a shot with Julie. When I started going out with her, one friend said, "Don't break her heart." I said, "She's gonna break mine." He said, "Yeah, you're right."

Patrick started dating Julie full steam ahead, begging her for more commitment, yet all the while knowing unconsciously that this very begging would sabotage their relationship. They did the dance of two Commitment-Phobes colluding with each other in an unspoken 'commitment' not to get too close.

I wanted more commitment, sooner, better, hotter. I tried to wear her down. I liked her too much and I was too available. But I couldn't help myself. Julie was smart, engaging, very self-confident, funny and interested in my stuff. We had our profession in common. It was easy and a pleasure to talk with her. She had lustrous brown hair and a perfect oval face with a strong chin. Some men might not have been attracted to her because she was about 20-25 pounds overweight, but I thought she was sexy. It was mostly her personality and her way about her. The woman I dated right before her wanted too much of me. Julie was independent, the opposite of intrusive and not remotely needy. We each had different lives in different cities.

Their first date was romantic. Patrick picked Julie up at her New York apartment and they walked in the rain to a restaurant she chose. When they got back, his kiss led to their sleeping together. The next day they drove out to the countryside. Since Patrick's work often brought him into the city, they saw each other at least once a week and their warm feelings towards each other grew. There was one problem that arose early on. Patrick had his children on alternate weekends and Julie did not want to meet them, so it meant less time that they could spend together.

I was eager to have her meet my kids because I took her seriously as a possible wife. It struck her as too much, too soon.

So Patrick suggested that she let him take her on vacation. She told him to surprise her. Since he knew she loved the theatre, he bought plane tickets and booked a hotel in London. About a week before they were supposed to leave, Julie got cold feet.

She broke up with me because she thought I was going too fast. She had mentioned a couple of times, "You're pushing this." And we had had some scuffles about me wanting more. On the phone, she told me she didn't want to go to London and didn't want to go out with me anymore. I said I was surprised and disappointed, but that I didn't want to push her if it feels wrong. What could I say? I offered her the tickets because they were non-refundable. When I hung up, I was sad. The next morning she surprised me. She called and said, "Have you figured out what restaurant you're taking me to in London?"

London was fabulous. They drank in pubs, drove out to the countryside, saw castles and took in several plays.

On the last night, when we were in bed at a bed and breakfast, Julie told me she loved me. It was the first time she said it. I had told her I loved her about a month into our relationship. Back then, she had kissed and hugged me, but said nothing and seemed uncomfortable.

When they got back home they were still warm and close.

Julie made a big deal of my birthday. She bought me an expensive watch and took me to a very nice restaurant. I got her a necklace with a diamond and gave it to her on my birthday. She wore it constantly.

One day, Julie asked, "Do vasectomies ever fail?" I said, "How late are you?" She said, "About a week and I'm never late." I had had a vasectomy during my marriage. I said, "It's very unusual, but occasionally there are slips. If you are pregnant, and if you would have me, I would marry you." She hugged me. Days later, she got her period and she cried.

But as the months passed, Julie still resisted Patrick's efforts to get her together with his family. Finally, six months after they'd started going out, he brought his children to Coney Island and she dropped by. They rode the Cyclone, billed as the scariest roller coaster in the world, but it was nothing compared to the roller-coaster ride of their relationship. For just as their feelings for each other seemed to reach a peak, there would always be the letdown.

We picked out puppies for her at a puppy farm. She got two because she couldn't choose.

But after this, a day filled with the type of cuddly puppy scene you'd see on a Hallmark card, Julie became distant. Patrick attributed it to problems she was having at work. She changed jobs. Then came her birthday.

We celebrated her birthday the day after. I screwed up. Everything was wrong – the wrong day, the wrong restaurant, the wrong gift. My first choice was a restaurant that was hard to get into, so I had a back-up plan – a nearby Italian place. But it turned out we were the only ones there because the food was terrible. I bought her a $300 cashmere sweater in rich purple. She usually wore black and gray but looked really great in colors. She was not excited about my gift. We did make love. There had been lots of uncomfortable silence. I planned to say that I noticed a developing distance between us, but I said nothing.

The next day I sent her an email: "I'm sorry about things that went wrong and that you were disappointed, but I hope you know how deeply I care about you. I see spending my future with you as my eventual wife, maybe making it permanent." She sent an email back: "We have to talk about this and us. It's burdensome feeling that you want so much more than I do. This isn't what I want."

The killer part was she wrote, "When I broke up with you before London, I was following my heart and I should have left it at that. I hope you know you're a really great guy." I was a total wreck.

The temperature of their relationship decreased drastically. One night, on the phone, Julie tried to explain why she had pulled away.

She said, "You were suffocating me. I felt smothered!" It was the first time she said anything like it.

Actually Julie had been saying this all along, just using gentler, more euphemistic words.

She admitted that she had abandonment issues because of her mother dying when she was so young. I tried explaining, "Your mom died and now you think everyone else will leave you, too."

They saw each other at the next meeting of their professional society and Julie invited herself along when Patrick went to get something to eat afterwards.

When we were done she said, "Want to see the puppies?" I came up. She was drunk and tired and fell asleep on me. So the sex was pleasurable for her and nothing for me. But I didn't mind. It was a pleasure for me to lie there holding her.

A few days later, at Julie's suggestion, they met at one of their favorite restaurants.

She said, "We don't have a future. I like your company and we have great sex, but you keep expecting more. Don't get too into me. You're not gonna get me. You can date other women if you want to. Probably one of us will get involved with someone else." So we began again. From the outside, it looked the same. I was beginning to get the impression that she just wasn't that into me. I hoped she would change if I gave her enough good experiences. In my head, I kept hearing her say, "I don't want to be with you," but I was still in love with her.

They saw each other once a week. Patrick took her to restaurants, Broadway shows, antiquing in the countryside, and other romantic places. He was enjoying her company, but not feeling terribly wanted by her. He took her on another trip, this time to the Bahamas. They made love every night. When they got home, she called to say, "Thank you," and then backed off again.

Patrick's birthday was coming up. He invited her to a family celebration at his home, where she'd only been twice in the past year and a half – the whole time they were dating.

After we got home, she disappeared. I got a couple of emails asking for my help with things, but nothing asking when she could see me or asking about celebrating my birthday. Then she wrote: "Hi, What's your dealio for this weekend?"

Patrick chose to interpret this as her forgetting or ignoring his birthday, rather than her wanting to discuss the details she would need to know in order to come to his party. He dashed off a nasty email in reply.

I was mad because she hadn't said she was coming. She wrote back, "You are incessantly needy. I just spent five days with you! Here you go again. I'm thinking things are going swimmingly and then you always throw a wrench in it!"

Julie's terms for our relationship were: fuck me, love me, don't ask anything of me. She'd say, "Why do I need to tell you 'I love you' – I'm with you, aren't I?"

In Julie's mind, her presence should have been enough for Patrick. It would have been enough for her if her mom had just been present and had not died when she was a little girl. It had been soul-destroying when her mother died. Julie kept pictures of her mom, who looked like Audrey Hepburn, all around her apartment. Her parents were both actors. After her mother died, her father became a reclusive alcoholic, neglecting Julie and her sisters. Julie's parents had been very much in love. Over the years she romanticized her parents' great love and keeps looking for one just like it. But it has been impossible to find, because no flesh and blood man could live up to the romantic script of her fantasies.

Shipwrecked

From the moment Scott saw Megan walking across the college campus, he wanted her to be his girlfriend. The only problem was that Megan already had a boyfriend. But Scott was more popular –

a senior and in the band. This apparently intrigued Megan because she broke up with her boyfriend and hooked up with Scott. Her ex was devastated.

A lot of my friends said she wasn't that amazing. I wanted to inoculate myself against their visions of her, so I dove in. I loved that she was into metal music. I'm into it and it's unusual to find a woman who likes metal. She had lip piercings in a snakebite arrangement. It was really sexy. Her outlook on life was the opposite of mine; she was fine not controlling anything. Megan was like the ocean – she didn't react to things on the surface, but she had undertows of emotions that you couldn't see. And when she touched me, I felt like she was burning my skin. It superseded reason.

Megan was a wild child. She had an alcohol problem and dabbled in drugs like Ritalin, Adderall and other uppers. Scott snuck her into bars. She'd never done this before because she was underage. And one time they almost drove to Mexico. It was all very exhilarating, except for Megan's refusal to pick just one boyfriend.

Her ex kept trying to win her back and she kept letting him. It drove me insane with jealousy. She'd break up with me for nothing. I sent steamy letters to her and tried to win her back. Megan would come back to me and then go back to him. She was totally quixotic. Her ex would show up crying. She'd console him and cancel plans with me. Then she would break up with him again and come back to me. When she broke up with me for the last time, our fun memories seemed to mean nothing to her. I had heard Megan had a history of doing this to guys. She'd lose interest and dump them. Before I dated her, I knew she made men fall in love with her, then broke up with them and ruined their life. But I thought it would be different with me!

Until she was 11, Megan grew up on a boat sailing around the Pacific. Her father had made a good deal of money, retired young and took his wife, Megan and her younger brother on a never-ending vacation. Megan said she commonly made friends at a port only to have to say good-bye to them.

It was no wonder Megan was such a Commitment-Phobe. She didn't want to get close to anyone because she was afraid of having to say good-bye to them.

I wanted to take a wild, unpredictable girl and tame her. I suspect she preferred her ex because he didn't push her into a deeper relationship. He was sort of her sidekick, content just to be a stowaway on her ship, no matter how troubled the waters.

Airport Insecurity

Ross, who we met in The Sex Siren chapter, has also dated Commitment-Phobes in his never-ending quest to find a "Ginger" from "Gilligan's Island."

When he met Kelly, his quest had taken him halfway around the world. Ross was on tour with a group in Southeast Asia. He had become a foster parent to a child there, who he supported with monthly donations. His plan was to visit the child after the tour. He noticed an attractive woman in their group and started chatting with her. At the next stop, when the group arrived at their hotel and were all going to meet for dinner, Ross told Kelly he would stop by her room to pick her up.

She met me at the door with a towel and said she was running late. Right there, she had me. We became a twosome and spent all our time together after that.

One day, the tour went to visit a summer palace. It was hot and Ross had eaten a big meal. He fainted. Kelly, a Scottish doctor who was practicing in England, ministered to him and accompanied him to the hospital. There they gave Ross an IV and discharged him.

After I got out of the hospital we made love for the first time. We spent the next couple of weeks together. I thought I'd found my soul mate. Kelly told me she was living with some guy, but I figured it couldn't be serious. She made me feel like Fabio. I just knew she was the girl I was gonna marry. At the end of the tour, we each had to go our separate ways. As the bus drove away, I put my hand over my heart to show her I loved her.

Ross and Kelly wrote and called each other for nine months. They spoke of their love and made plans for how she would transfer her medical practice to the U.S. They arranged for Ross to visit her and meet her parents. Besides her apartment, Kelly also had a room at the hospital where she worked.

She said I could stay there with her. I thought the guy would be history by then, anyway. I didn't call her the week before I left because everything seemed to be all set. I flew to London, expecting Kelly to fly into my arms, but when I got off the plane, I couldn't see her anywhere. I waited for hours. I finally had to admit that she'd left me stranded high and dry at Gatwick Airport. It got late, so I found a hotel. I called her hospital where the staff knew who I was from my having called there over the past months. The woman who answered said, "Kelly went to Scotland to visit her parents." She must have gotten cold feet. I sat in my hotel room and wrote a poison pen letter. When I finished, it was 5:00 A.M. I went down to the concierge and asked him to mail it. I didn't want to change my mind. I could've gone to Scotland to look for her. She lived in a small town and I could've probably found her.

But just like Kelly, his fear of commitment kept his cold feet firmly planted right where he was.

The next year someone left me a birthday message on my answering machine. It sounded like a Scottish brogue. I like to think it was Kelly.

Be Careful What You Wish For

Visual foreplay is what hooked Stan on Andrea. She lingered a minute longer when she returned his eye contact, creating a tension of mutual intrigue and he had a crush on her already. Stan had simply left the hotel to buy socks since he'd forgotten to pack them for his trip to the health care conference, when his elevator ride back to his room changed his life.

He was attracted to Andrea's bearing, poise, beautiful smile, dark hair, tan complexion, rosy cheeks, stature and stylish clothing – her whole look. When she asked questions at the seminar, a little later, he liked the way she comported herself.

We had a great time together that evening. There was a banquet and then some of us went out dancing and came back to sit by the swimming pool to chat. I think Andrea was afraid I'd rip her clothes off because she ran off without saying goodnight.

Stan and Andrea started dating exclusively and had a lot of fun together. They lived in Midwestern cities, about two hours apart. After a year, Andrea got a job in Stan's city, which was a more exciting place than where she lived. He found her a great corner apartment with a fireplace at a very reasonable rent.

Andrea took the apartment and I moved in with her. It was a casual conversation, not heavy or extended. "Would you like me to move in with you?" I said matter-of-factly. "Sure," she responded, "but I don't want my parents to know."

About three years into the relationship, when they were in their late twenties, Stan started talking about marriage.

Everything was great about the relationship. Andrea rocked my world. I initiated the talk about marriage because I was interested in having a family, I loved her, she loved me, and I felt like we could spend the rest of our lives together. I brought it up in a casual way, without a formal dinner or a ring. We were talking about future plans, but she told me she wasn't ready to settle down or have kids, that her job was tenuous, that I wasn't making enough money and that my career was unstable. Before this, making decisions together had always come so easy. This was the first time she pushed back. I decided I would give her some space. I told myself it was fine, we were still young. I tried not to take it as a rejection. But over time, it became increasingly frustrating. I told her, "Life has its ups and downs. Let's go through it together."

After the first time Stan mentioned marriage, they talked about it a couple of times a year. But Andrea kept bringing up the same arguments for why it wasn't a good idea. And she never specified that, if or when a certain landmark was reached, then they could get married.

She loved me, but not unconditionally. And she didn't want to become a partner with someone, to feel that her life was not totally her own, to give up a part of herself in a marriage. As long as she was not married, she still had control and the ability to say, "No."

Like a typical Commitment-Phobe, Andrea kept Stan dangling, but wouldn't agree to actually take the plunge and walk down the aisle to say, "I do." Finally, after eight years, Stan's patience had worn thin.

I was thinking, let's do this or I'm outta here. Shit or get off the pot. But in a loving way, I said, "I really want to have a family with you. If you wait until everything is perfect, we'll never get married. I would like you to make a decision and, if you don't, I need to make a decision about my life." It was the first time I had said that.

We went to a fabulous romantic place for dinner to celebrate our birthdays. At dinner, I casually, lovingly, brought it up. Andrea was very sweet about it. She said, "Let's do this." I had no misgivings. I was naïve. In hindsight, I realize she was not that into me. She didn't really want to get married. My sense of self wasn't good. I wasn't emotionally intelligent enough to say, "My God, if it's this much work...!"

Stan hadn't bought a ring because he was afraid Andrea would say "no" again – and because of his own unconscious fears of commitment. He got her one in the next few weeks and Andrea was delighted with it. They married three months later.

I'd asked her to make a decision or I'd move on. Big mistake. We married and I should have moved on.

Next came Stan's struggle to convince Andrea to get pregnant.

I said, "Andrea, you're almost 40. We gotta get going here."

Four years later, Andrea gave birth to a son.

She was not excited going into it. Once he came, she was delighted. Andrea thought he was the cat's meow. But our marriage really went downhill after he was born. I wasn't getting much time before we had a baby, and after the baby it was even less. It was like, "Can we have a date?" "No, go hunt and gather." Neither one of us felt loved.

Andrea and Stan separated after about 10 years of marriage and divorced shortly thereafter.

She started going out with a man whom she met at work. Andrea had talked about him before we separated. They've been engaged for at least five years. I lost track. When they originally got engaged, they were going to get married in two years. But now I'm back to calling him her "boyfriend." After three years, it's no longer her "fiancé." He's happy because he feels she's "under contract." She's happy because she feels she doesn't have to marry him.

From the time she was a little girl, Andrea had learned what marriage does to a woman as she watched her frustrated mother subjugating herself to her dad - a harsh man. Her mom sacrificed her own dreams, and her health to cook, clean, decorate, and take care of the family to please her husband. Andrea did not want to become her mother.

When Stan was growing up, his dad had been even harsher.

My dad never loved me. He was a pretty tough guy. It was his way or the highway. I was in the drum and bugle corps. It was a great way to get out of the house, go all over the country, and be accepted by my peers. My dad was against it because it wasn't what he picked. He thought it was stupid. If I would've taken up golf, he would have thought I was great. He always said golf was the perfect game.

Stan became increasingly frustrated trying to get acceptance from his father.

One day, I told him, "You just chase a little ball on the grass with a stick." I thought his head would explode. Eventually he said, "You can live at home or march with the corps!" So I chose the corps and left home at 18.

Stan's father had given him an ultimatum, just like Stan gave Andrea an ultimatum about marriage, but Stan's choice to leave home at 18 had more dire consequences, as we'll soon see.

I worked hard trying to get my dad to love me. He may have loved me inside, but he didn't make me feel loved.

Because of these childhood experiences, when Stan grew up, he became enmeshed in a repetition-compulsion scenario with Andrea. He kept trying to make her love him in the same way he'd kept trying to make his dad love him.

After my marriage broke up, I finally figured this out. You can't make someone love you.

Stan had felt very much loved by his mom, at least until he was about 11 years old, when she became mentally ill and it became hard to know who his mother was.

When she was in her early 40s, my mom had a hysterectomy. It caused hormone changes and she became mentally ill and unpredictable. She said strange things about other people. She kept calling the police because she felt people were out to get her. I thought it was a little unusual, but I didn't go "ding dong, mom's psycho." My dad was stressed-out about her behavior, and their relationship was stressful to her.

One day, when I was in my early teens, my father and I were downstairs. He had been instructed not to leave her alone. We heard a thump. She had slit her throat trying to commit suicide and went into my sister's closet to hide. There was a huge puddle of blood in the bathroom and the bedroom. I took her in an ambulance to the hospital. I was the only family member to go in the ambulance with her. She was conscious. I'll never forget the look in her eyes. My dad said he was going to stay home to clean up. It seemed like an odd choice. He came to the hospital later that day. I only know of this one attempt, but she continued being suicidal. She was hospitalized three times and was on heavy-duty medications. You could tell by her face and eyes that she was zombied out.

Stan's mother died when she was 49 years old.

She died in a car accident. There was heavy traffic and she was on a freeway ramp. A car hit her from behind, pushing her off the road into a ditch. She got out of the car and was hit by a semi truck. It might have been suicide. She was probably distraught about how my dad would react over the car, and because I had left home. The look on her face when I left was horrible. My mom died when I was 18... two months after I left.

Stan's response to his father's ultimatum would haunt him forever, not only because of guilt, but because of the fear it engendered – a fear of getting too close to a woman whom he might lose, like he did his mom.

The Runaway Bride

Before Nick met his Penthouse Pet, he was married twice. He married his second wife, Victoria, when he was 30 and it lasted three years.

It all started when he was working on the Eastern seaboard and decided to pursue his fantasy of playing Santa for Christmas.

I was a Santa at Montgomery Ward. I had an elf, a cute girl who soon asked to come into the changing room to help me get in and out of my costume. After we were going out for a couple of weeks, she brought her friend Victoria to meet me so she could get her opinion of me. Victoria destroyed their friendship of 18 years by stealing me away.

Victoria was very flashy. She flirted by sticking her boobs out. She wasn't as intellectual as my first wife, but she was creative. Her boyfriend before me was an activist. Victoria was the black sheep of her family. They were straight out of the Waltons. While her siblings were doing homework, she smoked a joint. Her family was very religious. Saturdays she went with them to religious retreats. Then Sundays we spent all day in bed.

Nick liked the fact that Victoria would be willing to destroy her friendship and rebel against her family in order to be with him because it seemed like proof of her love.

One day, we eloped. It was not a traditional wedding. There was no family there. We got married by a justice of the peace after lunch. We were kidding around saying he must have drank his lunch because he seemed drunk.

Because Victoria's parents disliked Nick, they moved to the South to get away from her family. She went to school to learn to be a bartender and got a job at a bar.

What I didn't know was that she was coming on to guys in the bar and had a relationship with the guy who taught her in bartending school. I was thinking everything was good, then one day Victoria called me to come to the bar. She introduced me to a couple who came into the bar periodically. They were swingers and had made an overture to invite us to get together. I said, "No," because I felt it came out of the blue sky and I didn't want our marriage to deteriorate.

Victoria and Nick moved around so he could take advantage of better job offers. When his agency was bought out and he lost his job, he took a job building racecars. They got an apartment across the street.

One morning, six weeks after we moved there, Victoria wanted to have sex. She was usually an afternoon and night sex person, so this struck me as a little odd, but I was happy to go along with it. Afterwards, I told her, "I'll come home for lunch." She said, "Don't, because I'm going downtown to look for a job." I decided to go home for lunch, anyway. I told my boss. He said, "No. You have to stay here because I want you to finish what you're working on. It has to be done today." He bought me lunch and brought it in. After work, I stopped at the florist to get her flowers since I thought she'd be down if she didn't get a job.

When I got home, the apartment was empty. Victoria took everything – even my underwear! I was so shocked. I thought, "Oh my God, somebody kidnapped her." All I had were the clothes on my back and my car. Despite my bad relationship with her parents, I called them to tell them Victoria was missing. They weren't as upset about it as they should have been, but my mind wasn't working right. I didn't call the police because I thought if I told them she had taken everything and her car was gone, they'd say she wasn't missing, she left me. How cold of her to have had sex with me when she knew she was leaving. I told my boss. He offered his sympathies and said if there was anything I needed to let him know.

Then I discovered she cleaned out our bank accounts. I toughed it out. I kept living in the empty apartment and kept going to work. I was working two jobs now – Pizza Hut and building racecars because I was trying to save money to move back where we came from. I kept calling her parents. About a month later, it was my birthday, which was the same day as hers. I called her parents again. I told them that if they knew where she was, to tell her I'd wait one more day and we could go back East together. I was still thinking she was helpless without me. I didn't want her hiding out. I felt obligated to bring her back to the bosom of her family. On my birthday, I sat in the empty apartment alone waiting for Victoria to come back.

This was pure torture for Nick. Since he was adopted, his birthday was always the most traumatic and desolate day of the year because it reminded him of having been rejected and abandoned by his biological mother. Yet there he was, abandoned by yet another woman, and waiting in an empty apartment for her to return to him, an endeavor that he suspected was useless. When Victoria didn't show up, Nick drove the 16 hours it took to get back to the East Coast.

It was an out-of-body experience. Why did I go back? Was I hoping to get her back? Maybe. Within a few months, I discovered that while she and I were living there, she had been having an affair with my ex-girlfriend, who lived in the same apartment complex as we did. Apparently, they got together when I was in other places, working or whatever.

But there was a bigger shock in store for Nick.

I found out that the day Victoria left me, my boss rushed to buy me lunch because his wife was helping my wife move out of our home and into theirs! Victoria was having an affair with both of them. How she had enough time privately to form a relationship with them, I don't know. She had gone out at night a few times and told me that she was having a girls' night out. She didn't mention that there would be a guy there, too. I guess she thought my boss was cute.

Unconsciously, Victoria may well have been trying to create a threesome, where Nick's boss and his wife were like her surrogate parents. In their home, she wouldn't have to share her 'parents' with so many brothers and sisters, and she wouldn't have to be the black sheep.

Then about a year later, I was with a friend who is an attorney. He asked me about the details of our marriage ceremony. I told him we were married by a justice of the peace who seemed like he was drunk. He asked, "Who witnessed it?" I told him there was nobody there. He called me later, after looking into it. "You were never married! The judge was drunk. There was no paperwork!" To Victoria, it was like it never happened, anyway. It was merely a fun thing to do for the afternoon. To her, our relationship was like an extended date. I don't think, in her heart of hearts, she ever felt married or committed. For her, divorce was sneaking away from our apartment.

Famous Commitment-Phobes

<u>Pamela Anderson</u> – Though Pam married Tommy Lee after knowing him for less than a week, their marriage was on-again, off-again. Pam has had similar on-again, off-again relationships with Kid Rock and several other men. She dips her toe into the water and then runs for shore when something is less than perfect.

<u>Alyssa Milano</u> – Before her most recent marriage, Alyssa played the field, literally, dating lots of professional athletes, as well as Hollywood types.

<u>Sienna Miller</u> – Sienna and Jude Law are both Commitment-

Phobes who have been doing the on-again, off-again relationship dance for years. After Jude had an affair with his children's nanny, he issued a public apology to Sienna, but these wounds take a lot of time to heal.

Kate Hudson – Flitting from one man to another, Kate is unconsciously acting out the message she got from her parents, that tying the knot is dangerous. She has chosen commitment-phobic men, like Alex Rodriguez and Lance Armstrong, and shied away from men like Owen Wilson, who wanted to commit to her so much that he became suicidal when she left him.

Sara Deever – In the movie "Sweet November," Sara (Charlize Theron) chooses a different man to be with each month. When Mr. November proposes, she turns him down and makes him leave; ultimately revealing that she has terminal cancer and doesn't want him to see her in her final days.

Cameron Diaz – Cameron admits that she's a Commitment-Phobe, telling the media, "I just hate committing myself to anything…. It probably comes from me being a total spoiled brat." The many Hollywood men she has dated can attest to this.

Sarah Lewis – In the film "Forces of Nature," Sarah (Sandra Bullock) appears to be a free spirit who doesn't want to stay with one man for the rest of her life. But it turns out that this is her protective mask, keeping love away because of her painful past.

The "You Don't Own Me" Girl – The Blow Monkeys' song "You Don't Own Me" describes the sentiments of a Commitment-Phobe: "Don't say I can't go with other boys…. Don't try to change me in any way…. Don't tie me down 'cause I'd never stay."

Tila Tequila – On "A Shot At Love with Tila Tequila," a bisexual reality TV show, Tila enjoyed being sought after by heterosexual men and lesbian women. In real life, she has yet to commit to one gender.

Heather Locklear – Heather has kept her boyfriend Jack Wagner dangling for years, wearing his diamond ring when she's with him and taking it off when she's not. Rumor has it that she may be hoping to reconcile with her former husband, Richie Sambora.

Jennifer Wilbanks – Known as the "runaway bride," Jennifer disappeared in order to avoid marrying her fiancé John Mason. After a nationwide search for her, she called him and claimed that she'd been kidnapped, later recanting that story and canceling her engagement.

Queen Latifah – Actress and singer Queen Latifah admits to having a "commitment issue" caused by having been sexually abused by a male babysitter. Since then she has kept people at arm's length.

Chapter 8
THE HUSBAND HUNTER AND TRAPPER

What does a Husband Hunter and Trapper want?

A Husband Hunter and Trapper wants a husband who will provide a house with a white picket fence, two children, a dog, the security of being taken care of and the status of being a 'married lady'.

Why? To fulfill the fantasy she has been taught since she was a little girl – that the only way she can live happily ever after is if she finds a prince who will marry her and walk with her, holding hands, into the sunset. The Husband Hunter and Trapper doesn't just wait for nature to take its course or for Cupid to sling his arrow. She takes matters into her own hands because deep down she suspects that it won't happen on its own since she's not a beautiful princess.

These bad girls fly in the face of history, where men were the hunters and trappers. The Husband Hunter's one goal in life is to beat the bushes to find an unsuspecting male whom she can trick into stepping right into her trap. Unlike The Gold-Digger, these women are not after a man's riches, but rather the sense of security he provides by mowing the lawn, taking out the trash, fixing her flat tire or doing anything else that makes her feel taken care of in the traditional way.

Despite the fact that we are living in another century now, there is still a pervasive nostalgia within our collective unconscious for the idyllic life that was portrayed in the 1950s TV shows. The wives in "Father Knows Best," "Leave It To Beaver," "Ozzie and Harriet," "I Love Lucy" and "Lassie" may have been repressed by modern feminist standards, but their husbands were always there for them to share the ups and downs and to provide help and comfort. Even when they sparred back and forth, it was all in good fun, and no one threatened divorce.

Despite all our supposed progress, there is still a stigma against single women. Just watch the claws come out whenever a married woman sees a single woman get closer to her husband than the 'invisible shield' is supposed to prevent. Then there are the dreaded "plus one" invitations that not only mean the single woman has to scurry about for a date to bring to the event, but the whole world knows there's no male name to inscribe next to hers. Wearing a wedding ring seems to convey proper standing in society. And if a woman says she's divorced, people jump to the conclusion that it must have been the husband who left her, rather than the other way around.

The Husband Hunter and Trapper is fiercely motivated because she is afraid of being single forever and looked down upon as damaged or not pretty enough or good enough. Though in these supposedly enlightened times, we use words like "bachelorette" to describe a single woman, instead of "spinster," "old maid," or "witch," the stereotypical image of a frumpy, prissy lady is still conjured up. And there remains a double standard. "Bachelor" does not have the same condescending or pitying aura to it. The longer a woman remains ring-less, the more people will wonder what's wrong with her and start to believe that there must be some reason that men have left her on the shelf. Besides, women are taught that they can have it all, so something definitely seems missing when there is no husband in the picture. It's no wonder this type of bad girl will say or do anything to trap a man.

Some Husband Hunters and Trappers are hoping to create the perfect fantasy family that they never had themselves when they were growing up. They are determined to make it better for their children. Others want to be married to solve a problem, such as their immigration status. And still other Husband Hunters have timetables in their heads. They've decided that they must be married by a certain age or before they reach a certain point in their career or before they're too old to have children. A woman's biological clock is a powerful motivator for marriage, even with today's ostensibly more open-minded attitude towards single women who have babies on their own. Ask any such woman about the stares and whispers she's had to endure from people who know her 'situation', and it is clear that we are not as tolerant as we would like to believe.

More than one Husband Hunter has cut a heart-shaped hole in her diaphragm to become pregnant in a bid to bag her catch. Once she finds herself pregnant, she goes on safari to snare the father of her child. We've all watched this scenario repeated on one soap opera after another. It's no wonder that it comes naturally to women feeling desperate for a husband. Almost unthinkingly, she plays out the scenes in real life that she has subliminally memorized from the soaps. It just seems like the normal thing to do. And if these gorgeous, sexy soap stars need to do it to trap a man, then what's the average husband-less woman to do?

In the Broadway musical "Funny Girl," Barbra Streisand, portraying Fanny Brice, sings the theme song of The Hunter and Trapper bad girl:

I'm Sadie, Sadie, married lady,
Bow when I go by.
I'm a corporation now,
Not me, myself and I.
Oh how that marriage license works
On chambermaids and hotel clerks....
I'm Sadie, Sadie, married lady,
Still in bed at noon,
Racking my brain deciding
Between orange juice and prune.
Nick says nothing is too good for me,
And who am I not to agree?
I'm Sadie, Sadie, married lady, that's me.
Meet a mortgagee,
The owner of an icebox
With a ten-year guarantee.
Oh, sit me in the softest seat,
Quick, a cushion for my feet.
Do for me, buy for me, lift me, carry me,
Finally got a guy to marry me!
I do my nails,
Read up on sales,
All day the records play.
Then he comes home, I tell him

Oy, what a day I had today!
I swear I'll do my wifely job,
Just sit at home, become a slob.
I'm Sadie, Sadie, married lady, that's me!

Why do men fall for Husband Hunters and Trappers?

The men who fall for Husband Hunters and Trappers are usually drifting blithely along without any preoccupying distraction or consuming goal. They are ripe for the picking because they are feeling lonely, have low self-esteem, and want to be wanted. When a Husband Hunter comes along and tells him, "You're the one for me, baby!" he doesn't have a quick or solid retort for why he isn't.

Some of these men are people pleasers, who feel uncomfortable or guilty if they have to tell a woman "no." They may have had manipulative mothers who used guilt to get them to do what they wanted when they were growing up, or to keep these men tied to their apron strings instead of letting them go free to find a wife.

Other men who fall for Husband Hunters and Trappers have successfully avoided marriage until now because they don't want a stormy and unhappy one like their parents had. Or they don't want children. Some of these men have even had vasectomies to avoid having children and to discourage women from wanting to marry them. But a Husband Hunter doesn't get discouraged easily. In fact, she is the only woman who can turn a marriage-resistant man around and drag him to the altar before he knows what's happened to him.

In "Sex and the City," Dr. Trey MacDougal, a Park Avenue

cardiologist with a wealthy pedigree, appears to be quite a catch. One wonders why he isn't married yet. It soon becomes clear that his mother, Bunny, has scared off any woman who threatened to take him from her side. That is, until Charlotte York, the prototypical Husband Hunter and Trapper, comes along and snatches him away. Refusing to wait until Trey pops the question, she catches him off-guard and proposes herself.

Charlotte: I proposed to myself!
Carrie: What?
Charlotte: Yes. I suggested he have a tomato salad, and then I suggested we get married.
Carrie: Wait. What exactly did he say?
Charlotte: "Alrighty!"
Carrie: "Alrighty?" He said, "Alrighty?" Now I'm thinking the upsetting thing isn't that you proposed, it's that you proposed to a guy that says "Alrighty."
Charlotte: Oh, Carrie, stop!
Carrie: Alrighty.

Real Stories from Men on the Dating Front

Dying to Get Married

Sam was working as a taxi driver in Minnesota, while searching for a job in his chosen field, computers. He had never been in a relationship before. So when Florence got into his cab, he was a sitting duck.

I had low self-esteem. I was a pretty naïve 23 year old – more like 16. I had a college degree, but I grew up on a farm. When I got the call from the dispatcher, I thought this was gonna be just another fare, but it wasn't.

Florence had called for a cab to pick her up at home. When she got in, she told Sam that the address she wanted to be driven to was her boyfriend's place. This didn't stop her from shamelessly flirting along the route, or from asking Sam to come back for her later.

I picked her up from her boyfriend's around midnight. She got in the front seat this time. I thought, "Okay, this could lead to something." She said, "Let's go for a drink." In the cab she was joking around. Neither one of us talked about her boyfriend. I dropped the cab off, turned my fares in and got my car. We went to a bowling alley bar, had some drinks and talked until the bar closed. Then I drove her home. There was some attraction on my part, but not much. I wasn't going to call her again and she didn't give me her phone number, anyway.

The next day Florence contacted the cab company and hunted Sam down. She talked to the dispatcher and found out more about him. She only knew his first name, but the dispatcher traced who Sam was by the time and place of her pick-up. She gave the dispatcher her phone number. Sam called her and asked her out. They went on an ordinary movie date. He liked her flirtatious conversation and sense of humor. They ended up at Sam's place.

Now Florence knew where I lived. Pretty soon, she was always there – even sometimes when I didn't want her to be. We had sex on the first date. It was good. Sex was the hook for why I continued seeing her. She'd come over and then we'd do something. She lived nearby, so we saw each other almost all the time. She made me feel good. I don't know what happened to her boyfriend. Maybe there was no boyfriend. She could have been visiting anyone and just told me it was her boyfriend.

Florence told Sam that she had run away from home with some guy she met. She'd followed him across country and somehow she ended up alone as a single mom in Minnesota. Florence had a two-year-old daughter, named Sheila. She began bringing Sheila with her when she went to Sam's. After a few months, they all moved in together.

I knew Florence had been in a car accident and was seeing a doctor. She'd shown me the scar on her arm. Soon after we began living together, Florence told me she had Hodgkin's lymphoma and only had six months left to live. I was devastated. I really cared about her. She gave me the doctor's name and told me what pills she was taking, so I took it as truth. I had no reason to doubt her. Then, less than a month after Florence told me she was dying, she brought up marriage. She wanted desperately to get married before she died. She told me she wanted Sheila to have someone to take care of her. She had no other family, and Sheila's father didn't want to have anything to do with her. I felt sorry for her. I said, "Okay, I can do this." I thought that this way it would be easier for me to adopt her child. We got married a month later by a justice of the peace.

Then a couple of months after they were married, Florence told Sam her cancer had gone into remission.

I thought it was great that she wouldn't die from cancer, but it was a whole new ballgame. There was no more mention of adoption. Whenever I brought it up, Florence would say, "You have nothing to say about it." Things changed.

The cancer wasn't terminal, however, their relationship was. Sam caught Florence in lies. She called with excuses for him to come home. She'd be up all night, drunk at 3:00 A.M. and bothering his mother with phone calls complaining about Sam.

The clincher was when I went with a guy friend on a business trip to Cincinnati. I'd gotten a job in computers by then. Florence called me and said my mom was in the hospital dying and I needed to come back right away. I was terribly upset and we drove all night to get back home. When I rushed in the door, Florence told me my mom wasn't in the hospital, after all. She just wanted me to come home. I was upset and we argued. She had been drinking. She drank all the time now.

After this, Sam still tried to work things out, but he couldn't take the lies and the fighting.

Florence started going to the bars drinking, and I don't know what else she was doing when the bars closed. Her last lie was when she was out all night until 6:00 A.M. I said, "That's it!" She tried to get me to stay, but I took my stuff and moved out. After I left home I didn't give her my phone number. I was done. I filed for divorce. I saw her at court and never again.

Florence seemed to have wanted a babysitter for herself and her daughter. Sam never was able to get a straight story or to find out if she ever did have Hodgkin's.

It was all sorta vague. I don't know if she did have it. I took her at her word, but almost everything else was not true. My father died young, two years before, and my uncles died young, too. So I figured that's the way things happen.

Sam tried to keep Florence and his mom apart, although he couldn't stop Florence from calling his mom and complaining about him.

It was not the best thing for Florence to do, since that did not endear her to my mother. My mom often mentioned to me that she did not want Florence calling her, so I know she did not like Florence.

My whole life, my mother was very manipulative. When I was a kid she would guilt me into things, like doing farm work. She always seemed to know when I was about to leave the yard. I could play in the yard unnoticed for hours, but as soon as I got the idea of grabbing my fishing pole and heading towards the creek, she came up with some chore for me to do. When I was around 11 years old, my two sisters were born a year apart. My mom didn't pay as much attention to me after that, but she still insisted on my staying home and made me feel guilty if I even thought about going out. When I grew up, it was, "How come you don't come to see me?" I lived 50 miles away, but she still expected me to go see her all the time.

Sam had married his mother. Just like his mom, Florence wanted him to be home with her all the time, even though when he was, he had to share her attention with the bottle, and then with the bars and other men.

After Sam's relationship with Florence ended, he saw a doctor of his own – to get a vasectomy.

I decided to have a vasectomy so a woman couldn't get pregnant and try to make me marry her. There'd be no trapping me into marriage ever again!

Timetable for Love

When Barry heard McKenna laugh at their socially inept math teacher's latest blunder, he turned around to check her out. He liked what he saw. He'd just transferred into the University of Utah, majoring in communications, after trying music and culinary arts at other colleges. He was new in town and trying to find himself. Things had been tough recently. The ski patrol had had to retrieve his dad from the slopes because of a ruptured aortic aneurysm. He survived, but Barry had had to be the strong one for his family, and it had worn him out. So when he met McKenna that day in class, he was emotionally exhausted. After class, she walked in his direction. They started talking and traded phone numbers.

She was very attractive, thin, with long brown hair, good skin and nice eyes. She had a fun attitude, like she was up for anything. I could see myself hanging out with her.

They started texting between classes. Math class met three times a week. It was not long before Barry asked her out for their first date. They went to a driving range to hit golf balls and then went to dinner. After a few weeks, McKenna made it clear that she wanted to be "boyfriend and girlfriend," exclusively.

I hadn't had any time for dates since I moved into town, so I was comfortable with that. We spent time together every day. It was nice to be back in the game.

McKenna brought up marriage a month after they started dating. At first she just mentioned it casually. Then Barry noticed that she had a stack of bridal magazines in her car.

When I asked her about them, she said, "I just like to look."

Then McKenna started bringing up marriage more often.

When she first brought up marriage, I told her, "I'll know when I'm ready. We're not finished with school and I don't have money." I had a little over a year left. She said, "I feel like a failure because I'm not married yet." McKenna was very strong-willed and knew what she wanted. She had a game plan for life, when everything was going to happen down to the month! She'd planned when she would graduate, marry, and go to grad school. This is not the way

I live. What happens, happens.

We'd be watching TV and she'd go, "So I've been thinking, if we got done with school, got engaged at the end of the year, and got married right away in the spring, then I could apply for grad school." When I didn't give her the green light, McKenna would become emotional and tell me she just knew I was The One for her. She'd said, "You make me happy, it feels like it works, and I know what I want. I'd say, "I enjoy being with you, we have a good thing going, but I'm not ready to make a commitment. It may be the next check mark on your to-do list, but I'm not ready." She'd get frustrated and upset.

After she began bringing up marriage, McKenna said they should have dinner with her parents. Barry went along with it. He had always been open to meeting a girl's parents. They always liked him. He came from a family with good values, and he had an education and a job. Along with school, McKenna was working as a receptionist for a med spa, where they did Botox and beauty treatments.

She had to look perfect and wore makeup all the time. She always made a big production to get ready. One day we were at Target. She said she could never buy clothes from there. I asked her, "If the exact same thing was $20 here and $60 at Abercrombie, which one would you buy?" She said she would buy the one at Abercrombie because otherwise she would know it came from Target. By the time we were dating, she was already on her second brand new car that her parents had bought her.

Barry started realizing that he was doing everything for her, from preparing their dinner to preparing her for the Graduate Record Exam, and from doing the dishes to doing her homework. McKenna would just sit on the couch. And when he brought it up one time, she said she never did these things before and it wasn't in her nature to help or to do things on her own.

Sex started out great, a lot of fun. But then she seemed to be less interested. It was not huge on her end. I dropped hints that I would like to do it more. She sighed, "Is that all you think about?" We had sex every one to two weeks. It was good when we did it. She made me feel like I was lucky for what I got. She implied that we could have great sex all the time if we got married and had our own place.

McKenna brought up marriage more and more frequently, from once a month to once a week. Each time she used a different strategy. Sometimes she would cry.

She tried to get my sympathy by saying, "Things never go right. I can never have what I want in life."

Other times she'd get angry and tell him there was no reason to delay it. Still other times, she'd give Barry a guilt trip.

She'd say, "This is what I want, is this not what you want?" "If we don't get married, we'll need to get two different apartments when I go out of town to grad school." She just assumed I would move with her wherever she wanted. She convinced me I could get a job just as easily somewhere else.

The more frequently they went to dinner with McKenna's parents, the more Barry started seeing red flags.

I watched how her mother treated her father. They were like two dogs. The mom was dominant and the dad was submissive, but they were still playing together. McKenna was trying to do the same to me. Her parents had a strange relationship. Her dad lived at a hotel. He came home for breakfast, went to work, came home, went out to dinner, and then he went back to his hotel. They had this arrangement because of her mother's obsessive-compulsive disorder that apparently made it difficult for her dad to stay home.

With her timetables for love and life, McKenna undoubtedly had inherited or copied some of her mom's obsessive compulsiveness. However, the greatest pressure to marry came from her being the eldest of three sisters. The youngest, a teenager, not only had a boyfriend, but they had exchanged promise rings and had made marriage plans. McKenna was desperate to marry before either of her younger sisters did.

Throughout their relationship, McKenna also used a subtle, but pervasive, threat to get Barry to the altar.

She kept bringing up this guy she dated before me. He was a car mechanic. She told me she was ready to marry him, but he didn't get on the ball fast enough, so she ended it. She kept implying that he missed the boat and that I would lose out, too, if I didn't agree soon enough to her marriage plans. I got the impression that McKenna didn't care who she married; she just wanted to get married.

Indeed, after they'd been dating for about 10 months, McKenna followed through with her threat. Barry's two best friends, Mason and Slider, moved to town. They had all played in their school band and had remained best buds. They went out for beers and had poker nights at Barry's place.

McKenna took a special shining to Mason. I noticed she was distant to me, but I tried to shrug it off by telling myself she was just having one of her funks. Then we went to a club one night: me, McKenna, Mason, Slider and Slider's girlfriend. McKenna ignored me. She was dancing behind Mason. When we got back to my place, I brought it up. "What's going on?" She confessed, "I'm attracted to somebody else." I said, "Mason?" She said, "How do you know?" How did I know? It was very obvious. She told me things were not good between us. She said, "You don't open up to me. You don't want to talk about marriage." I said, "We talked about it. It could happen, but I'm not ready. I'll work on it." I knew I needed to say, "I'll work on it," but I didn't know how. I was totally submissive at this point and really wanted to continue our relationship, but our trying to work on it lasted about two weeks.

Meanwhile, behind Barry's back, McKenna started going out to lunch with Mason. Sheepishly, she finally told Barry it was over between them.

She just said it flat-out, "I don't have feelings for you anymore.

I have them for Mason." The next day Mason came by. He said, "I told her I'm not ready for a relationship. I couldn't do this to you, buddy."

But about a week later, through Facebook and mutual friends, Barry found out that they were in a full-fledged relationship. He called each of them and left a message wishing them luck.

I told them, "I'm done with you because you had no respect for me." McKenna wrapped Mason around her little finger. He'd just moved to the area, like me when we'd started going out, so he hadn't gotten established here yet, and he had more free time to spend with her. McKenna ended our relationship in August and my former friend proposed in December. I wasn't surprised they got engaged so quickly, but I was hurt.

McKenna contacted Barry by phone and email at least once a month, even after she was engaged to Mason. She left messages asking Barry, "Can we talk, please?" But Barry never responded and never spoke to McKenna or Mason again.

A mutual friend told Barry that McKenna had wanted Mason as a back-up, in case Barry wouldn't marry her. Apparently, McKenna used to do the same thing with her mechanic boyfriend. She'd dump him, go off with some guy, then tell him she wanted to come back and he'd take her back. McKenna was hoping that the mechanic would then realize he had better marry her quickly or he would lose her. It didn't work with the mechanic, and it didn't work with Barry.

She'd had me hooked because I mistook lust for love. She was slowly breaking me down and it was working. But after it was over, I realized how much of a pleaser I am. With McKenna, 90 percent of the stuff I didn't like, but the 10 percent I did like kept it going, and I sucked up the rest.

McKenna had another obstacle to overcome in her race to get Barry to the altar. She should have recognized it the first time he took off his shirt. About a year before he'd met McKenna, Barry had gotten a tattoo. Over his heart it read, "Angela," his mom's first name. No wonder he couldn't consider marriage yet, his heart still belonged to Mama.

Green Card Marriage

My dad woke up at 27 years old with a house in the suburbs, a wife, three kids, and a mortgage. These were the last things he wanted. He let everyone know how unhappy he was by storming at my mom and cheating. When I was 12 years old, traveling with him to an out-of-town convention, I saw him kiss a woman. We never talked about it. You didn't question my father. My folks were mismatched and married for much too long. My childhood taught me to avoid marriage. I got "spayed" or "neutered" in my thirties because women's biological clocks were ticking all around me. That's how I sidestepped getting trapped by any of them and stayed single until I was 44 years old.

But Greg's luck ran out when he met Ming. She didn't care about children. She had something more utilitarian in mind. Greg was a successful consultant living on the West Coast when he went online to look for love and came across Ming's profile. They traded emails and phone calls.

Ming was adorable and funny. She had a self-deprecating sense of humor. She was extremely bright. Her English was just imperfect enough to be really charming. From our first email exchange, I could tell that she was very quick-witted, which was especially impressive because English was her third language. Her first was her local Chinese dialect and her second was Mandarin.

Greg doesn't remember where they went on their first date. Usually, he would take women he met online to coffee, lunch, dinner or a walk in the redwoods.

I do remember that Ming was seriously cute because of her petite size – less than five feet tall, her smile, and her pixie haircut. She was 30, but she looked about 12, with an ear-to-ear grin. She was more Sally Fields than Marilyn Monroe. I always found Sally Fields sexy.

They saw a good deal of each other and their relationship progressed quickly. Soon after they met, Greg helped her to get her deposit back from her landlord who was denying that she was entitled to it. Greg's imposing physical presence – six feet tall and muscular – facilitated matters. Ming was very impressed.

She liked the big guy-small girl thing. I suffered from a crippling congenital disorder: white knight syndrome. I had an ongoing pattern of riding to the rescue of damsels in distress and she had a way of bringing that out.

Indeed, had Ming not been a particularly determined Husband Hunter and Trapper, she might well have been considered an Ultimate Damsel in Distress type of bad girl. Greg helped her when she had a flat tire or her car broke down. He comforted her when something went wrong in her grad school classes or when her ongoing problems with her parents flared up. Greg had insecurities, as evidenced by his naming his little Pomeranian dog "Rambo." Despite his actual height and weight, he needed reassurance that he was a big man. So a little woman, who needed his help, made him feel more confident. She would be less likely to leave him than his first two girlfriends, who died suddenly. One had had a stroke and the other had been raped and murdered. Greg needed a woman he could count on. What he didn't count on was Ming's hidden agenda.

A month after they met, it was the third anniversary of Greg's mother's death.

We went to the cemetery where my mom was buried. I got emotional and Ming saw my tears. She put her arms around me and whispered, "Your mom sent me to take care of you." Looking back, I doubt Ming was sincere, but it certainly worked to reel me in.

Another month later after more complaining about her landlord issues, Ming moved in. That's when Greg learned she had other issues… with immigration.

I knew she was on a student visa, but I didn't know it had expired and she'd begun getting threatening letters about it. She'd counted on getting a job to extend her legal status, but she hadn't been able to find one. I walked in one day, right after she moved in, and found her sitting on the sofa and sobbing. "There are no jobs here. I'm going to be deported!" She didn't want to go back to China as a failure and have to live with her horrible parents again.

Greg had vaguely thought that they would live together and then see how it went. If, after a couple of years, they were still happy, he would have considered marriage. But now he felt pressured to do something about her situation – and fast.

Ming said, "You have to marry me! If we get married I can stay. Do you want to marry me?" I said, "I'm thinking about it. We've only been living together a few days. Let's spend some time and see how it works out." She kept crying and saying, "I don't have time. They're going to kick me out of the country!" It became the subtext of the relationship from then on. We kept talking about it and trying to figure out solutions. We went to an attorney who specialized in immigration. She got more and more stressed out.

A couple of months later, Greg succumbed. He took Ming to a romantic restaurant on the beach and gave her a ring.

Ming was the most ecstatic person I'd ever seen. I was in love, but it was too soon, so it was also because of my white knight syndrome. Seeing how happy she was, I felt I had rescued her and it felt good. I thought she was in love, too, although not madly.

A couple of months more and Greg and Ming were saying "I do" on a mountaintop in Hawaii in front of a justice of the peace.

It was sunset. It couldn't have been more romantic. She'd told her parents she was getting married. I think they were relieved. Ming had been married in China to a man they didn't like. He was busted for drugs and brought shame on the family, which is why she was encouraged to gallivant to the United States.

On our wedding night, we didn't have sex because we were too wiped out, but the next morning it was good. In general, the sex was okay. I thought it would get better as we got to know each other. She was willing to have sex, but she wasn't very responsive. I tried to get her to open up sexually and personally, but it was taking longer than I'd expected.

Then the newlyweds hit a rough patch. First, Greg lost just about all of his clients because there was a downturn in his field. Then he had a bad accident playing soccer. He had to have three back surgeries and had to pay for them out of his own pocket. So on their first wedding anniversary, he was disabled and rapidly heading for broke. Ming was not happy or supportive.

This was not the deal she bought into. Ming was a sourpuss most of the time. She did what a good wife is supposed to do – sat up all night in ICU and took care of things at home – though she was less than charmed about having to do it.

In fact, Ming wasn't always the "good wife."

She whacked me on my back when I was still recovering and sore. Ming got a charge out of being a little person making a big person wince. She jabbed me or poked me about a dozen times throughout our marriage. I told her, "The next time you do this, I'll slap you back." She did it again. I turned around and slapped her hand. This was the last time she ever did it. It was a parental relationship. Ming was like a child. It was like when you slap a child's hand when they reach for something they're not supposed to.

There were other problems, too. Ming became a less willing sexual partner. There was no sex from the time Greg got injured. It was impossible for six months, and after that Ming just didn't want to resume. So although he was recovering physically and financially, her immigration problems had not yet been resolved, and their relationship was still strained.

Sex never resumed to the same level as it had been before. We had sex every few weeks and it wasn't that great because she was closed off and mad at me for what happened. Being married to me was supposed to be her ticket to a less stressful life, but so far, it was more stressful.

Two years into the marriage, Ming finally got her green card. They took off for China, hoping that this trip would mark a turnaround in their relationship.

But she was a roaring bitch from the time she got off the plane. We were staying at her parents' house in Shanghai and from there

*we traveled all over the country. Her parents were nice to me and
nasty to her.*

Ming's parents had always been disappointed that she wasn't
a boy. Her mom had been in the Red Guard and was still tough.
Her dad ran a small manufacturing plant and saw his daughter's
purpose as that of raising his status. Ming had never been able to
win their approval.

*I loved China, but no matter where we went, Ming couldn't
stop herself from being cruel to me. We'd planned that she would
stay there awhile longer. When I left, I told her, "I don't care if
you come back or not." On the plane, I kept asking myself what
I had gotten into and why. I would not have been surprised if she
hadn't come back. Two weeks later she showed up looking like the
dog after I caught him peeing on the rug. She apologized, but the
pattern repeated every time we went to China. She was always a
bitch there.*

Things weren't much better back in the U.S. either. Ming
was never as sweet as she had been before Greg married her. He
helped her start a new career, applying her education in computer
software to architecture. She remodeled a historical landmark that
had burned to the ground. When the project was completed, Greg
flew her parents in from Shanghai for the commemoration. Ming
thought this was a wonderful idea because she wanted them to see
how well she had done for herself, living in a house, with a rose
garden, overlooking the ocean. While her parents were here, Greg
paid for a trip to Vegas for all of them.

It was probably the best time we had throughout the whole marriage. We'd worn her parents out and tucked them into bed. Ming and I had great sex that night. At 1:00 A.M. I went to the vending machine. I ran into her parents. They had been out having a wonderful time, collecting matchbooks from every hotel on the strip.

But after her parents left, things between Ming and Greg went back to being dull and disappointing. They both worked long hours and stopped paying attention to their marriage. Ming started paying attention to getting her citizenship and enlisted Greg's help. He filled out a lot of paperwork for her and gave her nightly pop quizzes, while they took a two-week drive up the coast. She was excited. They had a lot of fun stops and took long walks on the beach. They chased the dog over sand dunes and picnicked on the rocks. When they got back, Ming took her citizenship test and passed. Greg planned a party for two days after her ceremony. But Ming's decision to bail after she got her citizenship had been made long ago.

Later I found out that my party only delayed her departure for two days because she'd already written a check to a divorce lawyer and put a deposit on an apartment. She sat me down at the dinner table after she had become a citizen and told me, "I want a divorce." It was the first time divorce had ever been mentioned. She made it clear she had no interest in going to a marriage counselor. She'd paid a ridiculous amount to her divorce lawyer because she intended to fleece me. I never saw it coming. I felt pissed, upset, blindsided. I asked her a lot of questions, like,

"What are the problems?" "Where are you going?" "When did you decide?" "Why now?"

Ming never really answered, but it was obvious. She no longer needed Greg. Now that she was a citizen, she felt invulnerable. And as if this wasn't hurtful enough, she twisted the knife a little deeper by serving him with divorce papers on Valentine's Day.

The Oldest Trick in the Book

When Mike moved from the East Coast to the Pacific Northwest to begin a job as an engineer, he was 32 years old and looking for 'no-strings-attached' fun. One of his coworkers offered to set him up on a blind date.

He told me, "You might want to go out with my sister-in-law. She's easy."

Phoebe was a divorced mother of two. Although she was approaching 40, her biological clock was still ticking… at least as a means to an end. Mike called her up and they met at one of the singles scene restaurant-bars downtown.

As soon as I saw Phoebe, I was immediately turned off. First of all, she didn't take pains to spiff up for our blind date. I was used to women who wore makeup, did something nice with their hair, and dressed up to make a good impression on a date. She was below average to average in looks, and she was boring, not interested in anything but herself. She was a pre-school teacher. We had nothing in common.

Mike was disappointed. As he sat there, having drinks and snacks, he tried to think of ways to politely escape. After a couple of hours, he attempted his getaway. Although it was late in the evening, Phoebe told him she was going to go to a lookout point at the top of a hill where there was a nice view of the stars.

My parents taught me never to let a woman go into a dangerous situation alone, so I said, "Whoa. Are you sure that's safe?"

Mike couldn't fathom letting Phoebe go on alone, so he told her he would go with her. They each drove in separate cars and he followed her to the park, where they began walking under the stars.

Phoebe kept standing closer and closer to me. She was anxious and begging to be kissed, so I kissed her. I was disgusted with myself and the thought that I kissed her. She was a lousy kisser. We kissed for a few minutes. I finally put a stop to it and said good-bye.

Mike had been invited to a barbecue at the house of one of his coworkers. Everyone was bringing a spouse. He had often been the only single person at such parties and it was always awkward. But he knew no one to invite... except Phoebe. He called her and she eagerly accepted. After the barbecue, they both ended up in Mike's apartment. It was late, they were tired, had had a few drinks and Phoebe lived a half hour away. She asked if she could stay and Mike allowed himself to be persuaded by her yet again.

258

We were naked in the same bed. This was my twentieth mistake so far. I could've slept on the couch. In the middle of the night, she woke up pawing me. Phoebe was like a woman possessed. I thought, "Maybe if I have intercourse that will satisfy her and she'll go away." I'm a people pleaser. She wanted to be kissed. I did it. She wanted to be penetrated. I did it. I wore a condom or she had a sponge. I can't remember, but she didn't get pregnant that night.

Mike also can't remember how or why they continued dating, but they did. They saw each other two or three times a week and went to dinners, movies, and clubs where they listened to music.

I was so disgusted with myself. I was hoping she'd get tired of me and realize I was the wrong guy. On our first date, I made a point of telling Phoebe, "I'm playing the field and not interested in making any commitments, getting married or having kids." But she was as desperate as I was. Both of us hung around too long. At this point, I was feeling stuck.

On one occasion, Mike had invited Phoebe over for dinner. When dinner was ready, she still wasn't there and hadn't called. He called her and left messages. Two hours later, she showed up giggling. She had been with her sister and they had had a few drinks. Dinner was spoiled.

When she walked in, Phoebe just shrugged and said, "I was having a good time." There was no apology, not the slightest remorse. I said to myself, "Oh, well." I had no cojones.

Whenever we went out, we ended up at her place or mine. We had sex each time. She told me she was using a sponge. We'd have foreplay; then she'd disappear into the bathroom to put in a sponge. I didn't know much about the sponge, but I did research, and it didn't seem too reliable. I asked her, "What are you going to do if you get pregnant?" She said, "Don't worry about it. I've had four or five abortions. I'll take care of it." So I let myself be talked into having sex with a sponge.

It wasn't long before Mike started dating and having sex with another woman, and Phoebe started dating and having sex with another man. They each knew about the other.

It was no big deal because we weren't committed to each other. I was thinking that I had to end this, but she was so emotionally volatile. I knew I'd have to wait for the right moment, so she wouldn't turn into Jekyll or Hyde – whoever the bad one was.

Phoebe sensed that Mike wanted to get out of their relationship.

Even when she knew I wanted to stop seeing her, she insisted on having sex. In fact, it seemed like she wanted to have sex more often. I wanted to use a condom. She cried, "Don't use a condom! You can't!" Condoms solidified her fears of me wanting to leave. When I was trying not to ejaculate she said, "You have to come!" I thought it was weird but it never occurred to me she'd want to get pregnant.

One day, Phoebe called Mike and told him she felt as if she

might be pregnant.

I still hadn't put two and two together. I thought, "Shit, birth control failed." I didn't think she was purposely trying to get pregnant. But as it turned out, she was afraid of being abandoned. She didn't want to be alone. The other guy was not worth hanging onto and, apparently she thought I was too good to let go. I had had an ongoing fear of her getting pregnant. She kept saying, "Don't worry about it." I had said, "Okay, if you ever have to go for an abortion, I'll take care of it."

But when Phoebe did get pregnant, she refused to get an abortion. She explained to Mike that the doctor advised her to wait a certain number of weeks before getting the abortion. After this wait, Mike took her to an abortion clinic. When she came out, she told him that the first time was just a consultation to give her a chance to sleep on it. He was already an emotional wreck. They went back a week later.

I was expecting her to go through with it this time. When she came out of the doctor's office, she looked sad and teary. I said, "Did you get it done?" She started crying. "I can't kill this baby! I can't! I can't!" I was thinking, "You said you killed four or five others." I had been struggling with depression most of my life, and this situation was just exacerbating it. I didn't know what to say. All I knew was that I didn't want to be with her, whether she was having my baby or not.

Mike went to see a therapist who told him he needed to get

out of the relationship. He told the therapist he was a wimp and a people pleaser who couldn't hurt Phoebe. The therapist had sessions with them as individuals and as a couple, and still kept telling Mike to leave whether Phoebe had an abortion or not.

I told Phoebe that the therapist told me to leave. Phoebe just kept crying that I was abandoning her when she was pregnant. She offered me a deal. The deal was that if I stayed with her through her pregnancy and Lamaze classes until she had the baby, and then two more weeks to be sure she was okay, I could leave and have nothing more to do with her or the baby.

Caught between a rock and a hard place, Mike agreed. Meanwhile, the therapist got Phoebe to confess that she'd stopped using the sponge on purpose to get pregnant.

When the therapist told me this, I told her, "I don't believe you. It couldn't be true." But the therapist insisted Phoebe did it on purpose. When I asked Phoebe, she kept insisting it was an accident.

Mike wanted to believe Phoebe because he didn't want to acknowledge that he had let himself get trapped. It was something that only happened to other men, or so he had once believed. Eventually he faced the truth that the therapist was right. During the pregnancy, they never lived together, but Mike held to the bargain he'd made with the devil: to be there for Phoebe until two weeks after she had the baby.

Phoebe was getting nuttier because of the pregnancy hormones. She went from sweet thing to Tasmanian devil in a heartbeat. As her due date was coming closer, I was terrified and hoping this would just turn out to be a bad dream. I tried to be friendly and supportive because I knew it wasn't good for the fetus if the mother was on edge.

Finally Phoebe started having labor pains and they rushed to the hospital. Around 4:00 in the morning, the nurses took her into the delivery room.

Phoebe's sister, who probably didn't know about our deal, said, "So Mike, are you ready for proud papa-hood?" I was thinking, "I would like to kill this woman." I scowled. Then the baby started popping out. It was a healthy baby girl. We all went into a huge hug. Phoebe had assumed that when I saw the baby, my heart would melt and I'd want to marry her and live together happily ever after. But it wasn't about the baby. There was no way I wanted to spend my life with her.

Mike spent as much time as he could with Phoebe and the baby to make sure all was stable. At the end of the two weeks, they went to a Robin Williams show. They were still in agreement that this show would be their last night. They shared a lot of laughs and it seemed like the perfect way to end their time together.

That night I tried to be as gentle as I could, saying goodbye through our last sexual encounter. In the morning I was getting ready to leave. She was anxious and teary. Then she dropped the bomb. She begged me to stay for six months more. "Things will change, you'll see," she pleaded. I looked at her like I couldn't believe what she had just said. "Just give us six more months," she begged. I said, "We had an agreement." She was crying. I went to walk out. I turned around. There she was, looking after me, lonely and abandoned. I was bawling like I never did before, but I drove away.

Each step of the way, Phoebe had convinced Mike to stay long enough for her to persuade him to get to the next step. She realized she was losing her grasp, so she redoubled her efforts, calling him at all hours of the day and night, whining and crying. Finally he changed his phone number and moved, trying not to leave a trail. He wanted to become invisible.

One day, ding dong, the doorbell rang. It was Phoebe. She had gone to the county courthouse to see if there was a record of me buying a house. She said she needed to use the restroom. I said, "Okay." We talked. She left.

But she came back again, this time with the baby, and she wouldn't leave. I had to call the police to get her off my property. They talked to her. She left. She got my new number and kept calling and screaming that I wasn't taking responsibility for the baby, which meant, "Come back to me." I wrote her a letter saying, "I don't want anything to do with you or your baby." I put it in her mailbox so it would take less time to reach her. The next day at work, I got a subpoena for child support. I started thinking of killing myself or killing her. There was no chance I would've done it, but I couldn't stop fantasizing about it. I went to the emergency room and got a prescription for Valium to help me calm down and sleep.

Mike got an attorney who recommended a paternity test. The results came back with almost 100% probability that he was the father. He didn't want to be a deadbeat dad, but he felt as though he had been raped, or at least defrauded. When their court date arrived, the baby was almost three years old. He had only seen her once, when Phoebe brought her over as an infant. Mike agreed to a settlement for child support.

I felt terrible that the child didn't have a two-parent family, but I didn't want anything to do with Phoebe. And I thought her yelling and screaming at visitation exchanges would be worse than the child not having a father.

Mike heard nothing more until nine years later, when he received an envelope in the mail addressed to him in a child's handwriting. It was from his daughter. Mike happily began a correspondence with her, until Phoebe put a stop to it. She wrote, "You're going about this all wrong. You can't have a relationship with our daughter unless you have one with her mother."

This was the last thing Mike wanted, but he had been going to therapy on his own for depression and now wanted a relationship with his daughter more than he wanted to avoid Phoebe.

Mike's therapist had explained to him that the problem was that Mike couldn't say "no" to sex. Phoebe had made sex happen. Unconsciously, Mike had always felt that if he could get a woman to have sex with him, he could try to make himself believe that somebody loves him and that he's loveable.

Since Phoebe had full custody, he had to contend with her moods and whims as to when he could take his daughter to the park, or for ice-cream, or carousel rides. Phoebe was jealous and angry that he wanted to be close with their daughter, but not with her, so she purposely frustrated Mike's attempt to build a relationship with their daughter. She tried to stop him from sending a birthday card or calling.

I figured out a way around Phoebe's prohibitions. I sent money to the Jewish National Fund to buy my daughter trees and had them send her a card. Phoebe wrote back, "You can plant all the trees you want, but you can't have contact with our daughter, nor can anyone on your behalf."

And so began a chaotic mixture of restricted visitations with his daughter, court appearances, and custody evaluations – all the roadblocks Phoebe could muster to punish Mike for not wanting to marry her. After a lot of persistence and heartache, Mike finally got to see his daughter more and more frequently.

One day I got up the courage to ask my daughter, "Were you curious about where I'd been?" I admitted I was afraid of being a dad. "I didn't want to do the wrong thing. I didn't want to hurt you, but I know I did by not being there. I'm sorry." She nodded.

And so the pain of feeling unwanted and unloved gets passed down inadvertently from generation to generation. Like her daughter, Phoebe had been abandoned by her own father, a binge alcoholic who would disappear for days. Her childhood was filled with random and unpredictable chaos, which she unconsciously recreated in her adult life because it was familiar. Desperate not to lose another man, she tried every trick in the book to keep Mike permanently connected to her, ultimately relying on the oldest one – getting pregnant.

Mike's family looked like "Ozzie and Harriet" from the outside. His dad was a doctor and his mom a furrier. But on the inside, it was not a pretty picture. His volatile parents provided food on the table, but little love and attention to Mike's three older siblings and himself.

I got my brother's hand-me-downs. He was much bigger, so my pants kept falling down in gym. The gym teacher got a rope to hold them up. I was totally humiliated.

By seven or eight, I was starting down the road to depression. My brother tortured me relentlessly. He pulled my pajamas down, stuck his finger in my ear, called me a moron, and worse. We shared a room. Every night he'd jump on me, pin me down, put his butt in my face and pass gas. Then he'd take the pillow and smother my face. He'd fly over to his side of the room until he had some flatus ready and then jump back on top of me. I tried telling my parents, but no one believed me. Instead, they punished me for "instigating" him. I didn't know what "instigating" meant, but I knew they weren't protecting me.

Like Phoebe did later, Mike's parents were punishing him. They were letting Mike's brother act out their own anger for Mike's very existence. They had only wanted the three children they already had… and then Mike came along. When he was a teenager, his mother told him that he was an unwanted pregnancy. But in his heart, he already knew.

Famous Husband Hunters and Trappers

Nadya Suleman – Whereas a typical Husband Hunter will have one baby to get her man, Nadya has taken husband trapping to another level by having 14 of them. Though it has been generally assumed that she had her brood to garner fame and fortune, her underlying goal was to trap her elusive sperm donor into marrying her.

Jessica Simpson – Jessica was desperate to marry her quarterback Tony Romo. When she planned her birthday party with the theme of Ken and Barbie, not too subtly hinting that she wanted to play house, Tony finally had had enough and bailed.

Jamie Lynn Spears – At age 16, Jamie Lynn announced her pregnancy. The father, Casey Aldridge, was not ready to stop his teenage partying. Though they began living together, things fell apart, and he has not yet committed to marriage.

Sadie Hawkins – In the *L'il Abner* comic strip, when Sadie became a spinster at 35, her father declared "Sadie Hawkins Day," on which he held a foot race. When he fired his gun, all the bachelors in Dogpatch had to start running. The one who Sadie caught and dragged kicking and screaming across the finish line was supposed to become her husband. This started a trend in the strip and in real life.

<u>Nicole Richie</u> – Though Nicole had wanted to hold out for marriage to lead singer Joel Madden before having children with him, she gave in. She's hoping that each child will bring him closer to the altar.

<u>Eva Peron</u> – When Eva, an actress, affectionately known as Evita, met Colonel Juan Peron, a powerful politician, at a charity fundraiser, she knew that hitching her star to his would be a strategically brilliant move. When the gala was over, she walked out arm-in-arm with her prize.

<u>Kourtney Kardashian</u> – Kourtney hoped that having a baby with Scott Disick would push him towards the altar, but so far Scott, who has cheated on her before, hasn't altered his skirt-chasing ways.

Chapter 9
THE HUSBAND STEALER

What does a Husband Stealer want?

A Husband Stealer wants the satisfaction of knowing that she is able to steal a man away from his wife, proving that her beauty and charm is irresistible, even after a man has pledged his heart to another.

Why? To be victorious in a love triangle to make up for her defeat in her earliest love triangle – her rivalry with her mother for her father's love. Though these motives are unconscious, The Husband Stealer is very conscious of feeling validated and powerful when a man leaves his wife for her. It's this bad girl's way of proving that she is the most alluring of them all.

The Husband Stealer is not content with available men since there's not enough excitement in that. She gets her thrills by poaching another woman's guy because it's her way of getting revenge on her mother for the love and attention her mom 'stole' away from the bad girl's dad. When the husband leaves his wife, The Husband Stealer gets vicarious pleasure out of righting the perceived wrong of her childhood. She is symbolically showing her mother – and the world – that her dad (like the husband she steals) really preferred her, but was tied by societal convention to her mom. Since her father could never demonstrate his love by leaving her mom, The Husband Stealer gloats when she manages to get a husband to leave his wife.

In the modern era, where daddies often have affairs, sometimes The Husband Stealer's most powerful rival for Daddy's love has not been her mommy, but his mistress. This gives the bad girl extra satisfaction when she grows up, becomes a mistress herself, and successfully wins her man.

A wedding ring is like catnip to The Husband Stealer. It suddenly awakens the pleasure centers of her brain and brings out her claws. The married man is a greater challenge than a single man. *What do you mean I can't have you? We'll just see about this,* she thinks to herself.

History is replete with famous home wreckers, since the taboo factor makes these bad girls' conquests worthy of much tongue-wagging. From Scarlett O'Hara to Angelina Jolie, these women will stop at nothing to take the love they feel entitled to reclaim. The heart of a Husband Stealer beats faster, watching this memorable scene from "Gone with the Wind," as she identifies with Scarlett's agony when Ashley Wilkes rejects her for the much less glamorous Melanie:

Scarlett: You'd rather live with that silly little fool who can't open her mouth except to say "yes" or "no" and raise a passel of mealy-mouthed brats just like her.
Ashley: You mustn't say unkind things about Melanie.
Scarlett: Who are you to tell me I mustn't? You led me on... you made me believe you wanted to marry me.
Ashley: Now Scarlett, be fair. I never at any time...

Scarlett: You did, it's true, you did!

Scandalous Hollywood home wreckers have also included Elizabeth Taylor, who stole Eddie Fisher away from Debbie Reynolds and Richard Burton away from Sybil Williams, and Julia Roberts, who stole Danny Moder from his wife, Vera.

Famous Husband Stealers are found in all arenas. In politics, Camilla Bowles stole Prince Charles away from Princess Diana, and Rielle Hunter got pregnant to steal John Edwards away from his wife, Elizabeth (and from his chances of ever becoming president). In sports, Tiger Woods's many mistresses stole his heart, at least for the moment, away from his wife Elin Nordegren.

The unconscious psychological roots of The Husband Stealer are found in classical myths. In the feminine Oedipal Complex, also called the Electra Complex, the little girl wants to steal her daddy's love away from her rival, her mother. Oedipus cannot escape his destiny, prophesized before his birth: that he would kill his father and marry his mother. Out of her love for her father, Electra plotted revenge against her mother and had her killed.

The poet Sylvia Plath was consumed by her possessive love for her father and guilt over his untimely death when she'd just turned eight. Years later, she explained that her poem "Daddy" "is spoken by a girl with an Electra complex. Her father died while she thought he was God." In her poem "Electra on Azalea Path," Sylvia likens herself to Electra, both of them having mourned their father's death for the rest of their lives. Sylvia writes,

> *I brought my love to bear, and then you died....*
> *It was my love that did us both to death.*

Sylvia did not steal anyone's husband per se. But, ultimately, when she felt she was losing her daddy-substitute, Ted Hughes, to his mistress, Assia Wevill, Sylvia committed suicide.

Why do men fall for Husband Stealers?

Some Husband Stealers make stealing men away from their wives a sport. How is it that this hobby is so easy to engage in? A man who falls prey to such a bad girl is caught up in the illusion that the grass is always greener on the other side of the fence. He sees the flaws and failings of his wife every day, from menstrual cramps to morning breath, and bad moods to bathroom smells, while from afar, The Husband Stealer looks perfect.

The allure of The Husband Stealer is enhanced when the man, at risk of being stolen, is already angry at his wife. He could be angry at her because she's too critical of him or has let herself go and gotten fat, and is no longer arm candy for him. He could be resentful that his wife is not giving him something that The Husband Stealer seems to offer, like a baby, more attention, more sex, better cooking, a cleaner and better decorated house, or even more money.

And still other men are captivated by The Husband Stealer's charms because she seems to offer them an opportunity to escape from a life that they may no longer find satisfying and, indeed, may find frustrating and depressing. These men get caught up in the fantasy of being able to start over without the old responsibilities they had as a husband and father. Indeed, with this bad girl, the man's stolen kisses, renewed sexual drive, romance and passion are exhilarating. It's no wonder that such a man willingly dumps his flannel pajama-clad wife for a woman in Victoria's Secret or Frederick's of Hollywood lingerie, who feeds him strawberries and false promises of how it will all be different with her.

Real Stories from Men on the Dating Front

Ousting the Incumbent

Ever since he was a little boy, Mark dreamed of being the hero, fantasizing about being David in "David and Goliath," and then about being Luke Skywalker in "Star Wars."

Luke lived in a rural area, like I did, and was a dirt farmer, like many of the people in our town. He became a hero and that's what I wanted to be. When I was in Boy Scouts, I prayed I'd run across someone who needed a tourniquet. And I wanted to be the one to hit a home run at the bottom of the ninth.

So when Mark grew up, it's no wonder that he went into politics... and that he was vulnerable to Jennifer, a Husband Stealer, who made him feel like a hero.

They met at a political fundraiser. Jenni was a volunteer supporter for her friend Arlene, who was running for state office. And Mark was managing Arlene's campaign. They exchanged pleasantries. Jenni asked him to look her up when he was in her city because she'd won an election for something like dogcatcher or mosquito controller and thought she'd like to run for a higher office and might want to hire him to run her campaign. Mark didn't think much of it because people were always telling him this, and most of the time they weren't serious or, when they were, it was years later. Still, he thought Jenni seemed intelligent and fun.

Several weeks later they met again as the campaign trail took them to another event. Mark dropped Arlene off at her hotel and went with Jenni to a bar where everyone goes to see and be seen. At the end of the evening, he walked Jenni back to her hotel and said goodnight in the lobby at the elevator.

Arlene's election took place about a month later. She reserved hotel rooms: one for herself, one for Mark, and one that was designated as the "campaign room."

Jenni hadn't reserved a room for herself, but Arlene told her she could stay in the campaign room.

I said, "I'll be in there 'til 2:00 A.M. working on stuff." Jenni didn't have a problem with that, and she started helping me. The campaign had been draining. We were on our last lap, so having someone working alongside me helped keep the energy up. Suddenly Jenni grabbed my crotch, unzipped my fly, and started giving me oral sex. I was not expecting it. I thought, this is different. I got married at 19 and had had sex with only one person until that night – my wife.

Mark was in his mid-thirties and had been married to Joyce for 15 years. They had two sons. They also had marital problems, primarily stemming from his wife's chronic battles with depression.

After Jenni surprised and satisfied Mark with oral sex, he left the campaign room to Xerox some flyers for the election. When he hit the cold night air, he tried to process what had just happened.

He thought Jenni was attractive, but on a scale of one to ten, she would be one point below his wife. As far as flirtatiousness, however, Joyce didn't come close.

I'm a flirty guy, but women usually viewed me as harmless, like a gay guy, because I married my high school sweetheart. I've never been around someone like Jenni before. Wow.

The next day Arlene won the election and they all stayed in town to celebrate with drinks and dinner. Then some of them got a 12-pack of beer and went back to the campaign room. As the night wore on, they started leaving, one by one.

My buddy was trying to be helpful by getting me out of there so that I wouldn't give in to the temptation of having sex with Jenni. He was saying, "C'mon Mark, let's go." I said, "I'm gonna hang around for a while." I figured I made a mistake once, so I might as well do it again. I didn't think I was horrible and I wasn't thinking that I'd leave my wife.

Jenni was very active and very talkative in bed. My wife was not. Jenni said things like, "Oh, you look so good, you feel so good" – all those things you want to hear. She was making a lot of noise when we had intercourse and she had an orgasm. My wife did not, and she never performed oral sex on me.

The next morning Mark asked Jenni if he could contact her. He swears that he was just trying to be polite, and he wasn't thinking about pursuing their relationship, but he admits that, of course, he liked what had gone on between them. About a year before,

Mark had begun thinking that he and his wife weren't going to be together forever. He wanted to stay married at least until his kids were grown, but he and Joyce were more like friends than lovers.

My marriage wasn't totally sexless, but almost. We had some periods of six to eight months without sex. Usually it was once a month in the missionary position – not very exciting. And Joyce never cooked and didn't keep the house clean; she didn't even do basic household chores.

After Arlene won the election, she hired Jenni, which now made Mark Jenni's direct supervisor. Their next assignment took them out of town together for 10 days. They spent 12 to 15 hours a day working on the campaign and sleeping in each other's rooms.

I started falling for her. We began telling each other we were in love. We said we'd both be better off without our spouses. My wife was not politically-oriented. She was more of a drag on my career. Jenni was politically savvy. She was totally into my career and was trying to push me forward. She knew if I climbed the ladder, she would go with me. I thought Jenni would be a plus for my career, but she turned out to be a minus.

As the months went on, Mark and Jenni's love grew, as did their political clout. He was promoted and, in turn, she was promoted to fill his position. They continued traveling together along the campaign trail. People suspected they were having an affair, but no one had proof.

After a while, Jenni grew impatient for Mark to leave his wife. When Arlene held a major meeting of all her campaign staff, Jenni cornered Mark and gave him an ultimatum.

She tried to break it off because I was not making a commitment to divorce my wife. Jenni told me, "This is not going to work!" She was trying to push me away or force me to make a commitment. After the meeting, I went home to my wife and said, "I'm getting my own apartment." Joyce asked, "Are you having an affair?" I admitted, "I fell for someone else." My wife was upset. We had a big family discussion with our kids. My 13-year-old son was pissed. My 11-year-old son was sad.

When I got my apartment, it was the catalyst for everything to change. My boss Arlene said, "You and Jenni are not doing this on my watch! One of you has to go!" Arlene hated that I moved out to pursue my relationship with Jenni. It was a woman thing. She was really upset with Jenni. She took it as a personal affront and told me, "We've got to get Jenni out." But when Jenni heard about this, she said, "I'm not gonna be the 'other woman' who's run out of town on a rail!" Arlene had thought Jenni would resign to save me. I offered to resign so she could stay on, still get a paycheck, or I would stay on and use my position to get her a job somewhere else. But part of Jenni's strategy was to get me to resign so that I would be beholden to her. She didn't have a ton of money, but she had more liquid assets than I had. It never crossed my mind to depend on her.

When I had my apartment, I spent the nights at Jenni's house with her and her children. I was in love with her, but it was tumultuous financially, professionally, and personally – like being in the path of a tornado. Jenni was a powerful personality. She'd always say, "The two of us can conquer the world! Screw everybody! We can make money and own politics. As long as we stick together, we can do anything!"

Mark started looking around to see if there was some other political position he could transition into. When he called one colleague, he didn't find a job, but he found new insights about his boss, Arlene. This colleague had had an affair with her and told Mark that he was sure she had planned to have one with him, too. Mark had never looked at Arlene that way. She was much older, married, and had a son about his age. He began reflecting on all the red flags he had missed.

In politics, you hug. I didn't take it to mean anything. Arlene was very friendly and she frequently offered, "You can stay at my house when you're in the neighborhood." I thought nothing of it. Come to think of it, Arlene probably purposely didn't arrange for a hotel room for Jenni that first night when we were campaigning. Afterwards, she kept sending Jenni and me on trips together when she didn't need to. I told Arlene I didn't think it was necessary and asked her why she was sending her. She said it was because she didn't think I'd be there forever and she wanted me to show Jenni the ropes. One of the last conversations I had with Arlene was disturbing. She put her hand on my knee and said, "If you're going to divorce Joyce, there are other options...." I said, "I'm in love with Jenni."

It became clearer and clearer to Mark that his boss had wanted to hook up with him.

Arlene thought Jenni was a playgirl, that she wanted to have sex, but wouldn't get divorced. So my boss figured Jenni would get me to get divorced, then she would leave the picture, and then Arlene would have me to herself. But as all of this was happening, it was not on my radar.

Mark's boss was a politician, a strategizer. She wanted to win the 'seat' in his heart, so she had planned out all the moves. Indeed, Mark's boss was a Husband Stealer-by-proxy.

Meanwhile, when Jenni wouldn't resign to save Mark's political position, it was a turning point in his feelings towards her, too. He had not only been swept away by their physical relationship, but also the promise of her being a boon to his political aspirations. In the end, they both resigned.

By this time, Joyce had seen a divorce attorney. Mark had seen a divorce attorney. And Jenni was further down the road. She'd already seen an attorney and had her ducks in a row to finalize her divorce. All she needed was the commitment from Mark, and she was getting more impatient. Jenni arranged for Mark to "meet the parents," a rite of passage on the way to the altar. Her parents had had a long marriage, about 40 years. Jenni had been jealous of their love for each other and their strong bond.

It was the end of October, almost a year since Mark and Jenni had first laid eyes on each other. A perfect storm was brewing. And the waves were heading straight towards Mark, as events conspired all at once to persuade him to leave her.

First, my good friend who knew about my affair drove all the way from our hometown to tell me to go back to my wife. He said, "Jenni is the flavor of the month. It's too volatile for you, politically, to be with her. People have idealized your marriage with Joyce because you were high school sweethearts. It is not going down well that you left her." Then Jenni's husband called me. He said, "I'm pissed at you. But besides that, if you want a relationship with your sons, you'd better not marry Jenni." She'd stolen him from his wife and now he only saw his sons once a year. That night, I was reading Jenni's daughter a story. Jenni leaned over and whispered sweetly, "You're gonna make such a good father to my kids and Joyce will find a good father for yours."

Later that night, Joyce called Mark to make arrangements for Halloween. Both of them wanted to take their boys trick-or-treating. Joyce put her foot down and said that the only way he could take them would be if he came back home. On his way over to see Joyce to try to work out the Halloween arrangements, he was mad because she was trying to dictate the situation.

I was thinking, "This is crap. I'm gonna go over there to fix it."

When he got there, it was dark. He and Joyce sat cross-legged on the front lawn in the cul-de-sac and talked for almost three hours.

Joyce said, "I'm gonna take these kids so far away you'll never see them again!" How far? I didn't think she'd really kill the kids or herself, but I couldn't be certain. She'd never threatened to kill herself before, but she was depressed. In the back of my mind, I wondered if she could have meant that. Joyce finished by saying, "If you go back to her, we're through. This is a one-time offer. I'll take you back."

Mark drove back to Jenni's house with Joyce's threats still ringing in his ears and sending chills down his spine. He wondered whether she could really harm their children. He felt bad for the harm he had already caused them by moving out. But the main thing that kept bugging him was what Jenni had said about how he would make "such a good father" to her children, while Joyce would find one for his children. She had meant it to be a sweet remark, but it had made him queasy.

When Mark reached Jenni's house, she came to the door to greet him with a kiss and casually asked, "Did you work things out for Halloween?"

I said, "I've gotten something worked out... I'm going back to my wife." When I told her this she was in the kitchen with her arms crossed. She said, "Get out! Get all your crap and leave! Tell Joyce she doesn't have to worry about me coming after you. She won!" Jenni had always felt victorious over Joyce. She was winning... until the end. When I went to see Joyce, I had no idea I was going to leave Jenni. By Halloween, I'd moved back into my house. I'm still upset that I left my tools and grill at Jenni's house.

Mark's sudden turnaround and his unanticipated pronouncement to Jenni that he was going back to his wife were a bit harsh.

As is often the case with husbands who have been on the precipice of being 'stolen', when they hightail it back to the security of their wives, they become hostile towards The would-be Husband Stealer. These men are fearful of changing their minds again because of the temptation that still exists to run off with her.

I'd made the decision. It was not a time for hand-holding. I was making a logical decision to leave. I'd been in love with Jenni. It was hard. But if I sit on the couch and hold her hand... it prolongs the agony. I expected anger – and that's what I got. Jenni didn't cry. I had to be cold because there was still that attraction. It's like firing someone. It's better to rip the band-aid off quickly.

When I'd moved out, I told my kids that I had fallen in love with someone else. When I moved back in, I told them that I loved them and that both their mother and I loved our family, so we were going to try to make sure that we kept it together. I've been tempted to call Jenni, but I've resisted the temptation.

Jenni hadn't realized what she was up against when she tried to steal Mark away from Joyce. The bloom was definitely off the rose of his marriage, but he and Joyce had a history rooted in childhood, growing up in a very small rural town. They met at age 10 in middle school and began a friendship. They started dating when they were juniors in high school. After high school graduation, it was customary to stay in the same town and live there forever.

You were supposed to pick a person in your class, or the class before or after you, and marry them. Joyce was one of the prettiest

*girls in the school. I was infatuated with her since middle school –
partly because she wouldn't give me the time of day. She was with
the popular crowd; I was not. We became "Mr. and Mrs. High
School." She was from one of the historic families who founded
the town; I was from the other side of the tracks.*

Mark's father was a minister. Before they settled in this rural
town, his family had had to live in parsonages and move every two
or three years.

*Churches are very political and Dad never liked the politics.
He lost more than he won. So he had to keep moving to have a
congregation. We were like the Griswolds in those Chevy Chase
movies, with the transmission breaking down. When my dad finally
gave up the ministry, he got depressed. Even though he was a
college graduate, he ended up pumping gas at a truck stop for
years until he found a job ministering to the sick.*

When Mark and Joyce were 16 years old after dating for six
months, they began having sex. It was his first sexual experience,
but not hers.

*I initiated it. Afterwards, Joyce said she'd had sex before
and was on the pill, but she wasn't having sex with just anyone
who took her out for dinner. It was ingrained in us that sex is a
bad thing. I grew up in a very religious home, where you're not
supposed to have sex before marriage. To my mother, everything
was bad. If you had any alcohol you would become drunk and get
sick; if you had sex you'd catch diseases and get pregnant; if you*

masturbated then sex wouldn't be as much fun when you had it years in the future. I'm not sure why I bought into it – the idea of marrying one's high school sweetheart. We married at 19 and had kids by our early twenties. Maybe I married Joyce because I felt guilty for having premarital sex.

When Mark left Jenni and returned to Joyce with his tail between his legs, she made a lot of demands.

She told me I had to go to counseling and cut off all communication with Jenni. I did both. She asked me, "How did this happen? I want to know how another woman got my husband's pants off!"

Joyce began getting increasingly depressed.

She lived on the couch for four or five weeks, literally, just watching movies and doing nothing else.

Eventually Joyce began going to therapy, which started uncovering her past.

It came out that, when they were growing up, her brother had made her give him oral sex.

It was no wonder that she had not wanted to do this with Mark, and that she had always had conflicted feelings about sex.

Then Joyce told the counselor that she been holding a knife to

*her wrists, but couldn't go through with it because of the children.
The counselor called me and we spoke with her. Joyce said she still
had suicidal thoughts and wasn't sure if she could restrain herself
one hundred percent of the time. We persuaded her to check into
the hospital.*

Joyce started on the road to recovery, but Mark couldn't help
feeling those chills down his spine again, remembering her threats
before Halloween. She'd warned him if he didn't come back to
her, "I'm gonna take these kids so far away you'll never see them
again." Maybe she would have done it....

Curiosity Killed the Cat

Remember Nick – and his Penthouse Pet, Kimberly and
Commitment-Phobe, Victoria? Well, before he met them, he was
involved with a Husband Stealer – a bad girl who stole him from
his first wife, a mistake he still regrets. Nick has been married
three times. Each time he has run into Husband Stealers, but after
the first one wrecked his home, he learned how to spot them.

*I'm certainly no Brad Pitt, but whenever I've been married, the
girls I'd meet from day to day would come on hot and heavy. Being
married is like coming to a party with a woman. If you come to a
party alone, women aren't that interested. But if you bring a date,
women suddenly flock around and give you their phone numbers.
I didn't talk about being married, but I had a ring on. The first
thing women did was look for a ring. If I'd decline their advances,
pointing out that I'm married, their comeback would be, "I didn't
say I wanted to marry you. I said I wanted to fuck you!"*

When Nick married his first wife Paulette, she was a virgin. They were both in art school in New York. Nick was studying interior design, Paulette was studying fashion, and Sarah, The Husband Stealer, was studying fine arts. Paulette was smart and in the top 10 percent of the class. She was also sweet and beautiful.

Paulette was a real trophy wife. Sarah was not as pretty as Paulette at all, but Sarah either had a larger-than-life view of herself or she didn't care. What Sarah lacked in looks, she made up for with her free spirit.

Sarah's parents were old-school and were married for what seemed like forever, so Sarah had to keep proving that if she couldn't win her father away from her mother, she would win other men away from their wives.

Sarah broke up with the guy she was dating and went after me because she was bored and it was a tempting challenge for her. She was not madly in love with me. I got caught up in the heady feeling of having two women competing over me.

In his senior year of art school, Nick managed a local camera shop. He liked the status it gave him. Sarah "dropped in" five or six times a day to flirt with him.

Sarah kept asking me, "Why don't you come over sometime?" I'd tell her I was married. Every time she came into the photo shop she had one more button of her blouse unbuttoned. I blew it off. Then one day, after she'd been coming on to me for five months, I thought, "I can do this – for one shot." Then it became one or two times a week. I felt guilty. I was too immature to be married, and having two women willing to give me sex was exhilarating.

I told Paulette, "There's this girl trying to pick me up. She keeps coming into the shop five or six times a day." Paulette said, "Why don't you just tell her not to come in?" I said, "I can't, it's a store." Then she'd ask, "Is she cute?" "No," I'd answer, "I can't believe you think I'd be interested in another woman. If you don't trust me maybe this relationship is over!" Then she would say, "Oh, honey, I didn't mean to make you feel bad, like I don't trust you." And the conversation would be over. This is the way we guys change things around to make the woman feel bad.

As aggressive as Sarah was in relentlessly pursuing Nick, she was even more aggressive in bed.

Sarah was very animalistic in bed. She would say, "If you did that two inches to the left it would feel a lot better." She never worried about my feelings or if I'd be insulted. She was always suggesting different positions – like anal sex. I didn't even know what that was. Afterwards, I thought, "Hmm... this is cool!" Paulette was like a librarian. She only knew missionary position. After having tried different positions with Sarah, I suggested to Paulette, "Let's do this on your hands and knees." Paulette would always say, "I'm not interested." This gave me another excuse to be with Sarah.

After several months of clandestine rendezvous, Nick started sleeping over at Sarah's place one or two nights a week. He would simply tell Paulette he wasn't coming home and left her to wonder why not. Nick and Paulette lived on the 17th floor of a Manhattan high-rise near school.

One night when I was sleeping over at Sarah's, Paulette put on her wedding gown. She sat and stared at herself in the mirror, thinking of happier times or wondering why she married me. We had a kitten. We kept the window open a crack for ventilation. That night, while Paulette was staring in the mirror, the kitten crept out the window and fell 17 floors. Paulette had to go down and find the dead kitten in the bushes. I showed up at 7:00 A.M. and saw her in her wedding gown, stained with mud. I've just been the biggest asshole on the planet.

As we learned before, Nick was adopted.

I've always felt I needed back-up. My biological mother didn't want me. And at three days old, I didn't know I'd be adopted. Then when I was adopted I always worried I wasn't good enough – and they would return me for a refund! When I was dating Sarah and married to Paulette, it wasn't about showing that I was a stud. It was that if one of them didn't want me anymore, there would always be the other one. I had girlfriends starting at age 13. Each time we broke up, it felt like another abandonment. It had to do with my feelings of abandonment from being given up for adoption. If a woman had a pulse, it was all I needed. I still ask myself, "What could I have done that was so bad that my mother would walk away?"

Nick started wondering if he'd made the right decision to marry Paulette. Her father kept putting pressure on her to divorce him, which always made Nick nervous that one day she would listen to her dad and leave him. Paulette's father was an executive of a steel company.

He called me an "artiste." He worked with his hands, like me. But he did it with steel and I did it with a paintbrush. He thought I was effeminate, not a real man.

Nick had confided in Sarah about his problems with Paulette's parents. Sarah took advantage of this by playing on his insecurities. At the end of his senior year, both girls still had one more year of college to go. Sarah was afraid that if Nick stayed in New York after graduation, she would never pry him away from Paulette.

Sarah wanted to separate me from Paulette so if I got bored with Sarah, Paulette wouldn't be around to go back to. Sarah was from Washington, D.C. Her brother got me a job as a White House photographer.

Sarah knew Nick wouldn't be able to turn down a job offer like that. She planned to visit him in D.C. on the weekends – and have him all to herself.

I never said to Paulette, "You're coming, right?" And she never said, "I'm coming, too." I confessed to Paulette, "I've been messing around with a girl." Paulette asked, "Are you in love with her? Do you want to be with her?" The more I was honest with her about Sarah, the more Paulette was angry and willing for me

290

to leave.

Nick wanted to be with Sarah, or so he thought at the time.

Paulette kept forwarding my magazines to me in D.C., and she penciled in the margins: "I miss you," "I love you," "Come home." I just kept thinking, "Don't mark up my magazines."

Nick was angry at Paulette, not only because of the rejection he anticipated when she would finally listen to her dad, but because she gave him up too easily.

I wanted Paulette to fight for me. I wondered why she didn't insist on coming with me to show me the marriage was most important.

After Nick was in D.C. for several months, he began to hear rumors that Sarah was involved with other guys. And her weekend visits trickled down to nothing. Their relationship fell apart. After a while, he invited Paulette to come down for the weekend.

We had a wonderfully romantic weekend: candlelight dinners, car racing, and sex. Paulette seemed like she was trying to rekindle our relationship. She told me her dad wanted to make it up to me and accept me. We still loved each other. Then she went back to school. She only had a few months left. I kept waiting for her to come back to me. But it was like "The Twilight Zone." The weekend had everything but the payoff.

A couple of months after Paulette came down, I had an epiphany. I realized that Sarah was the biggest mistake of my life! I called Paulette to tell her I wanted to get back together. But instead of calling her, I accidentally called my parents in the Hamptons. My parents loved Paulette and I was going to tell them about my epiphany.

But before he could do that, Nick's parents put Paulette on the phone. It turned out that his parents hadn't wanted her to be alone, so they had been having her come visit them on the weekends.

I told Paulette, "I want to get back together." She said, "It won't work because I got the divorce papers the other day, and you're supposed to sign them." I protested, "We had such a great time." She said, "It's too late." Paulette had gotten the divorce papers because I didn't say something that weekend she came down and didn't call the next day to say I wanted to get back together.

Of all the things I could do over in my life, that phone call is it. I didn't immediately get on a plane or get in my car and go to my parents' home to patch it up and tell her to tear up the divorce papers. Instead, I said, "Okay, fine, if that's the way you feel, then fine. Just know I was ready to patch it up." Why didn't I say, "Put Mom or Dad on the phone" and get them to convince her? Paulette wanted me to try harder, to say, "Don't do it. Tear up the papers!"

But Nick didn't do this because he was afraid. Nick had found the experience of having two women fight for him terribly seductive because his biological mother had never fought to keep him; she simply gave him up for adoption. When Paulette didn't go to great lengths to fight to keep him, it made him feel that she was just like his biological mother. They were both too willing to give him up. He was afraid that Paulette would ultimately reject him, as his birth-mother had done.

Even when Nick was adopted, he never received the hugs, kisses and praise he craved. His adoptive parents had had an extensive military career and maintained their tough attitude towards his upbringing.

My adoptive mother was a tough broad. She grew up in a poor Pennsylvania coal-mining family. When she was a little girl, she had to earn her own money for food. She walked for miles, alongside the hobos, carrying big wicker baskets, collecting body parts to be buried in Potter's field. So when she adopted me, she couldn't tolerate my sensitivity or artistic temperament. She was not huggy or kissy, which was what I needed. I always felt I was a disappointment to her.

My adoptive parents dealt with my adoption by doing nothing more than handing me a book, "The Adopted Baby." It was written like "Dick and Jane." It said, "You're special because you were picked out." When I went to kindergarten and anyone asked about my parents, I'd say, "I'm special because I was picked out."

But Nick didn't really feel special at all.

In recent years, Nick tracked down Sarah. She had become a designer. He emailed her.

I wrote, "I can't believe what you did to break up my marriage." She emailed back, "I don't bear any guilt because you wouldn't have left if you didn't want to. I have no remorse." But I still do.

Famous Husband Stealers

<u>Scarlett O'Hara</u> – Scarlett's obsession with stealing Ashley away from his wife, Melanie, ruined all of their lives. Though a part of Ashley longed for Scarlett, he stayed married, much to her consternation. Her Husband Hunting ultimately prevented her from falling in love with the dashing Rhett Butler, until it was too late, and he uttered the famous line, "Frankly my dear, I don't give a damn."

<u>Angelina Jolie</u> – The "sexiest woman in the world" set her sights on the "sexiest man in the world," Brad Pitt, and just had to have him. Brad, angry at Jennifer Aniston for not giving him babies, was a vulnerable target. But he soon found out that the grass was not really greener with Angelina.

<u>Lara </u> – In the film "Dr. Zhivago," Lara steals Yuri Zhivago away from his wife, Tonya. Yuri becomes obsessed with Lara and dies of a heart attack – literally, a broken heart – in a Moscow street, chasing after a woman he believes to be his beloved Lara.

<u>Elizabeth Taylor</u> – Liz made Husband Hunting a hobby that made headlines. First, she heisted Eddie Fisher from Debbie Reynolds, and then Richard Burton from Sybil Williams. Her passionate romances were like car accidents – even though there were casualties, people couldn't take their eyes off of them.

<u>Julia Roberts</u> – Danny Moder's wife Vera didn't stand a chance when Julia noticed Danny, the cute guy behind the camera, and decided that "Pretty Woman" wanted him for herself. It was hard enough to compete with Julia's feminine wiles, but the 'promotion' she offered was too much to resist.

Julianne Potter – Ironically, Julia Roberts (as Julianne) plays a Husband Stealer in the movie "My Best Friend's Wedding." The tagline for the movie is that Julianne fell in love with her best friend the day he decided to marry someone else.

Camilla Bowles – It boggled everyone's mind, from the Royal Family to the lowest commoner, how Prince Charles could prefer Camilla to Princess Diana. Camilla finally captured her Prince, but then became a 'royal' pain.

Rielle Hunter – On the road to the presidency, John Edwards was led astray when Rielle approached him at a bar, flattered his ego, and got him into bed long enough to impregnate her. Elizabeth stood by her man far longer than she should have, but finally gave up the ghost and moved on.

Tiger Woods's Harem – Countless women have put a 'Tiger in their tank', hoping to hijack him for more than one night of pleasure. This wild man is now realizing he made the mistake of his life, since Elin will no longer be in the clubhouse when he gets off the fairway.

Fantasia Barrino – This "American Idol" winner is not winning fans now ever since she moved a married man, Antwaun Cook, into her home and had his name tattooed on her shoulder. Her sad suicide attempt is a harbinger of disappointment to come.

Leann Rimes – Married songbird Leann made a play for married actor Eddie Cibrian when they played lovers in the Lifetime TV movie "Northern Lights." The action didn't stop when the movie wrapped and both their marriages headed towards divorce.

Denise Richards – Hollywood home wrecker Denise wrecked Heather Locklear's marriage to Richie Sambora and wrecked her 'BFF' friendship with Heather. Ultimately, Denise's relationship with Richie was brief and not worth the grief.

Sarah Symonds – Sarah has made a career out of husband stealing. She's bedded celebrity chef Gordon Ramsay, among others, as 'research' for her handbook for the other woman.

Barbara Walters – In Barbara's memoir, she confessed to having affairs with married men, including Senator Edward Brooke and catering guru Claude Philippe, bragging that these affairs were luscious because they were "forbidden fruit."

Nancy Bacon – On assignment, Nancy, a Hollywood journalist, was sent to the set of "Butch Cassidy and the Sundance Kid." She got more than a story out of it. She and Paul Newman began an affair that caused him to separate from his wife, Joanne Woodward, until he realized he loved Joanne more.

Abbie Cornish – Abbie met Ryan Phillippe on the set of "Stop-Loss," but that didn't stop her from stealing him away from Reese Witherspoon and his two children, breaking Reese's heart.

Georgia O'Keeffe – Photographer Alfred Stieglitz staged a photo shoot of Georgia at his home, knowing that his wife, Emmy, might well return home and that a confrontation would free him to marry Georgia. It did, and after Georgia married Alfred, she suffered from his ongoing affairs with younger women.

Stephanie Birkitt – "Late Show" staffer Stephanie kept a diary of her tryst with David Letterman, which continued after Letterman wed his long-term live-in girlfriend Regina Lasko. Stephanie simultaneously carried on a relationship with producer Robert 'Joe' Halderman who allegedly tried to extort money over the affair.

Chapter 10
THE ULTIMATE DAMSEL IN DISTRESS

What does an Ultimate Damsel in Distress want?

An Ultimate Damsel in Distress wants to be rescued from the fire-breathing dragon outside her turret, which today means anything from poverty to physical abuse, depression to disability, or loneliness to a low credit score.

Why? To feel safe and secure, knowing that her 'knight in shining armor' is eternally at her side to take care of all her needs, free her from life's hassles and protect her from danger.

One of the most duplicitous types of bad girls is The Ultimate Damsel in Distress. Appearing weak, helpless and in need of a big strong man to rescue her, she is particularly enticing to knights looking to feel powerful and worthy. She knows just how to wrap a man around her little finger, while shedding crocodile tears. Though she may, in fact, be in some genuine distress, she's fond of using melodrama to manipulate a man to come to her aid.

Blanche DuBois, in Tennessee Williams's play "A Streetcar Named Desire," is the prototypical Ultimate Damsel in Distress. Blanche arrives at her sister Stella's home at the end of her rope, having lost everything: her family to fatal illnesses, her husband to suicide, her ancestral home to creditors, her position as an English teacher, her battle with alcoholism, her morals, her standing in society, her self-respect, and her pride. Stanley, Stella's husband, sees through Blanche's affectations and has little sympathy for her. Desperate to find a man who will rescue her from her plight, Blanche musters her feminine wiles and fancy finery to entice Stanley's friend, Mitch, to marry her. But before Blanche entraps Mitch in her web, Stanley reveals her sordid past and sends Mitch running for the hills. Her last hope seemingly dashed, Blanche loses touch with reality and a doctor is called to take her to the asylum. In the last scene, we realize that this Ultimate Damsel in Distress may, in fact, have found a knight to rescue her after all.

Doctor: Miss DuBois. (Blanche stares at him with desperate pleading. He smiles.... Blanche extends her hands toward the doctor. He draws her up gently and supports her with his arm and leads her through the portieres.)
Blanche: Whoever you are – I have always depended on the kindness of strangers.

Underneath her ultra-feminine façade, The Ultimate Damsel in Distress is dangerous. She not only exploits her knight's need to feel heroic by finding endless quests for him to pursue on her behalf, but even after he fulfills them, she ends up breaking his heart. Some Damsels may even put a man's very life in danger. Just look at Tinker Bell, who almost did Peter Pan in because of his involvement with Wendy.

Few women could seem more helpless than tiny Tinker Bell with her fragile gossamer wings. Yet her jealousy of Wendy allows Captain Hook to ensnare her in his plot to kill Peter. Hook pretends to conspire to shanghai Wendy and take her to sea, if only he could find Peter Pan's lair. Tinker Bell, thrilled at the promise of Wendy being led away by the pirates, points out the way on a map of Never Land. Hook leaves Peter a "present" of a bomb. Though "Tink" tries to warn Peter, the bomb explodes and he barely survives. Peter ends up searching desperately in the rubble to rescue her.

Don't you understand, Tink? You mean more to me than anything in this whole world!

The Ultimate Damsel in Distress is a broken-winged woman, who has always wanted to be 'daddy's little girl', but whose father did not rescue her from 'dragons' while she was growing up. Daddy either wasn't around, wasn't the rescuing type, or may have been a 'dragon' himself. So The Damsel is still searching for this feeling of safety and security that an ideal daddy would provide.

If The Damsel is a waif, she may want someone to guide her towards fulfilling her dreams. If she's disabled, she may want a caretaker. If she's poor, she may want a man to take care of her bills. If she's being beaten, she may want a strong man to frighten her abusers. If she's misunderstood, she may want sympathy and a shoulder to cry on. If she's frightened of bankruptcy and losing her socialite status, she may want a man who's willing to beg, borrow, lie, cheat and steal to help maintain her illusion. Whatever the plight of The Ultimate Damsel in Distress, she holds out eternal hope that a man she can coerce into becoming her 'knight in shining armor' is just around the corner.

To some degree, all bad girls are damsels in distress because they all have wants, borne out of a deprivation or danger that they want to be rescued from, but those in this chapter are The Ultimate Damsels in Distress.

Why do men fall for Ultimate Damsels in Distress?

Men who fall for Damsels are often living out their own rescue fantasies, but this time they play the knight, instead of the wimp who watches from the sidelines. Such a man wanted to rescue his mother when he was little, but did not have the power to save her from her psychological demons, his father's temper, poverty or whatever other dragons were outside their door. Or, the man may have wanted to rescue his sister from being abused, but couldn't because he was too little and too scared, himself. On the other hand, sometimes a man who falls for Damsels has had lots of practice as a child caring for a mother who depended on him, such as one who was chronically ill, so he learned that caretaking was the way to a woman's heart.

Many times, men who fall for Ultimate Damsels in Distress are secretly or unconsciously wishing that they themselves would have been rescued as little boys from their 'dragon-mother' who neglected or mistreated them. They feel that it's unmanly to acknowledge these long-hidden, but still smoldering yearnings, so they repress them and act them out by rescuing a Damsel, instead. But underneath, they're still longing for someone to call 911 for them.

The fairytale "Rapunzel" incorporates these seemingly para-doxical wishes to save and be saved. When Rapunzel became a young damsel, with splendid long hair, a sorceress locked her in a tower that had only a little window at the top.

When the sorceress wanted to enter, she stood below and called out:

"Rapunzel, Rapunzel, let down your hair to me."

One day, a prince passed by and, charmed by Rapunzel's sweet song, fell in love with her. When he saw that the sorceress reached her by using her long hair to climb up to the tower, he called to Rapunzel to let down her hair and he climbed up in the same way and began visiting her. She told him to bring a strand of silk each time he came so that she could weave a ladder and escape. But when the sorceress discovered this, she cut off Rapunzel's hair and banished her to the forest. Tying the hair to a hook, the sorceress fooled the prince into climbing up as usual. When the prince saw that Rapunzel was no longer there, he threw himself from the tower and fell upon thorns that blinded him. Eventually, after wandering in the forest for a very long time, he heard Rapunzel's song and was drawn to her. When she saw him, she threw her arms around him.

Two of Rapunzel's tears fell into his eyes. They became clear once again, and he could see as well as before.

So although the prince wanted to rescue Rapunzel from a distressful life alone in the tower, she ended up rescuing him from a distressful life of blindness.

The most compelling reason that men, even those who make

reluctant knights, mount their steed and go off in search of Damsels in Distress, is that they believe that distressed women will accept them – with their flaws - whereas more self-sufficient women will not. The more dependent The Damsel, the more reassured a man can feel that she is unlikely to abandon him, as other fair maidens have done. These men think that they need to rescue a Damsel in order to earn affection that she would otherwise not bestow upon him. In fact, once such a man has rescued his Damsel, he sometimes seems to lose interest. This is because, unconsciously, he becomes frightened that she will leave him since she doesn't need him anymore.

Real Stories from Men on the Dating Front

Pas de Deux

We met Ross, the self-admitted "Ginger" addict, in the chapters about Sex Sirens and Commitment-Phobes. After those dating disasters, he met Belle, an Ultimate Damsel in Distress who has left a deeper hole in his heart. But let's see how this all began.

When Ross was 10 years old, "Gilligan's Island" became his favorite TV show. Farm girl Mary Ann seemed wholesome, sweet and kind, but movie starlet Ginger was sexy, conniving and hot, filling his little boy's head with lustful fantasies that became a bad girl addiction later on. Also, during his childhood, he read *Archie* comic books and yearned for the capricious, spoiled Veronica, rather than girl-next-door Betty. When he was 11 years old, his parents took him to see "Dr. Zhivago" and he fell in love with Lara.

At that age, I didn't understand the politics or history, but I was captivated by Dr. Zhivago's choice. His love for Lara ruined his life and he ended up dying in the street chasing after her. He had an adorable wife, but Julie Christie was breathtaking. I could see why he chose her and it made a big impression on me.

Indeed it did. Ross has remained stuck in "Dr. Zhivago" and the rest of these stories from his childhood. His never-ending search for these fantasy women – Ginger, Veronica, Lara, and others – has gotten in the way of his finding a real soul mate and real love. Pop culture has perpetuated his search for elusive bad girls, who have been breaking his heart every step of the way.

In 'reel life', Ross was the leading man who got the girl, but in 'real life' the story didn't have such a happy ending. Ross's first big heartbreak occurred when he was a senior in high school and met Vanessa, a sophomore. She was his real life "Veronica."

I was always excited about the first day of school because I got to see the girls in my class. On the first day, you notice the drop-dead gorgeous ones, the second day, the very pretty ones, and on the third day, the pretty ones. I went after girls like these. No one told me what kind of girl I should go after. I wasn't the captain of the high school football team, but I was a cheerleader finalist. I didn't make it to cheerleader.

Vanessa was beautiful, with long dark hair and an exquisite body. She was wealthy, demanding, selfish, and immature. We dated my whole senior year. She was a virgin. I got towards third base, but she was getting scared, so I stopped. I was sorta fatherly. I took Vanessa to the prom in June. Afterwards, she became distant and things began to fall apart. When I confronted her on my birthday, in July, she broke up with me. She'd gotten tired of our relationship and had started seeing another guy. I was in tears for weeks. Even though her older sister tried to comfort me, it still took me two years to get over Vanessa. Maybe I've never grown up.

Vanessa was Ross's first bad girl. For a sophomore girl, being invited to senior prom was a coup. Though he was too caught up in his fantasy to pick up on her manipulative ways, it's likely that Vanessa hung in there until prom night, then started dating someone else and looking for her opening to break up with Ross.

When Ross was about 40 years old and still obsessed with bad girls of pop culture, he saw the movie, "Beautiful Girls." In the movie, a friend of Timothy Hutton's character, with posters of supermodels in his room, won't commit to his girlfriend because he's still looking for a supermodel. His girlfriend finally dumps him. The movie is a coming-of-age story about guys getting past childhood fantasies in order to deal with reality and appreciate life.

I am the Timothy Hutton character, Willie Conway. He's in his thirties. He moves back home with his family and meets an underage Natalie Portman. They're skating together and take a tumble. There's some sexual tension. He knows a relationship with her would be frowned upon. He tells her about how she'll outgrow him like she outgrew Winnie the Pooh, and that's why he can't see her.

The movie turned out to be prophetic, as Ross soon discovered when he met Belle, his ballerina.

It's the best 'meeting' story ever. I was in Blockbuster with my date on a Saturday night at 8:30 P.M., when I saw a vision of loveliness. She was a young Audrey Hepburn look-alike. My date and I wanted to rent "The American President." We went over to that section and Belle was holding the last tape. She said, "You can have it. I watched it already." My date was next to me, so there was nothing I could do. Belle left. For the next three Saturday nights, I went to Blockbuster at 8:30 P.M., but Belle never showed up. Then one day I was walking in the street and I saw her walking dogs. I went up to her. She didn't remember me from Blockbuster. She said she was house-sitting for my neighbor. I said, "Give me a call if you'd like to get sushi." She was my Natalie Portman. I bought the 1957 movie "Funny Face" with Fred Astaire and Audrey Hepburn. He was in his late 50s and she was 22. They were having a relationship. I left it at my neighbor's house for her. She never called. Then about a year later I was in Safeway. She walked past. By the time I got one more item, she was gone. I didn't know if she was 16 or 30. The next week I saw her drive by in an alleyway. It was Kismet. I took down her license. At the time you could go to the DMV and get the person's name, address and telephone number. She lived close by. I sent her a nice card. She called me at work. I went over.

When Ross got to her apartment there were warning signs all over the place, but he didn't heed any of them. Belle, who turned out to be 20 years old, had pictures of herself in every room. She mentioned that she was lying to her mother, having told her mom to keep sending her money for tuition at the university, though she was really using the money to attend a ballet academy and for living expenses. Belle told Ross she didn't want children because she would never want anyone to treat her like she was treating her mom, who struggled with two jobs to scrape together the money she sent her. Belle's father had abandoned them when she was an infant. All Belle had left of him was a couple of timeworn photos, anger towards men, a need to be rescued, and a pervasive sense of entitlement.

Ross and Belle began a relationship, spending the weekends together and going out to expensive restaurants. Belle was a virgin when they started making love. For two years Ross couldn't believe his good fortune.

She was my fantasy – a young Audrey Hepburn ballet dancer.

But then Ross realized that he had gotten in too deep and was in dangerous territory.

When I saw that Belle had a shower curtain with Winnie the Pooh on it, it blew me away. It was just like the movie, "Beautiful Girls," where Timothy Hutton told Natalie Portman she would outgrow him like Pooh. I started holding back because I was afraid of getting my heart broken. One time, Luciano Pavarotti was gonna be in town. I knew she would expect me to buy tickets, but I thought, "I'll be damned if I'm gonna buy tickets for her." I refused. I realized the writing was on the wall.

Ross couldn't get himself to make love to her anymore, either.

I could never feel secure with her. I knew if I lost my job or got sick she wouldn't stick around.

Then Belle got accepted for the summer session at a renowned ballet academy on the East coast. Ross paid for her tuition.

At the end of summer when she came back, I knew I'd lost her. She had changed. Soon she said she wanted to break up. We hadn't made love for two years. She found out she got accepted to the East coast ballet academy for the fall. I'd bought her a black cocker spaniel that she wanted. I was upset that I'd lose the dog, too. I paid the tuition, and hoped she might give me the dog back.

When the semester began, Belle kissed Ross on the cheek and danced out of his life. She did give him the dog back, but kept his heart.

I'm still not over her. Belle was the most self-absorbed woman I had ever met, but I still grieve and dream about her. I took over where her mother left off. She never even thanked me, but I wish I would've tried harder.

Belle danced for one year, then got injured and couldn't audition for a ballet company. It was the end of her dancing career, but the beginning of a yoga career.

She poses and performs everywhere. She's posted thousands of photos of herself on Facebook. "Here I am posing in front of the Louvre. Here I am posing in front of...." She's like that Travelocity gnome who goes all over the world. She lives 'the life of Riley'. I'm jealous and depressed. When I was a kid, I was in the local "Nutcracker" performance, but I never became a famous performer.

Belle was a waif when Ross rode up on his steed to rescue her. He supported her financially and emotionally through ballet schools, only to see her go on to find fame and leave him in the dust. Indeed, Ross seems to have given up early in life, somehow fearing that real life was bound to be a disappointment compared to the fairytales and fantasies that captivated him.

My mom was June Cleaver without the pearls. When I was a little boy, she would take me with her when she went to the beauty parlor. She told me to sit in the corner with crayons and I did. Sometimes she says she wished I would've thrown a few rocks.

But Ross was on his way towards becoming a 'good boy', not the type who would have thrown rocks. Ross's intimidating dad didn't approve, either, of his quiet and unassertive nature.

My dad had a temper. At dinner, he wanted me to tell him about my day, but I couldn't, so he slapped me. He never struck my mom, but he yelled at her. He was like Ralph Cramden from "The Honeymooners", shouting, "To the moon, Alice." Then, after a while, he'd say, "Alice, you're the greatest." I never stuck up for my mom. I just withdrew.

It would have been too scary for little Ross to try to rescue his mom, since he sensed how much frustration his dad had bottled up inside.

My dad was an insurance salesman, but he'd wanted to be a foreign correspondent. I wanted to be a baseball player.

When his dad was disappointed in him and lost his temper, Ross's mom never rescued Ross, either. These early years of living in a sitcom world, inhibited Ross later in his relationships with women.

When I meet a new woman, I can strike a match under myself and be charming, the life of the party, but it's not natural, not like Eddie Haskell saying, "What a lovely dress, Mrs. Cleaver."

Even after Belle, Ross continued holding out for a "Ginger." He tried Internet dating, dating services like Great Expectations and It's Just Lunch, mail order brides, everything, but his love life has been a vast wasteland. Ironically, his Ginger addiction has caused him to wind up on an island, where, like Gilligan, he's lost and stranded – but living with his aging mother instead of a starlet. Heartbroken one too many times, Ross has hopefully reached bottom.

"I keep being burned. I guess it's time to go after Mary Ann instead of Ginger."

The Knight Errant
Both before and after Alan's relationship with The Addict,

Felicity, he found himself trying to rescue Ultimate Damsels in Distress. There were four such damsels who came on to him at various times, weeping crocodile tears.

These relationships are all a blur now. They were one woman with four different names. They were beaten by their father or by boyfriends, and most by both: first their father, and then other men. My 'knight in shining armor' came out. I wanted to treat them like queens and rescue them from the horrors of their past lives. I wined them, dined them, opened doors for them, all the proper ways to treat a lady.

At first these damsels appreciated Alan's chivalrous treatment, but then there were problems.

If I said, "I love you," to one of these women who was used to getting punched afterwards, she didn't believe I loved her if I didn't follow it with a punch. They antagonized me to try to get me to punch them, either to validate their expectations or to prove I wasn't the genuine article. They would find things to argue about and escalate the argument from 0 to 60 in one second, getting in my face and trying to provoke me.

Sometimes there were violent ex-boyfriends lurking in the shadows, which made Alan's knightly jousting all the more challenging and satisfying because of the shadows in his own past.

My parents were divorced when I was three years old. After that, my relationship with my dad was fairly non-existent. When I was 12 and my father died, my mother confessed that he used to beat her.

Either these beatings happened when Alan wasn't around or he repressed the memories of them.

Upon learning of his violent history with my mother, I became extremely frustrated. He was dead, so I couldn't confront him or exact any kind of revenge on behalf of my mom. I suppose that's what led me to want to play the role of 'knight in shining armor' to the women in my life.

The One That Couldn't Get Away

Kevin was in his mid-twenties and he had been unlucky in love all his life. One awkward pseudo-relationship was more disappointing than the next. But that was before he met Jolene.

I was in love with a girl in high school. She was an honor student and really cool. A lot of us guys liked her. I had a couple of dates with her – nothing sexual. We had fun, but she was dating other guys at the same time. I bought her little gifts, like a costume jewelry ring and Harley Davidson underwear. Then she told me, "These two dates were awesome, but I don't think this is going anywhere romantic, so let's just be friends." I still had feelings for her, so it really hurt.

Next Kevin tried finding a girlfriend by scouring lists of potential pen-pals. He found a girl in a neighboring state and corresponded with her for a few months.

I didn't have the skills to talk to girls, so I tried writing to one. Then we had phone conversations and decided we loved each other. We agreed to go on a date to see if it could work. I met her and her friends, and we continued on to the amusement park. As we were driving there, she'd blurt out the exact same thoughts I was having, like, "Isn't that a strange-looking dog in the driveway?" I was dumbfounded. I said nothing. The next day she called me. She said, "If you can't talk to me, our relationship can't go anywhere." I was so distraught. I didn't know what to tell her, so we broke up.

Next Kevin joined a theatre group, hoping they might need him to be their stagehand. During rehearsal, he started flirting with a blonde actress.

I asked her to see "West Side Story" and we started dating. I fell in love with her. I thought she was in love with me. We dated for a couple of months. Then she said she was going to see a play with her mom. I said, "Want to go with me, instead?" She said, "No." She wanted to break up with me. She was an acting major, looking forward to exploring the world. I was looking forward to setting down roots.

After this, Kevin turned to an Internet dating site. The women he'd been matched with so far, according to their answers to questions, had a 70 percent compatibility factor with him.

They didn't pan out. Suddenly I logged in one night and I was

matched with Jolene, a girl who the system said was 99 percent
compatible with me.

Kevin and Jolene were both interested in fantasy and sci fi, not much to build a relationship on, but they were both desperate to find love, as well. They began to get to know each other through email.

It's not like I fell head over heels. I thought she was interesting. In an email, she explained that she'd been disabled from birth because her muscles didn't develop properly in the womb. She said she had very little strength in any part of her body, couldn't walk at all, and used a wheelchair to get around. But she was able to have kids and didn't need home help. Her disability didn't bother me. She was shy and hesitant to have a phone conversation because her voice was high-pitched. I said, "It doesn't matter."

After a couple of phone conversations, Jolene and Kevin decided to meet at the zoo.

I was just thinking that I wanted to be friends. She came with her sister and her sister's fiance. When I saw her, my first thought was, "She's very pretty." My second thought was, "She's in a wheelchair."

Unconsciously, Kevin was also thinking that at least Jolene couldn't 'walk away' like the previous heartbreakers he'd sort of dated, and she would be less likely to hurt him since she seemed to need him more. They got along well. The next week they chatted online. Jolene lived 55 miles away from the city where Kevin lived and worked, but he began traveling to see her every weekend.

I still just wanted to be friends because I didn't feel a great attraction to her, and it wasn't practical to try to have a relationship because she lived so far away. I told her, "We're just friends." But Jolene wanted to be more than friends. She told me, "Think about it."

Fortuitously for Jolene, Kevin had been feeling stuck in a situation that he wanted to get out of very badly.

If you think of the typical overbearing mother as a small ship, my mother was the Titanic. My parents had begun splitting up. My mom had gotten me to buy a house that she and I could live in together. Living with mom was really miserable. So for me it was: boy living with mother in bad situation happens to see girl over there who might possibly put him in a situation that could be better. Jolene kept telling me, "I think we have something good here." So I finally gave in.

The next time Kevin visited Jolene, he gave her a handwritten note telling her that they could be more than friends.

I wrote it on lined loose-leaf paper, like from grade school. It was my feeble attempt to be romantic. She was ecstatic.

Jolene was living in her father's house. Six weeks after they met, Kevin moved in and he commuted to work. Although theirs was still a fledgling relationship, Jolene pressed her advantage and told him, "You need to choose between your mother and me." Kevin began giving hints to his mother that she had to move.

I felt horrible. I told my mom I wanted to be a cop and cops don't make much money, so I couldn't afford my house anymore. My mom was working odd jobs. She went back to live with my dad in a crappy apartment in a bad part of the city. He was still having bad luck with jobs. My mom was a cat collector. Her cats had caused so much damage to my house that it sat there, unsold, for months, and I had to take a loss.

Six months after they met, Jolene went on the pill and they started having intercourse. Although they had engaged in some sexual activity before this, they had waited to consummate their relationship.

I was always a prude. Jolene was the first woman I had intercourse with. She said she was a virgin and I have no reason not to believe her. I wanted to wait to be sure that if she accidentally got pregnant, I would be okay having a child with her. During this time, we thought we were in love, but now I realize it was just that we were having more experiences together.

Two years into the relationship, they had come to assume they would get married. Kevin ordered an engagement ring. When it arrived, however, he didn't formally propose.

Our relationship was not lovey-dovey, but good enough. There was no getting down on my knee. I said, "Your ring came today." Jolene said, "Does this mean we're engaged?" I said, "Yeah." She said, "Okay, cool." But we never set an actual wedding date.

When they were first living together, Jolene was in college and had interesting things to talk about. After graduation she sent out countless resumes, but couldn't find a job. She became discouraged. Then her father got into a bad motorcycle accident, and Jolene had to take care of him. This brought up old wounds, since she'd always known deep down that, because of her disability, her dad had never wanted her. When Jolene was a little girl, her dad made her mom move out and take Jolene with her so that he didn't have to be reminded of her imperfections, which made him feel guilty and inadequate. But when her mom became involved with abusive men, Jolene's dad took Jolene back in. Now he was the one who needed looking after. As her future prospects became dimmer by the day, Jolene became more and more depressed.

Our intimacy went to zero. Jolene said she was too distraught to have sex and that her birth control pills lowered her libido.

When he was on the mend, Jolene's father let them know that he wanted them to move out. They found the perfect house. Kevin hoped that the privacy and romantic notion of setting up house would re-ignite their sex life, but there was still no real intimacy. Instead, Jolene became more demanding of him.

She always wanted to be right. I never had the courage to say she was wrong because she always brought her disability into it to manipulate me. Since it was a hassle for her to go out into the world, she wanted me to stay home with her. If there was one snowflake, she'd say, "You need to work from home today because you could spin out on the icy overpass and die." In the summer, she'd tell me I had to stay home in case there was a thunderstorm. I was forever capitulating to her. But whenever I was home, she had the TV on 24/7. "I want to be with you," meant taking TV as an IV drip while sitting in the living room ostensibly together.

For a while Kevin felt flattered that Jolene wanted him around, since neither one of his parents had cared whether he was around or not.

I was never close with my dad and my mother was harsh and neglectful. I never figured out what she was so angry about but when I was growing up, she was on medication, and every Christmas she landed in the psych ward. She saw the bad in everything. Jolene is just like my mom. They both have to be right all the time, and they throw fits if you don't do what they want.

My parents were hoarders, so our house was always a disaster area. When I was nine years old, there was a knock on the door. A repairman must have called Child Protective Services. My parents were working and I was home alone with my little brother. The social worker asked, "Can I come in and talk to you?" I said, "You need to come back with a police officer and get a search warrant," and I shut the door. I called a friend who lived nearby. In the next eight hours, my friend and I filled up trash bags of clutter and put them in the basement. The place was spotless.

When my mom came home, she freaked out and said, "What in the hell happened? All that stuff was important; what did you do with it?" I told my mom CPS came. She made me get the trash bags and dump everything out again. The social worker came back. She said, "We'll put the kids in foster care until this is cleaned up." People from the church helped my mom clean it up. After the social worker stopped coming, boom - the house was back to being a mess again! My mom is a perfectionist, but there were so many things that were out of her control. My father kept losing his job and they never had enough money. If she couldn't have the perfect living situation, she would have a perfect disaster.

From the time he was in kindergarten, Kevin liked to watch TV shows about saving people's lives. His favorites were "Rescue," which was about a man who drove an ambulance, and "Adam 12," which was about two L.A. cops. He dreamed of being an emergency medical technician. When he was a boy, Kevin wished he could rescue his mom from whatever was making her sad and angry, even though he bore the brunt of her discontent. When he grew up, he rescued her from the streets when he had her come live with him. But then he met Jolene, a Damsel in Distress who was in even greater need of being rescued. And though Jolene's demands were oppressive, they served to reassure him that, unlike the other women in his life, she is less likely to reject or run away from him.

The Knight in Prison Garb

When Christopher spotted Chloe at the crowded airport waiting to board the same flight to Europe, it was love at first sight.

I was mesmerized. I like little women. She was 5'1." I'm 6 feet. She was cute, skinny with large green eyes and blonde hair. I'd never gone out with a blonde. Later I found out it was dyed. All the girls I went out with before had dark hair, dark eyes, and were buxom; she wasn't. She seemed to have boundless energy and lots of friends milling about, seeing her off. But I especially liked her classy image and her sophisticated family.

Chloe and Christopher were 20 years old and off to a multi-city summer vacation in Europe. Once on the plane, Christopher struck up a conversation and Chloe told him her itinerary. He followed it and chased after her all over Europe. They landed in London, where she let him carry her on his shoulders because she was tired from the flight. But in Amsterdam, Chloe told the *housefrau* not to let Christopher stay in the same hostel. Rejected, he went off on his own. Three weeks later he ran into her on a street in Salzburg. When she saw him, Chloe turned to her girlfriend and said, "Oh my God, he's here, too!" Christopher took the last room in Chloe's hotel. It was the attic with ceilings that were only five feet high.

Part of the romance was the chase. I asked her to come to Innsbruck to go skiing with me. She told me she would come. I was waiting for her on the platform. Train after train passed by. I had always wanted to go skiing in Innsbruck. Instead, I wasted the day waiting for her to arrive. I was disappointed and mad, but I was attracted to her attitude; she didn't care. Years later, I found out she'd told her girlfriend she couldn't stand me.

Indeed, the faster Chloe ran away, the more determined Christopher was to pursue her and catch what seemed like a prize. On the outside, Christopher looked like quite a prize, too. He was a model who wore the best designer clothes, had a gentleman's manners, intelligence and just enough arrogance to be intriguing – except when Chloe was bringing him to his knees. But Christopher hadn't always been this debonair.

I was a chubby nerd until I was 11 years old. I used to watch "Star Trek" and eat chips. The kids made fun of me because I was fat. My mom bought me Husky clothes. I hated them. Then that summer, I went to camp at 5'3" and 165 pounds and, by the end, I was 5'8" and 135 pounds. One girl at camp grabbed my leg and wouldn't let go. I got to first base with a 17-year-old counselor. After camp, I went back to school in skin-tight jeans, boots and sunglasses. I dropped my nerdy friends and entered into the "sub-cool" category. You can never become really cool. You have to be born into it. At least I became "sub-cool." I was still a nerd inside, but I was practicing to be a pompous hottie on the outside. Even though girls started throwing themselves at me, I was still nervous around them.

Christopher had given Chloe his contact information. When she got back from Europe, she called him. She wanted him to introduce her to people he knew so she could expand her network.

On our first date, before she got to our table at the restaurant, I put a rose on it and told her how much I wanted to be with her. We dated on and off. She was not that into me. She would say, "We'll go out, but you have to come with my friends and family." There was always a condition I had to meet.

As Christopher got to know her, he began to see that, under a superficial layer of perfection, she was masking a lot of insecurities and psychological problems. When they finally had sex, Christopher discovered that she had intimacy issues.

She didn't snuggle and didn't like me to touch her affectionately. We got along, but there was a sense of unfamiliarity. She had body image issues. She didn't want me to see her naked. I found out later she had an eating disorder.

Chloe was fat until she was 11 years old – like me. Her father would put her down. He'd say, "I'll love you even if you can't fit through the door." Finally, she starved herself and lost weight. When I met her, she was anorexic and bulimic. She ate cakes and ice cream and then threw up. At first, Chloe tried to hide her eating disorder. She ate Caesar salads, but told the server to put everything on the side except the lettuce, so she was just eating lettuce. Finally, she confessed, "I have a problem." Then I tried to help her eat better and I watched her. Whenever she went to the bathroom, I worried that she was sticking her head in the toilet.

Christopher and Chloe continued dating for three and a half years. He catered to her every whim. She maintained an air of disinterest because she knew it would keep him hooked on the chase. But sometimes she seemed so fragile and needy. If he didn't rescue her, she would surely have found some other knight who would. After he got his MBA and Chloe had begun to count on him being around – like a comfortable shoe – he felt he had to go on to the next stage and marry her.

I'm from a well-respected family. My father had a chain of gift shops where people would list their bridal registries. So after a while, Chloe decided I was a decent catch. I attached a ring to the bell of a Gund stuffed cow, took her to a romantic French restaurant, and when she opened the gift box, I asked her, "Will you marry me?" The week before, I had asked her father for her hand. It was a perfect beginning to a disastrous marriage.

Ironically, Christopher chose a cow as the animal that would bare the engagement ring. Unconsciously, he may well have been trying to entice her into saying, "Yes," by assuring her he would be providing a lot of warm milk. But little did he know just how much milk Chloe would squeeze out of him.

They were married five years after that fateful European vacation. Since Chloe's parents' *raison d'etre* was putting on airs, and they fancied themselves as socialites, the wedding had to be an elegant affair. The bride wore a designer wedding gown, and her parents boasted to the 350 wedding guests that Christopher was a banker.

I got a job offer at Goldman Sachs. But Chloe wanted to be nearer to her family, so I turned it down. It was my biggest mistake, aside from marrying Chloe. I got a job at a bank and set to work. I was supposed to provide for the life Chloe was supposed to become accustomed to. During our first years of marriage, it was clear that she was unhappy. I found her crying in the stairwell of our apartment. This was the first sign we'd made a mistake. She'd be on the phone with her friends and carelessly toss me spaghetti for dinner.

Christopher climbed the ladder of success in the financial world and eventually they moved to Manhattan.

Chloe insisted that we rent a $4,000-a-month apartment. All my money went to the rent. She fell in love with the New York lifestyle and its frenetic energy. I got another investment banking job making twice the money. But $300,000 a year is poverty on the Upper East Side. I kept trying to buy my way into her heart.

But it wasn't working. Even after they were married, Christopher still had to jump through hoops to keep her interested and try to get some affection. He never got hugs or massages. Sometimes Chloe wouldn't want to have sex for six months to a year. They were married six years before they had children.

Then I began doing things that were illegal. I was running a hedge fund. I put my chips with the wrong people – those who were offering me quick bucks, instead of the slow climb to the top. I saw people transferring $500,000, $1 million into my trading accounts. The money was just sitting there.

A few years later, I made $1 million – but we spent $2 million. All Chloe cared about was hanging out with the crème de la crème of the social world. She needed more and more to keep up. I bought $12,000 pieces of art, ruby rings and diamond tennis bracelets. I kept two cars in Manhattan, paying exorbitant monthly fees to *park the Mercedes that I couldn't afford. I had to hire a nanny and a cook, and send cars to pick up Chloe all over the city. We lived the glamorous, expensive New York lifestyle. We were flying everywhere. We gave a $4,000 birthday party for our one year old.*

We moved about once a year. Because Chloe wasn't happy, I was always looking for something better or brighter. I began to suspect that she was never going to be happy because she wasn't happy with herself. Finally, we moved into the $3 million condo she wanted and I couldn't afford, especially after I lost my job when my company went bankrupt. I was getting scared. She didn't want to hear that we had no money. She just kept watching her soap operas. I was on the treadmill to ruin, always trying to make more. Millions weren't enough for her. Chloe was desperate to keep up appearances and relationships with the shallow socialites that she befriended.

And Christopher was desperate to survive. Angry at his wife, he fell prey to Linda, a wealthy, well-connected attorney-friend of Chloe's. After he ended their brief affair, Linda told Chloe that Christopher was cheating, but didn't say that it was with her. Linda's husband found an email. He told Chloe, and she told Christopher to leave. They separated after 12 years of marriage.

People were shocked to hear that we separated because we were looked upon as the 'golden couple' – literally. We seemed to have it all, a perfect life hobnobbing with the rich in the lap of luxury. I had stolen money to maintain our lifestyle and I hadn't told Chloe. By this point, I loathed my life and myself. I had thought about jumping off a building. I was really tired. There were lies everywhere. I just wished someone would take me away.

Christopher's wishes came true. It wasn't long before the FBI came looking for him.

When I got a call from the FBI, I was half terrified and half relieved. I told them what I had done because I wanted them to take me away. I was looking forward to prison.

Christopher lived under a cloud while they investigated. Eventually he was arrested and it all fell apart. They had to sell their condo and hock everything else they owned.

It only became evident when I was sitting in a courtroom, ready to be charged with a felony and be given a prison sentence that Chloe had a sickness I couldn't cure, no matter how many millions of dollars I spent on her or tears I cried. Chloe told the judge that I never gave her any of the money. She wanted to punish me because I hadn't kept her in the lifestyle she felt entitled to and I'd hurt her socialite image.

Christopher was sentenced to three years in prison.

The judge didn't think I was sorry enough. I ended up sharing a cell with a 245-pound tough guy from Cincinnati.

In prison Christopher got involved in a drug prevention program, which lessened his sentence to one and a half years.

During this time Chloe took their last $250,000 from the sale of their property and spent it – leaving Christopher destitute when he got out.

I often told Chloe that I was her knight, and I had come on a white horse to save her. She loved that image. This is wonderful for fairytales, but not for a real life. I was trying to rescue Chloe from herself and from her family. She was part of a magnificent family – or so it seemed. They lived in a nice part of town, indulged themselves in luxuries and pretended to be regal. When people asked her parents, "What do you do?" they'd answer, "I'm a socialite," as if being a socialite is an occupation.

But Chloe's parents' regal socialite lifestyle was an illusion built on a house of cards. They knew it and she knew it. When Chloe was a little girl, her father, a merchant banker who wore British vintage suits and drove a Jaguar, had gone bankrupt. Since he'd never saved any money, the family's lifestyle suddenly went from hobnobbing with the rich to living leanly in a small apartment. Since then, his fortune has had its ups and downs, causing Chloe to live in fear that money, and the fancy life it could buy, would suddenly, and inexplicably be gone. So she felt she needed to flaunt it while she had it. As long as she could keep her husband on the treadmill making more money, she would be safe.

My job was to save her, to help her resolve the mental illness that was driving her to keep up the pretense of being perfect and a socialite.

Christopher tried to use money to make up for what he felt she regretted in marrying him. Regardless of his having become a model and then a successful financier, he still felt like the little fat nerd. And Chloe, knowing she could get him to do anything to keep her, took advantage of his fears.

Christopher had tried to rescue his mom when he was growing up. She had waited 10 long years for his debonair father – considered a great catch – to come back and ask for her hand in marriage. Once they married, she devoted herself to him and spent long hours helping his dad build his empire.

My mom would work her tail off. She only ate when I brought her a sandwich from the shop next door. It gave me pleasure to bring food to her and try to save her from my father's harsh demands. I tried to make sure Chloe ate enough, too. My mom was only the daughter of a poor tailor, but she had been good enough to date William Shatner. My dad should have appreciated her more.

His father was a depression-era baby, who loved to go on about how his family never had food during this period and how his mother would feed marrow to the children.

My dad was the millionaire-next-door. He never flaunted his wealth. He drove an Olds or a Pontiac. He was an angry man, always barking or screaming. He worked very hard and never played with me. I was never good enough for him – just like I was never good enough for Chloe – and I'd hide behind my mom when he went after me with the belt.

When I was modeling I wanted to have the newest designer clothes – Versace and all the rest. I bought $300 shoes. My father told me that he remembered when he paid $300 for a car. In his mind he never moved out of the depression era. When I got married and on the treadmill, my dad thought I should go to jail because of how frivolously I was spending money. He died before he knew that I committed a real crime.

When Christopher was growing up, his parents never set boundaries.

My friends got punished. I had to punish myself. My parents had bags of money around the house, but they were not around enough themselves because they were always working. The first time I was punished was when I was put in prison.

These days Christopher is a convicted felon who is still on probation. Chloe, not unlike Blanche DuBois, has become a shadow of her former self, tenuously holding onto reality. Instead of her stylish designer clothes, she now wears the same clothes every day – a black t-shirt, frilly skirt and leggings, from a bygone age. And she lives on the edge of eviction.

Chloe was once a skinny little blonde-haired, green-eyed girl, who pretended to be such a helpless thing, but my God, she was like a boa constrictor using her coils to squeeze every ounce of humanity out of me. I'm lucky to be alive.

Famous Ultimate Damsels in Distress

Madonna's "Rescue Me" – This is a theme song of Damsels in Distress: "Rescue me. Your love has given me hope. Rescue me. I'm drowning, baby throw out your rope."

Dulcinea – Don Quixote tilts at windmills and fights off dragons to protect the honor of his Damsel, Dulcinea. Though only a peasant girl, actually named Aldonza, Quixote believes her to be the most beautiful princess in the land and in need of rescue by a knight errant such as himself.

Susan Mayer - In the TV show "Desperate Housewives," Susan (Teri Hatcher) is the accident-prone, unlucky, self-sabotaging resident of Wisteria Lane. However, underneath, she's tougher than she seems and knows how to wrap men around her finger.

Leticia Musgrove – In the movie "Monster's Ball," things look bleak for Leticia (Halle Berry) after her husband is executed, her son is struck by a car, and her financial problems are mounting. Then in walks Hank (Billy Bob Thornton) to rescue her, and in so doing, rescues himself.

Enrique Iglesias's "Hero" – These are the words a Damsel likes to hear: "I can be your hero baby. I can kiss away the pain. I will stand by you forever. You can take my breath away."

Alice Bowman – In the movie "Proof of Life," Alice (Meg Ryan) is at total loose ends when her husband is ambushed and held hostage in a South American country. Terry (Russell Crowe) negotiates with the kidnappers and rescues Alice's husband, despite his having fallen in love with her, himself.

Bonnie Tyler's "I Need A Hero" – Another theme song of

Damsels in Distress: "Isn't there a white knight upon a fiery steed? Late at night, I toss and I turn, and I dream of what I need. I need a hero…. It's gonna take a Superman to sweep me off my feet."

Rachel Marron - In the film "The Bodyguard," Rachel (Whitney Houston) is a music star, endangered by a stalker. The bodyguard (Kevin Costner) sacrifices his love for her in order to better rescue her.

Candy Kendall – In the movie "The Cider House Rules," we first meet Candy (Charlize Theron) when she is pregnant and needs an abortion. Homer (Tobey Maguire), an orphan, leaves the orphanage with Candy and her boyfriend, who goes off to war. While her boyfriend is away, Homer takes care of Candy, only to lose her when he returns.

Chapter 11
THE COUGAR

What does a Cougar want?

A Cougar wants a boy-toy to play with, a personal fountain of youth, to help her turn back the clock so that she still feels desired and desirable and still has power over men.

Why? To match the age and libido that she has inside. The Cougar feels like a young sexy woman stuck in an older woman's body – and she wants to get out and roar. Cunning Cougars are not an endangered species. In fact, they are becoming more popular, if not more domesticated. These wild women know how to take a bite out of prime – men, that is. They need young flesh in order to shore up their sagging self-esteem and to stave off their fear of getting old.

The Cougar wants to walk into a room and still make heads turn - those that would have otherwise ignored her because of her age. With a young thing on her arm, she knows that women will be jealous and men will fantasize about the sexual safaris she must take her lovers on to pleasure them in ways that keep them coming back for more.

Some Cougars were insecure earlier in their dating life and didn't attract the amorous attentions of the captain of the football team, or the CEO of their company. Since then, they've done work on themselves (or had it done…), feel more confident, and are ready to attract the man of their dreams. But there are fewer men in their own age group, and those that are single are carrying a lot of baggage. So Cougars turn to younger guys and start making up for all the hotshots they missed along the way.

The cunning Cougar is not just after good sex, but great sex with young guys who don't yet have hang-ups about their bodies or their performance. She wants a man to be a man and lustily devour her. Let's face it, as men get older, and especially if they've been hurt by bad girls who have stomped all over them, they lose confidence in their erections, which, in turn, causes them to lose their lust. Cougars want to put the lust back into sex, and if an older man is too egotistical or too tired to try harder, what else is a woman to do? So yes, The Cougar sees a man as a sex object… and, she's proud of it.

Flaunting society's rules is great fun for a Cougar, who licks her lips just thinking of the scandalous stir she causes. Why should the sight of an older man with a girl young-enough-to-be-his-daughter not raise eyebrows, but the sight of a Mrs. Robinson with her beau cause the room to fall silent? The Cougar is on a mission to change these obsolete stereotypes and amuse herself in the process.

Before the term "cougar" became popular, an older woman who seduced a younger man was called "Mrs. Robinson," from the novel and movie of the 1960s, "The Graduate." Though this was not the first time in history an older woman bedded a younger man, it brought this controversial concept to the attention of modern society.

Ben (played by Dustin Hoffman in the movie) has just been

graduated from college and is at a loss as to what to do next. But Mrs. Robinson (Anne Bancroft) knows just what his future should hold, and it's not "plastics," as one of the other guests at Ben's graduation party suggests.

Benjamin: For God's sake, Mrs. Robinson. Here we are. You got me into your house. You give me a drink. You... put on music. Now you start opening up your personal life to me and tell me your husband won't be home for hours.
Mrs. Robinson: So?
Benjamin: Mrs. Robinson, you're trying to seduce me.
Mrs. Robinson: [laughs]
Benjamin: Aren't you?

Mrs. Robinson eventually does seduce the at-first-reluctant Benjamin, and they begin having an affair. She extracts a promise out of him never to date her lovely daughter, Elaine (Katharine Ross). Though he tries to avoid doing so, circumstances push Ben and Elaine together and he falls in love with her. Under threat of exposure by Mrs. Robinson, Ben confesses to Elaine that he has been having an affair with her mother. Elaine angrily refuses to see him ever again and, despite Ben's relentless pursuit of her, gets engaged to another man. The story ends with Ben pounding on the glass of the church, interrupting the wedding in the nick of time, and running off with Elaine, who still loves him. Mother and daughter exchange poignant final words:

Mrs. Robinson: Elaine, it's too late.
Elaine: Not for me.

Just like Mrs. Robinson and Elaine, often the trigger for a woman to become a Cougar is when she realizes that her daughter has begun to blossom, while she has begun to fade. Consciously or unconsciously, the mother decides it's time to show who's the Queen of the Jungle, and she goes prowling for conquests.

Some Cougars – when they were little cubs – had bad experiences with dangerous men and grew up fearing them. By choosing a very young and very gentle man to be with, a Cougar can feel less intimidated by his aggressive or sexual impulses and more in control and safe.

Why do men fall for Cougars?

The Cougar is the 'new black'. She's the latest accessory. Everybody's got one – or so it seems.

Many men who fall for Cougars are looking for the good mothering they never had enough of, or never had at all. They want to be nurtured and fed. They appreciate the perks that a Cougar may bring towards propelling their aspirations. Her wisdom, experience, time or money can give them a leg up, so to speak.

It's an alluring challenge for these boy-toys to try to satisfy the sexual needs of a hungry, more experienced Cougar, and an exhilarating rush once they conquer her. Many have the hot fantasy of ripping off a professional woman's power suit and tasting her wild side. Secretly, these men are hoping that The Cougar is more willing to look past their flaws if they satisfy her in bed.

A man who falls for a Cougar doesn't want the responsibility of children or a woman who is dependent upon him. If a Cougar has children, they are usually old enough not to need intensive parenting, but often she has already decided that she doesn't want children either, or has passed childbearing age.

Some men are attracted to Cougars because they have the same obsession of wanting to push back the clock, and now have a partner to share in running, biking, hiking, marathons, and Botox parties.

But problems creep into the relationship when The Cougar comes to realize that she not only wants hot sex, but also wants her toy-boy to play a more traditional role and take care of her. The younger man is thinking this is not what he signed up for, since part of The Cougar's attraction was her ability to provide nurturing to him, or at least an equal partnership. Problems also creep in when The Cougar's insecurities start showing. Her underlying fear of her young man leaving her when she gets too old, can cause her to sabotage the relationship and make this a self-fulfilling prophecy. This is when these May-December relationships start winding down and getting messy.

Rod Stewart's song "Maggie May" is based upon his own experience with a Cougar who stole his innocence and his heart when he was a teenager. Stewart is quoted as saying, "Maggie May was more or less a true story about the first woman I had sex with, at the Beaulieu Jazz Festival." This song touched a nerve when it became a hit in the early 1970s, just as "Mrs. Robinson" had done in the preceding years. As years passed, The Cougar breeding season was getting underway.

Wake up Maggie, I think I got something to say to you.

It's late September and I really should be back at school.
I know I keep you amused, but I feel I'm being used.
Oh Maggie, I couldn't have tried any more.
You lured me away from home, just to save you from being alone.
You stole my heart and that's what really hurts.
The morning sun, when it's in your face, really shows your age
But that don't worry me none, in my eyes you're ev'rything.
I laughed at all of your jokes, my love you didn't need to coax....
You stole my soul, and that's a pain I can do without.
All I needed was a friend to lend a guiding hand
But you turned into a lover and Mother what a lover, you wore me out.
All you did was wreck my bed, and in the morning kick me in the head....
You stole my heart. I couldn't leave you if I tried.
I suppose I could collect my books and get on back to school.
Or steal my daddy's cue and make a living out of playing pool.
Or find myself a rock and roll band that needs a helpin' hand.
Oh Maggie, I wish I'd never seen your face.
You made a first-class fool out of me, but I'm as blind as a fool can be.
You stole my heart, but I love you anyway....

Real Stories from Men on the Dating Front

The Magic of the White Rose

Warren jumped at the chance to be on a reality dating show that purported to match up singles with unique jobs, who are unable to find love through normal channels. Since Warren's a magician with no time for 'bunnies' – unless they're in his hat – he thought he'd give the show a try. It didn't work out. There was no love connection with the women they introduced him to on his episode. But when the series was about to air, Warren watched the promo that featured singles from other episodes, and he was mesmerized by Melissa.

I was a sucker for blondes and I had the sense she was a genuine person. It was her laugh that really got me. In the commercial, Melissa was at a party. Someone told her a joke and she laughed. She had lovely hazel blue eyes. And she had her teacup poodle with her because that's her unique job – managing her celebrity dog, who acts, models and appears at charity events. I love animals, and especially dogs.

Warren watched her episode and liked Melissa even more. The fact that she was older didn't matter. She called her dog "Purity Poodle" because her rule was that anyone who can't accept her dog or doesn't meet with the dog's approval doesn't get to have a lasting relationship with her. Melissa was as obsessed with her dog as Warren was with magic, and it was getting in the way of their love lives. Warren found her on the Internet and contacted her.

They met in a chic café and spent two hours over coffee and dessert. She'd left her poodle at home. When Warren was on the reality show, the host gave him tips on how to meet women. The first tip was not to hide behind magic tricks, but to try to get to know the women. So when Warren met Melissa, he struggled to avoid bringing up his magic.

I was dying to do magic. I was trying not to, but she wanted me to do a trick for her, so I folded a cocktail napkin and made it into a white rose. It had a huge impact; she smiled and blushed. Later I learned it was because she has a profound connection to white roses. She'd always wanted white roses from men, but had only gotten red ones. She never told anyone. She's into the law of attraction and metaphysical stuff, so it made her feel that I was 'The One'.

Melissa had gone to a Renaissance Festival years before and saw men dressed as knights kneeling before women and handing them white roses. Since then, she fantasized about a man giving her a white rose, especially after she read a poem about how the white rose symbolizes love that is pure. She'd been meditating and visualizing a white rose in order to attract it to her. When Warren presented her with one, she was taken aback and allowed this mystical manifestation to override her concerns about the age difference, at least enough to see him again.

After the café, Warren and Melissa continued on to a restaurant and then started going to dinner at least twice a week.

We had sex around the third week, after one of our dinners. I had been to her place once before to visit the dog. I always made a point to show her that I liked the dog. The sex was very passionate because we had a great connection. It wasn't a quick encounter like the sexual experiences I've had with prior women.

Ironically, that night, right before they had sex, they watched the movie "Driving Miss Daisy," about an older woman whose closest companion was her younger chauffeur. Then, after more dates and more sex, Warren worked up the courage to have 'the talk' about age.

I was very afraid. I wanted to be sure that our relationship was sealed before telling her my age. I wanted her to be so overjoyed with my presence, that it wouldn't make a difference. Weekly, I sent white rose bouquets to her office. This night, I cooked her dinner at her place, and I don't cook. Melissa mentioned that her birthday was coming up. Then she asked, "How old are you?" Age was constantly on our minds. We'd played a guessing game. I thought she was about 38. She thought I was close to 30, and I let her think that. I thought she was it – and I didn't want age to be a factor. We were joking around and then I said, testing the waters, "I could be 25." When I admitted that I was 23, she burst out laughing hysterically, "Whoa-ho!" By her reaction, I knew she must be in her forties. I was the youngest person she'd ever dated. She said, "Oh, I'm a cougar! I'm 45."

Now that it was out in the open, they'd finally broken through the age barrier.

Being seen in public with a more mature woman was a big step for me. It didn't click with people that we were dating. Women would come on to me when I was with her because they thought I was available. When I took Melissa on an out-of-town getaway for her birthday, people started to realize we were more than just friends.

Melissa made Warren's birthday special, too, in a way that none of his previous dates had done. She made reservations at his favorite restaurant and treated him to dinner. Knowing he loves ties, she gave him a cool tie – and a little bed and dog bowl for his place. It was her way of showing that she entrusted her precious dog to him and that she expected the relationship to continue. But what pleased Warren most was that all her surprises showed that she was paying attention to what he liked.

Some of my friends say I'm whipped, but Melissa is the top woman I've ever been with. I've hinted at marriage. If I'm holding her left hand, I say, "This doesn't have a ring on it." She jokes back with a laugh and a smile. She always says, "Maybe" or "We'll see," and she gets real red in the face. We've talked about children. We love them, but we don't want any. Melissa never wanted children. She's never been married before. She said every man she has ever met has wanted children, so they left her.

Melissa never wanted a marriage like her parents' marriage. Her mother was an artist and her father was a scientist who, her siblings suspected, may have had affairs. They bickered a lot. Her mom would tell her that she sacrificed her art in order to raise four children and became a teacher to help support them, so Melissa always felt that children were a burden and a hindrance to one's free spirit.

Melissa worries whether I'll still love her as the years go by. She says, "In a couple of years I'm going to be old and wrinkly." I tell her, "I'll be a millionaire, so I can pay for your plastic surgery." She brings this up a lot. She says she'll be an old bag.

On at least one occasion, they've been mistaken for mother

and son.

She goes to a little grocery in her neighborhood. One day, when I went in for her, the man behind the counter asked me, "Who's that blonde girl, your mother?" I got annoyed. I said, "She's probably my future wife." He started choking. He didn't want me to take my business elsewhere, so he said he must be thinking of a different lady. I stormed out.

Not coincidentally, Melissa is the exact same age as Warren's mother, but far more nurturing.

My mother is "Mommy Dearest." She was a Gucci model who always accused me of ruining her modeling career because I ruined her figure, or because I'd sit backstage when she did runway modeling, or because of my very existence. She quit when I was five years old. My father was a model, too, but he quit when I was born to take a job like Tom Hanks had in "Castaway." He had to travel a lot, so it was just "Mommy" and me at home, and it was very lonely. She degraded me, threw me in the closet, and slapped me because she blamed me for her having to sit home instead of being on the glamorous runways.

My mom would terrorize me with a Chuckie doll from the movie "Child's Play." She told me Chuckie would get me if I wasn't good. When I was five years old, right when she quit modeling, she came after me with a knife. My dad and I were sitting in the living room. My mom came in with a knife in her hand and pounced on me, saying, "It's Chuckie with a knife!" It scared the shit out of me. I had nightmares of Chuckie and I woke up crying and screaming.

Warren's mother may have taken her frustration out on their dogs, as well, since they all seemed to die or disappear under strange circumstances.

My mom said that our two cocker spaniels were kidnapped by a senator who she met in the park. She claimed that when she chased after our terrier romping in the park, she saw our cocker spaniels in the back of their car as the senator and his wife drove away. I tried researching which senator it could have been and even showed her photos, but she couldn't identify him. My dad and I thought that she must have poisoned the dogs or just left them somewhere because they were too much of a hassle for her. I'd bought one of the cocker spaniels for her for Valentine's Day, so it felt like she wanted to poison or lose me. We had other dogs and cats that died mysteriously, too.

It's no wonder that part of Melissa's allure was her devotion to nurturing dogs. Right before Warren met Melissa, his mother filed for divorce. He hasn't spoken to his mother in over six months because, on top of everything else, she disapproves of his relationship with Melissa.

I'd mentioned I was seeing someone. I didn't mention her age, but I sent a photo. My mom sent back a text saying, "Don't get involved with her. Older women will be more trouble." I replied, "You're dating someone who could be my grandfather."

When Melissa was in her twenties, she was too busy being

insecure to actually be in a healthy relationship. After years of doing work on herself, she feels deserving and capable of attracting someone worthwhile. But she found fewer available men in her age range, and the ones who were available had ex-wives, kids and other baggage. Then she thought about how her gay friends were getting married, and suddenly it struck her that marriage is being redefined. If two people of the same sex can marry, why should age make a difference?

Melissa had been having a recurring image of a magician who had told her in a meditation that he was, 'The One'. She had assumed it was symbolic of the type of person who is good at manifesting things from spiritual form into physical reality – like the magician card in the tarot is supposed to represent. It had never occurred to her that he might literally be a magician. Then Warren came into her life. He's not only a magician... he's now 'top dog'.

Patron of the Arts

When Jane was 44 years old, after four marriages and one 24-year-old son, she went on an Internet dating site to find her next catch. Unlike many women who give up after too many of their relationships end in heartbreak, Cougars know what they want and go for it.

Jane had more hooks in her tackle box than a hundred fishermen, and they were all loaded with bait when she contacted Dennis. She told him that she had never initiated contact with any other man on the dating site, but that he intrigued her. She said that her preferences had been set for men from 40-60 years old, but that on the day she contacted him, she'd thrown out her criteria. Dennis was 30. His preferred age range had been set to 25-45 years old.

Jane just squeaked in under the wire.

Jane wrote that she thought I was "interesting." She wanted to know if I wanted to "hang out." She said she would be leaving the West Coast and moving out of the country, so she didn't want a serious relationship. She was just looking to have "a good time."

Jane knew all the right things to say, so Dennis started nibbling.

She wasn't the first woman in her forties I dated. I always connect with older women more because they have their stuff together. They're more comfortable with who they are, so they don't play games or do the dance. And they either had kids already or don't want any.

Children are a big sacrifice. I was in a couple of relationships where, when we had unprotected sex there were a few days when I wasn't sure if the woman was pregnant. I realized that if I were a father, the child would come before everything. The women my age have ticking biological clocks. I had to be leery of them. They'd tell me, "This is not gonna work if you don't want kids." I don't want kids. I'm too selfish. I'm committed to my art and I want to experience a lot in life.

But the root of Dennis's decision not to have children goes deeper.

Part of me did fear that some of my dad's temper lay dormant in me and that it might come out if I were a parent. One time, when

I was about six years old, we went for ice cream – my dad, mom, little sister and me. We'd just gotten the ice cream and started to drive home. My dad suddenly got out of the car. He said, "Fuck this, I'm out of here!" My mom was crying and she got into the driver's seat. My dad wouldn't get in. As she drove the car slowly, following my dad, I leaned out the window and begged him to get in the car. "Please come home with us." Eventually he did.

In Jane's email, she suggested that they meet for wine and cheese. She knew that the kind of man who would fall for a Cougar might appreciate sophistication, and the wine would loosen his inhibitions – at least for more comfortable conversation, if not for sex.

We had a great conversation sitting by a fountain, but I felt Jane was out of my league. She did a local spot on TV, she'd been to leadership programs, and was trained as a yoga teacher. I was a graphic designer and I hadn't accomplished much. I walked with her to her car. She had a shiny black sports Mercedes convertible – and all I had was a Honda Civic hatchback. She asked, "Want a ride to your car?" I thought, "Oh no, she's gonna see that I have a crappy car." But then I thought, "This is who I am."

Jane didn't care about his car. She told Dennis she had front-row tickets to a concert and hotel reservations for a fund-raising weekend in Palm Springs, and she invited him to come along.

It took me aback because I'd only seen her once. She said, "I'll drive. All you have to do is show up." I thought, "How can I refuse?" She picked me up. It was a two-hour drive. I had no idea if there were going to be two rooms or two beds. She opened the door and there was only one big bed! From a guy's perspective, this was alright! We had a great weekend – an opening night party at the museum, a concert, she taught yoga and I took a sketch pad. On the way home, we pulled up to a gas station. One of her tires was flat. As I went to put air in it, I told her, "I totally feel like your pool boy!" She laughed. She gave me grief because I didn't kiss her on our first date. She said, "I didn't think you liked me." I made up for it on this second date. She told me I was awesome.

Next Jane invited Dennis to go out with her for New Year's Eve. She was going to a cool party at an airplane hangar that she knew he couldn't resist. Indeed, even though Dennis injured his knee playing basketball, he went. Then he found out that his knee required surgery.

I was gonna ask her to take me to the hospital. It was a leap, but I thought she would do it. Before I asked, Jane offered. She said, "I want to be there for you." She saw me at my worst. I couldn't walk. It put us in a more intimate place. We bonded.

Dennis's birthday was approaching. On their first date Jane had told him that in the spring she was going to go to Italy to open a yoga studio.

Right before my birthday, I felt things were getting serious. I didn't want to get too attached if she was leaving. I told Jane, "I need to know what's going on." She said she was waiting for my birthday, but since I brought it up now, she would give me my present on the spot: "Do you want to go to Italy with me?" How could I say no? Once we decided that I would go, too, we started pricing things out.

Jane was a cunning Cougar, indeed. She obviously had not made arrangements for her trip or her yoga studio. It had been more of a fantasy – and more bait to lure Dennis in. By telling him, from day one, that she was leaving, it made her seem more elusive and calmed his fears that she was looking for a commitment just long enough to hook him on the idea of going off on an adventure together. They wound up choosing South America instead, but it had the same desired effect of taking him out of his comfort zone, isolating him, and making him more dependent upon her. Dennis quit his job at the ad agency and they were off. Once they got to their destination, they bought an apartment and he started following his true passion, painting, while Jane taught yoga.

For 10 years, I've been working as a graphic artist by day and dreaming of being a full-time painter. I have tremendous gratitude to Jane for this opportunity. She says she doesn't want my talent to go to waste.

Was Jane referring to his talent on canvas or in the bedroom? That's the question. What isn't in doubt is that using her money to fund her man's dream was another hook – and it worked. They had a big opening night at their home, which they'd turned into an art gallery of sorts. Dennis was thrilled.

I sold a few paintings. It was nowhere near enough money, but my painting is taking off. I like to be self-sufficient. For me to live off Jane's money is not something I like, so I work hard at what I do, hoping to make more. Jane is amazing. She's very nurturing and motherly. We have sex almost every day. She has a high sex drive and I'm in my prime, so it helps to balance out our ages. In my past relationships, I was always helping the woman figure things out in the relationship and in life. This is the first relationship where I don't have to have this burden. Jane has taken the lead.

But there is some trouble in paradise.

It's important to me to have alone time as an artist. Our home is one grand room with my easels in the middle of it. I'll say, "I'm going to work now." It's supposed to be a hint that I want Jane to leave me alone so that I can work, but she keeps interrupting me. And sometimes the artist in me closes up and goes inside my head while she wants me to share more. And sometimes Jane gets jealous. On opening night, an artist in her late twenties came to see my work. She invited me to see her work. Jane was not on board with this. My perspective was that the girl was a friend and another artist, and I thought it was no big deal. Jane said it was a big deal for her. I didn't initially ask Jane to go, but she could have gone. In the end, I didn't go. Jane says, "When you give me affection and time, I feel secure, but when you don't, I feel insecure about younger women." Jane's fear is that I'll leave her. We both believe nothing lasts forever. A few times a week, I pick out a song for her and we slow dance in the living room. Yesterday, I played a song that had lyrics that said, "We'll grow old together." It put a smile on her face.

Dennis acknowledges that 'The Cougar and her toy-boy' is a stereotype that people may think they fit, especially those who have never been in such a relationship, but, like other men who are with Cougars, he says that his relationship with Jane is deep, meaningful, and goes far beyond the stereotype.

When I joked about being her pool boy that weekend in Palm Springs, I was calling out the elephant in the room so that it would be easier to talk about it. But sometimes it gets sensitive. One of my coworkers referred to Jane as my "sugar mama." He said it in a lighthearted way. When I told her, she was very offended.

And there have been a few times since they've been in South America when cab drivers making small talk have asked whether Dennis was Jane's son.

They were interested in her, so they were trying to figure out my role. They were making a power play, giving me a jab so that they could be the dominant male. When something like this happens, I give Jane a big hug and kiss.

From the first time he picked up a crayon, Dennis's mother always supported his art, but she was suffocating, which is why he feels suffocated these days when Jane doesn't give him enough space to be alone at his easel. Dennis's father had wanted him to go into computers because it had more earning potential, but he'd flunked computer science and continued pursuing his bliss. Dennis's dad was a pessimistic, controlling, unpredictable man, frustrated with his wife, who was much less educated than himself, and frustrated with his life in general.

Things never got physical beyond him pounding his fist on the kitchen table. I always feared it would, though. The more he drank, the more he would have temper outbursts.

Jane's father divorced her mother and abandoned them when she was a little girl, never to be heard from again. Her mother became a civil rights organizer, which meant that they had to move from state to state when Jane was growing up.

The sheriff would come in the middle of the night and knock on their door. He'd tell them, "I can't vouch for your safety in the morning." Her mom would hand Jane two bags: one for clothes and one for toys so that she could throw her stuff into them and they could run away by dawn. Jane despised this life on the run that always made her feel like an outsider.

It is no wonder that Jane longed to be with a gentle younger man who she could control, and then finally stop running.

Innocence Lost: Bagged on a Bus

When Oliver stepped on the New York Transit Authority bus, he was an innocent 13 year old helping his mom take their dog to the vet. When he got off, he was a 43-year-old Cougar's prey.

She leaned into me when the bus moved, not just with her

shoulder, but with her breast. Her body didn't stop when the bus did. I was trying to figure out what was going on and whether it was real. My mother started to get off. The woman turned to me and whispered, "Meet me at this bus stop in one hour."

Oliver told his mom that he was going out to meet a friend. Instead, he took a cab to the Upper East Side bus stop where the woman had indicated. He wanted to get there as quickly as possible because he was afraid she'd be gone. She greeted him with, "Oh good, you're on time. Follow me." She took him up to her apartment a couple of blocks away.

I was self-conscious when we walked in past the doorman. He looked at me like he knew what was going on. That made one of us. I couldn't believe my luck, but I was also thinking, "What's going on?" I'd seen a movie with a young Patrick Dempsey, where he played a pizza delivery boy who had sex with an older woman. I'd thought, "What a great job." This movie kept going through my head. She looked like the wife of Chevy Chase in the National Lampoon movies, Beverly D'Angelo. It was difficult for me to pass up this opportunity – not just for sex – but to relate to someone on an intimate level.

She'd had a boob job and the body of a dancer, with only a couple of minor crow's feet. She was taller than me, with a very, very curvy body, broad shoulders and narrow hips. So many things were going through my head. What if she's a psycho? What if she's a guy? She asked if I wanted a glass of water. I said no because what if she put something in it?

His Cougar had photos and programs around her apartment that announced she was in burlesque on Broadway. She also had pictures of her husband, who was in the Navy. Oliver hoped that her husband was on a ship right now, but worried that he might be in the closet, or might even be filming him. She told Oliver to lie down on the bed. Then she directed him on how to pleasure her.

I was one big hormone. I disappeared when she laid back on the bed and her breasts didn't move. It was my first experience with saline. She was completely shaved below the waist. She said, "Do this, do that." She showed me what to do with my hands and my tongue. She was careful about explaining how much speed and pressure I should use and where. This was our only conversation. It was all in a dream state. We went from 0 to 160 in a couple of hours.

She'd obviously done this before and was comfortable with it. There was no wasted time. She knew what she wanted. The second it was done, she wanted me to leave. She asked how old I was. I told her I was 13. She said, "Oh, I thought you were 16." She asked if she could have my number, but she was not willing to give me hers. I was like, "When can we do this again?" On the next outings I had with my parents, I kept scanning the crowd. They asked, "What are you looking for?"

But The Cougar never called him. A year and a half later, when Oliver was with his mother at Serendipity, a chic ice cream parlor, he saw her. She was with a friend. She looked up and started checking him out. Then she got that look in her eye, like, "Oh, yeah, I remember you." The Cougar left abruptly and Oliver began chasing after her in the street. He tried to arrange another rendezvous. He recited his phone number and she repeated it, but she never called. Oliver wants to believe that she just couldn't remember his number, but it is more likely that the sight of his mother and the realization that she was this close to going to jail for statutory rape made her cross Oliver off her list of prey. Today, Oliver is in his forties, but the scars from his first Cougar are still with him.

Now that Oliver had "seen Paree" he did not want to be kept down on the proverbial "farm." When he was 16, he started having girlfriends, but they were not sexually experienced and would get funny looks on their faces when he tried to do those things that The Cougar had taught him. "Where did you learn that?" They'd want to know.

When I was fooling around with my first girlfriend, I asked her, "Don't you people shave down there?" Because of the bus woman, I had no concept of foreplay or the emotional side that goes along with sex. It was a weird perspective. In some ways, being more experienced gave me confidence, but I had none of the maturity and wisdom to go along with it. It was like being able to drive fast in a sports car and knowing how to gun it – but the streets and traffic lights gave me difficulty. I had a lot of problems with girls because of my expectations. As a teenager, you're supposed to go through that stage, "I'll show you mine if you show me yours," but I wanted to bypass it. I'd say, "Can we just get naked?" The girl would say, "No!"

The girls Oliver was dating at 16 would be nothing like the bus

Cougar. So, out of frustration, he started saving money to have a night with a prostitute. Because he was tall for his age, he hung out with older kids.

The night I called the prostitute, I had been out drinking and carousing with my friends. First, we went to Jackson Hole and then to a buddy's apartment, who lives off the park. His parents were at a party. They had a well-stacked liquor cabinet that wasn't locked. We were four kids with a bottle of old Grey Goose.

When Oliver got home and his hormones were raging, he called a prostitute at 2:00 A.M. to come to his parents' apartment. When the woman walked in, his dogs ran out and were jumping around in the hallway. Fortunately, by the time his sleepy-eyed father opened his bedroom door to see what the ruckus was about, the prostitute was already in Oliver's room. But it made her nervous to know that his dad was prowling about. "This will have to be really quick," she said. She made Oliver put on a condom. Between his father, the condom and having to rush, Oliver lost steam.

She was very kind and patient and tried to help me keep my erection and have an orgasm, but I couldn't finish. I was sorta in a trance. I kept wondering what the penalty would be for this if my parents found out. It would have to be off the charts. After she was there for a while, she started to get more of a reaction out of me, but she was worried that if she stayed longer, her agency would call my parents' apartment. So I never reached orgasm. I was devastated. I just spent $250 for nothing, except humiliation.

After this, Oliver never called another prostitute and he developed a phobia against condoms. When the Cougar from the bus had seduced him, she hadn't made him wear one.

When he was all grown up, he had a few other relationships with Cougars. The one that stands out is Sandra. He was in his early twenties and she was in her mid-thirties when she set her sights on him at work. Like his early life experiences, it was also 'forbidden' since, at the time, Oliver was living with a girlfriend who expected him to marry her.

Sandra made her move at the company Christmas party. She knew Oliver had a girlfriend. She didn't want a boyfriend (or so she said). She didn't want to come to work the next day and find a 'puppy' sitting at her desk with flowers and chocolate. What she did want was sex, and Oliver was happy to oblige. They had a secret steamy relationship for months. It was as surreal to him as his earlier Cougar trysts.

He was really turned on when Sandra would answer her door naked except for a towel, pretending that she wasn't dressed because she had been running late. And he liked that she didn't have stuffed animals on her bed like the younger girls he had dated.

I didn't know what to name it. The term "Cougar" hadn't been invented yet, but I knew I had a tiger by its tail. Sandra was a young girl in an older woman's body. She taught me more on a rainy Saturday afternoon than some women have in entire relationships. I behaved differently around her, always the gentleman. Unlike girls closer to my age, I was always on my A-game with Sandra.

All the while, Oliver's unsuspecting girlfriend was sitting at home dreaming of wedding dresses and white picket fences. But Oliver wasn't ready. When he was offered a job in another city, it provided him with an escape. Sandra had begun to seem bored with him and his high-maintenance live-in girlfriend was tired of waiting for him to commit. So he moved on.

I was always clear I never wanted kids. I was afraid of being as much of a disappointment to my kids as my father was to me. Women I dated eventually wanted kids. I might get there one day. If I wait any longer, I'll be like Tony Randall.

I was an unintended consequence of one-too-many margaritas. My parents went to Acapulco on their honeymoon. My mother didn't want children. My father did. But he liked the idea of having children better than he liked actually being a dad. We butted heads from the time I was born, which is why I was sent away to boarding school at age nine and took the train home only on weekends. Not long before I met the woman on the bus, my dad had had an affair. I was always encouraging my mom to get a divorce.

My mother's views on sex were very European because of the way she was raised. She was like Jenny in the book and movie, "The World According To Garp." Jenny paid for her son to visit a prostitute.

Unthinkingly, Oliver made this comparison without realizing how revealing it was. In the book, Garp's prostitute is an older woman who had a son his age. Oliver's reason for following The Cougar from the bus had not just been for sex, but for intimacy – an intimacy he was missing with his own mother after having been sent away at nine years old.

Famous Cougars

<u>Gabrielle Solis</u> – In the TV show "Desperate Housewives," Gaby (Eva Longoria Parker) has an affair with her young gardener because he is more loving than her husband and she is feeling neglected.

<u>Cher</u> – An award-winning singer and actress, Cher has dated several younger men, but her relationship with Rob Camilletti, who was scandalously called "the bagel boy," made the most headlines. She is said to have met him on her 40th birthday, when he was 22. They lived together for three passionate years.

<u>Mary Kay Letourneau</u> – Mary Kay took Cougar-ing a bit too far, snaring an underage boy-toy who was still playing with toys himself. She began a sexual relationship with Vili Fualaau when he was 12 years old and served time in prison for statutory rape. To this day, she continues to hold him under her spell.

<u>Demi Moore</u> – One of the most seemingly successful marriages in Hollywood is Demi and Ashton Kutcher, despite their 16-year age difference. It is clear that Demi is a young hot babe inside an older woman's body – that still looks hot. Though rumors of Ashton's cheating with a younger woman have rattled Demi, she's still an inspiration for Cougars everywhere.

<u>Susan Sarandon</u> – Susan, an Academy Award-winning actress and social activist, met Tim Robbins when they both filmed "Bull Durham." Ironically, she played a Cougar and mentor to Tim, a rookie baseball player. They had two sons and their relationship lasted 11 years.

<u>Desiree</u> – In this song by Neil Diamond, he sings, "I became

a man at the hands of a girl almost twice my age.... Somehow I knew I could only have you 'til the morning light.... She was there and gone without one regret, but she continues on like the words of a song I could not forget."

Courtney Cox – Courtney is a Cougar and proud of it. Her husband, David Arquette, is 7 years younger. And Courtney stars in the TV show, "Cougar Town," as Jules Cobb, a divorced single mom who tries to get back into the dating scene by way of younger men to make up for time she has lost.

Pamela Morris – In the "Queen of the Nile" episode of "The Twilight Zone" TV show, Pamela is a famous movie star. A reporter comes to interview her and learns that the secret to her youthful beauty is poisoning young men like him and then using a scarab beetle to drain his vitality and transfer it into her.

Jeanine Stifler – In the film "American Pie," Stifler's mom (Jennifer Coolidge) is considered a 'MILF' (Mom I'd Like to Fuck) and lusted after by all the high school boys. At the prom after-party at Stifler's house, she has sex with Paul, one of the four boys who made a pact to lose their virginity by graduation.

Stella Payne – In the movie "How Stella Got Her Groove Back," Stella (Angela Bassett), a successful single mom, takes a vacation in Jamaica and falls in love with a man 20 years her junior. She confronts the challenges of combining love with her responsibilities to her career and her son.

Stacy's Mom – In this song by Fountains of Wayne, an adolescent boy is trying to convince his female friend that he's grown up enough for her sexy single mom. He sings, "Stacy's mom has got it goin' on.... I could tell she liked me from the way she stared.... I know it might be wrong, but I'm in love with

Stacy's mom."

<u>Rosie Hanson</u> – In the movie "I Could Never Be Your Woman," Rosie (Michelle Pfeiffer) is a TV scriptwriter who falls for a younger man at the same time that her daughter has her first romantic crush.

<u>Barbra Streisand</u> – Andre Agassi served up some steamy romance when he answered Babs' love songs, despite there being a 28-year age gap. But when it came to marriage, this Cougar turned in her claws and picked someone closer to her own age.

<u>Mariah Carey</u> – Mariah scooped Nick Cannon out of his baby carriage and got him to say, "I do," after dating only six weeks. She continues to wear the pants in the family and gets him to cater to her every whim.

<u>Linda Bollea</u> – The ex-wife of pro-wrestler Hulk Hogan is dating Charlie Hill, 30 years her junior, who reportedly went to school with her son. There has been talk of an engagement and a wedding on the horizon.

Chapter 12
THE BALL-BUSTER

What does a Ball-Buster want?

A Ball-Buster wants a man to prove he loves her by perpetually scrambling to meet her insatiable demands and surrendering to her control.

Why? To restore the sense of having control over her destiny that was snatched away during her childhood. If you scratch the surface of the angry, controlling, rebellious Ball-Buster, you find a hurt and depressed little girl. The more pain and resentment she has towards men from her past – especially her father – the more belligerent she appears. Her past experiences have made her overly sensitive to being controlled by a man and she is now unwilling to let any man tell her what to do.

Helen Reddy wrote the song "I Am Woman" based upon her own life. She had seen women in her family experience hardships and had experienced hardships herself. Her father, an alcoholic vaudevillian, was sent to entertain troops in New Guinea when Helen was a little girl. She expected him to come home that night and felt confused and abandoned when he didn't. He had been disappointed that she was a girl. Helen admits that she's lived her life as if she were a man, refusing to let men hold her back from reaching her dreams.

I am woman, hear me roar
In numbers too big to ignore
And I know too much to go back and pretend
'Cause I've heard it all before
And I've been down there on the floor
No one's ever gonna keep me down again.
Oh yes, I am wise
But it's wisdom born of pain
Yes, I've paid the price
But look how much I gained
If I have to, I can do anything
I am strong, I am invincible, I am woman.

The Ball-Buster's unending list of insatiable demands will emasculate any man until he is whimpering at her feet. The problem with Ball-Busters is that no matter how many times they break their man's balls, they still never feel loved. At best, they just feel obeyed. They doubt that a man could truly love them because their father never did. So each time her man cowers and gives in, it only soothes this bad girl's insecurities temporarily until she remembers that she has manipulated him into this corner – and that he has not gone willingly or lovingly.

Ball-Busters have the sense that if they don't control their man and their life, it will all fall apart, as it once did when they were little. Their early experiences make them obsessive-compulsive and passive-aggressive. Ball-Busters are particularly controlling over their man when it comes to sex and money.

Many a Ball-Buster has been schooled at the heels of her mother, who has worn the pants in the family and served as her role model. She has observed the panoply of techniques that her mom has used to control her dad and has committed them to memory for her own use in the future.

Some Ball-Busters take their title literally and underscore their verbal demands with physical abuse. Domestic violence, perpetrated by women, has increased over the years, though many men are still too ashamed to report it.

The movie "Thelma and Louise" jolted audiences with its bold portrayal of women who transformed themselves from being victims of men to Ball-Busters. Thelma (Geena Davis) is an acquiescent housewife married to an emotionally abusive husband. Louise (Susan Sarandon) is a single woman scarred from having been raped in her past. When a stranger attempts to rape Thelma in the parking lot of the cowboy bar, Louise's memories of her rape are 'triggered', and she shoots and kills him.

Louise: Get off her or I'm gonna splatter your brains all over this nice car.

Harlan: [Getting off of Thelma] Easy, we're just having a little fun.

Louise: Sounds like you got a real fucked up idea of fun. Turn around. In the future, when a woman's crying like that, she isn't having any fun!

Harlan: Bitch! I shoulda gone ahead and fucked her!

Louise: What did you say?

Harlan: I said suck my cock.

[Louise shoots him]

Now on the run, Thelma and Louise show that a woman with a gun, a phallic symbol, can be just as powerful as a man. Indeed, they become progressively more ruthless and empowered. Ultimately, they chose to take a 'leap' into oblivion, eluding their pursuers by driving off a cliff, rather than be abused and subjugated by more men.

Why do men fall for Ball-Busters?

Men who fall for Ball-Busters are unconsciously drawn to scenarios that are familiar to them from childhood, where one parent was powerful, intimidating and sometimes physically brutal. Although this home life made the little boy miserable or frightened, he finds himself drawn into it again. His underlying wish this time is to transform himself from the kid cowering in the corner or the placating lap dog into a grown man who is listened to and respected. But this wish doesn't get fulfilled when he's in a relationship with a Ball-Buster.

These childhood scenarios consist of a father who is a strict disciplinarian, often using physical punishment or abuse to teach his son life lessons. This son grows up angry and rebellious, but tries hard to deny these feelings. Other childhood scenarios have gone to the other extreme – that of a Ball-Busting mother who has defeated his disheartened dad and browbeaten him into submission. This son feels shame towards his dad for allowing his mom to walk all over him. In either case, the little boys live under threat of explosive conflict erupting, whether directed towards them or towards their dad. It creates a repetition compulsion where, as adults, they again end up sacrificing their own needs and wants to try to avoid conflict in the home.

Men who marry Ball-Busters worry whether their sons will wind up marrying a Ball-Buster themselves or wind up trying to avoid women because their mom, the only woman they have known, was too threatening. A Ball-Busting mother commandeers her offspring and caters to them in order to win them over to her side so that she will have allies against their dad. When her offspring are sons and she smothers them by spoon-feeding them long after they're old enough to feed themselves, or by taking them shopping with her, the result is often metro-sexual, self-indulgent men unable to form romantic connections to women.

Real Stories from Men on the Dating Front

The Woman Who Took Ball-Busting Literally

My adoptive parents went to the pound and found me. They had to donate three books of postage stamps and it was a done deal. My biological father was a mutt and my adoptive father was a Kentucky coon hound.

This gloomy and self-deprecating description of his ancestry, birth and adoption, is a reflection of Gary's low sense of self-worth. Is it any wonder that he fell prey to bad girls who hooked him by playing on his need to feel wanted?

The day after his high school graduation, Gary left home at 17 and joined the Marines. He went from one strict authoritarian environment, where he was constantly under threat by his adoptive father, to another. He found it safer to release his pent-up anger and rebelliousness once he was in the military because the Marines couldn't return him to the pound.

I knew I wanted to go wild at that age and get out of my house before I did it. My first couple of years in the Corps are a blur of booze, bar fights, and liaisons with strippers.

Then, at age 20, while in the service, he decided to settle down and get married. Still unconsciously drawn to an authoritarian environment, he married Alice, a Ball-Buster-in-the-making because, although it wasn't pleasant, it was familiar to him.

When she was angry at something I did, Alice would retaliate by putting Nair in my shampoo. It made clumps of my hair fall out. Or when I was sleeping, she would paint my toenails pink, which made it pretty tough for me when I had to take showers at the Marine base. Or when I worked the night crew and came home in the dark, she'd leave cabinet doors open so that I'd hit my head. I could hear her laughing from the bedroom.

After four years of marriage and too many months of his serving in the Gulf War, they drifted apart and divorced.

After living in a tent in the middle of the desert during a war, your tolerance for wasting time is much lower because you're very aware of your mortality. You don't have much of a stomach for complaining by people who really don't know what a bad life is all about. That was probably my Achilles heel in my second marriage. I just had no tolerance for bitching and I married a woman who bitched like it was an Olympic event. It was how she manipulated me. She knew I'd do anything just to not have to hear it.

Indeed, Alice was merely a prankster compared to Gary's second wife, Donna, the real Ball-Buster. He met her when he was 27 years old and was taking a break from being a stockbroker by working as a captain on a yacht, moored on the West Coast. Donna sauntered over to him as he was having a beer with a buddy in a bar. Gary thought she was good-looking and confident, but it was only a faux-confidence that masked deep childhood insecurities. He was wearing a shirt with a picture of the yacht on it.

She said, "What's with the boat?" I wasn't a rich guy, but she saw my earning potential and it piqued her interest. We hung out that night. She was living with a guy, so she didn't give me her number. We ran into each other at the same bar a couple of weeks later. She was cute and fun to be around. She was aggressive and let it be known that she was interested in me. She came back to my place. We fooled around a little, but nothing serious. Eventually it did get physical. I wasn't hung up on the fact that she was still living with the guy.

But it should have been a red flag to make this captain steer away from Donna and head for waters that were not infested with bad girls. If she was willing to cheat on the guy she was living with, she might well cheat on Gary or have ulterior motives for being with him. By now, Gary was working for a company teaching investing. They had an opening for a telemarketer, so he jumped at the opportunity to get Donna more involved with his life by inviting her to interview for the job. His plan worked. She started

368

working there and they started going out more. Then she moved out of her boyfriend's place. After six months, she convinced Gary that they should get a place together. She had been living with a roommate and he was living on a 30-foot sailboat that he owned.

After we were living together for three weeks, Donna freaked out and left. She said we were moving too fast. Now I'm off my boat with a shiny new lease. I was stunned.

Donna and Gary continued seeing each other. Her prior live-in boyfriend wasn't letting go and was trying to win her back. She told Gary she would end it with the boyfriend. One night she and Gary went to a birthday party. Donna disappeared. Gary found her at the club next door, which was where she used to hang out with her boyfriend. She was with her boyfriend again that night. It turned out that she was using Gary to make her boyfriend jealous because the boyfriend was taking too long to make a commitment. Although competing with her ex had been part of her attraction, by now Gary had had it.

I told her, "Come pick up your trash from my apartment and leave." She left. We were done. Since we were working in different places now, I didn't see her for months. Then she started showing up at my apartment at 1:00 in the morning. She was drunk, beating on my door, and telling me I was a son of a bitch.

When Donna had gone back to her boyfriend, Gary started going out with a sweet single mom.

But there was no drama with the single mom. There was something about the drama that kept me hooked.

Like many men hooked on the drama of bad girls, Gary was hooked by Donna's out-of-control behavior because it made him feel like she was so in love with him that she couldn't help herself. He'd always felt unwanted, ever since he was left at the orphanage. Now here was a woman who seemed to love him so much that she was pounding on his door in the middle of the night. Gary let Donna move back in with him and, one year after they met, they were on the marriage track.

She liked to party and the sex was good. It was not a relationship I had to spend time thinking about. She made herself available when I needed her, but didn't crowd me when I was working. I'm a workaholic, so she seemed perfect. She had the inexplicable allure of the woman you absolutely know you should not be with, so I asked her to marry me.

Before the wedding there were many more red flags. Donna always needed to be the center of attention. She was uncontrollably emotional and had a violent temper. She was cavalier with money, as long as it was Gary's money. She insisted upon a big wedding, but since neither she nor her family could pay for it, Gary ended up footing the whole bill.

Once we reached the zero hour, during the planning stage of our wedding, I got a glimpse of what she was really like. It was apparent that this marriage wouldn't last. Her attitude was "do it my way or I'm gonna throw a fit." I tolerated it because I couldn't afford distraction from my work. It was easier to write a check than to spend time arguing with her.

As a surprise, I got us a suite for our wedding night at the best hotel in the city. We would get there by limo. The night before the wedding, I went to the hotel to drop a car off so that we could get home the morning after the wedding. My groomsmen met me at the hotel to have a few beers. Donna called over 20 bars looking for me before she happened to hit this hotel bar. It wasn't a bachelor party with strippers. Donna went berserk. The guys in the bar gave me a hard time, asking why I'm marrying someone like this. I'd been thinking of calling it off, but my friends and family had made such an effort to be there. At the wedding I was miserable. My best man told me to run. When I saw her coming down the aisle, I was thinking, "I wonder how long it will last?" My mouth got so dry in front of the preacher I almost threw up.

After the wedding Gary started keeping a journal.

After we got married she was pissed off about something every day. I made a conscious decision to write down every transgression, like her tantrums, so I could explain why I was divorcing her. It was a journal to justify why I couldn't stay married. I discontinued it because I got depressed every time I had to write something down. She got extremely spoiled very quickly. It was easier to give her what she wanted. I was focused on my career, so I kept throwing money at the problem.

I had to take a pass on my closest friend's bachelor party because she said, "If you go, I'm gonna make your life miserable."

She was always afraid I'd be with other women. If a woman was friendly towards me, her claws came out. She was extremely insecure. I never cheated.

Donna was obsessed with worry about Gary cheating because she had cheated and projected her own proclivities onto him. Any time Gary did something she disapproved of, she'd sulk, complain, and make his life a living hell.

My friends used to call her "Columbo" because of her knack for tracking me down wherever we were having a few drinks. She would call a place and page one of my buddies because she knew I wasn't dumb enough to answer a page. Then when he'd answer, she'd know where to find us.

Then came the literal ball-busting.

Donna was wrapping presents one night. I nudged her playfully. She grabbed scissors and jammed them into my arm. I started sleeping with one eye open after that. Another time, I used the last piece of toilet paper and didn't put in a new roll. She stormed out of the bathroom and kicked me in my crotch – all because I didn't replace the toilet paper. To her, slapping me in the face, hitting me in the arm, kicking me in the crotch, or stabbing me were all justified retribution for some unspeakable transgression on my part.

Donna thought that she could literally bust his balls and Gary would never walk out. She was wrong. After three years of marriage, he ended the misery.

September 11th was a wake-up call. I realized I could go to work and someone could fly a plane into my building. I didn't want to spend the rest of my life like this. When I decided to tell her, I felt like a kid with a bad report card who waits until Sunday night to give it to his parents. Like the kid, in order not to spoil the weekend, I waited until Sunday night to tell her I was leaving.

That weekend Gary took Donna sailing and out to lovely dinners. Then, when they were sitting in candlelight on the balcony of their condo, he broke the news. Donna flew into a rage.

She picked up the glass candle and winged it at me. Luckily, it didn't hit me. But it was not so lucky for the guy riding his bike below. He skidded out. The first thing the next morning, my phone was ringing off the hook. It was my buddies. She'd sent an email blast to everyone, saying I was leaving her and that I had never been any good to her. She made it easier because now there was no going back. She wanted to know why. I wished I'd kept my journal so I could tell her. I said, "I don't enjoy being with you. You're too high maintenance. I'm done and I'm moving." I barricaded myself in the guest room. I was scared. She was crazy.

The next day Gary gave her whatever cash and property he had and moved out. Donna tracked him down at his new address and left countless messages on his answering machine. She also got several subscriptions to gay porn magazines and had them mailed to him, hoping that his neighbors or any new girlfriends would see them. After a while, he never heard from her again.

She wanted out, but she wanted to be the one to pull the trigger. She hated that I did. She didn't have somewhere else to go yet. She wouldn't take her foot off first base until she had a clear path to second – like she did with me when she was living with the first guy.

Donna's need to control came from her having been unable to control her father. He divorced her mom when she was three years old. Since then, he only sent her Christmas cards every few years. When she married Gary, her father became angry upon hearing that she was having her mom walk her down the aisle instead of him, so he didn't show up.

Donna's mother taught her, early in life, how to be a Ball-Buster. She was an unhappy woman who walked all over the next man she married. Donna had outright disdain for her stepfather because he was a total doormat for her mom.

Gary admits to being a mama's boy. He was devoted to his adoptive mother because she protected him from his strict and punitive adoptive dad.

I was not allowed to go to parties because they didn't want me to get a girl pregnant. It was nothing for me to be grounded for an entire semester in high school for bringing home bad grades. I was punished physically when my dad thought the transgression was appropriately severe.

374

My dad and I had it out one day when I was 16, and we brawled from room to room in the house until my screaming mom threatened to call the cops. It all started because I wasn't allowed to drive, so I had to rely on my parents to get me to and from my job. My dad kept me out all day running menial errands and I kept telling him he was going to make me late for work. We finally got back home and I was pretty pissed. I told him I needed to leave right that minute and he told me he just wasn't going to take me. I was enraged, and he saw me ball-up a fist. He asked me, "Are you gonna hit me, boy?" And before I could do anything, he nailed me right in the jaw and sent me sprawling backwards into the bathroom where I conked my head on the toilet. That was the last straw. I came out swinging and we went from room to room. We both took our licks, and it ended up being a sort of rite of passage for me. It was high drama.

Gary had ambivalent feelings about his dad. On the one hand he had a great deal of respect for him, bordering on idol worship, because his dad was a war hero with medals to prove it. Plus, he worked three jobs to support his family. But on the other hand, his dad was brutal. It mirrored the ambivalent feelings Gary had towards Donna, and she took over where his dad left off.

Aside from living under the threat of his dad's wrath, Gary's childhood was dull and boring because of the many restrictions and prohibitions his parents put on his life. Ever since he was a little boy reading *Treasure Island* and *Swiss Family Robinson*, he yearned for adventure.

I wanted to live a life of daring. In fact, a large part of the reason I joined the Marines was for the training because I knew, for the life I wanted to lead, I'd better be able to take care of myself when things got intense. The Marines imbued me with survival skills that I've relied upon time and time again.

Indeed, when he was married to Donna, he needed all the survival skills he'd learned.

I was hooked on the drama with Donna. Actually, it wasn't as much an attraction to drama as it was an attraction to adventure. There was never a dull moment. Sex with a crazy girl is the best. She convinced me to turn my life around from my quiet life on the boat and then it got crazier from there. There are girls you screw and girls you marry. Donna was a girl you screw that I messed up and married.

Being a Marine was high adventure, especially in the Gulf War and the other hellholes they put me in. I got used to the adrenaline rush. That's why I became a trader to have the jolt all the time. I lived a life of high stakes. I put my life on the line in the war zone, my fortune on the line in the money markets, and my heart on the line being married to a crazy girl.

Master Emasculator

People would always tell Larry, "You're such a nice guy. I don't understand why you're not in a relationship." That's because they didn't know how shy and insecure he was when it came to relating to women, and how it all stemmed from dodging conflict with his disciplinarian parents. Growing up, he befriended kids who were not part of the in-crowd. He didn't date much throughout junior high or high school. His first relationship that lasted at least a year was as a freshman in college. When Larry was in his twenties, he dated a girl for a year with a lot of medical issues.

We didn't have much in common. My friends asked me why I was still with her because it didn't seem like I was so into her. I felt sorry for her, and I would have felt guilty if I had ended the relationship while she was struggling with her health. She didn't have the energy to go to parties or movies, so I went over to cook dinner and keep her company. That way she wouldn't feel as bad about being stuck in her house.

Larry's love life was going nowhere, and his grueling schedule at CNN Sports wasn't helping. He switched to the mortgage industry and started looking to settle down. He met his wife online.

She was one of the few people who could make me laugh and we always had a great time together. Before we got married I was so smitten that I heard what I wanted to hear. She'd said, "I'll have children if you want." After we got married and I started pushing, she said she didn't want children after all. It was difficult to decide whether to stay married, but after five years I realized she was not going to change her mind. Even the day we got divorced, we were sitting in the back of the courtroom cracking up at the quirky judge. Nobody would've thought we were getting a divorce. I was hurt and really disappointed because I was still in love with her.

Larry moved to the Gulf Coast and started working in management at a finance corporation. His eagerness to put his disappointment behind him and to start a family made him vulnerable to Janet, a bad girl who could spot a nice guy a mile away. They met at work and flirted for a few weeks.

I dipped my toes in the water by calling her at work and leaving a message asking her if there was a happy hour that people from the company went to. She called me on a Saturday to say, "No, not really." We danced around. She said, "I just called to see what you were doing." She surprised me because she was calling on a Saturday. I asked her out for drinks that evening.

Just like bad girls bring alcohol into the mix to make it easier for them to seduce their prey, men bring alcohol into it, too, when they - at some level - know they're about to do something stupid..

Janet was very attractive, friendly, outgoing, confident, and independent, with a strong personality. It was very refreshing to be with someone who I could have a more open conversation with on the first date. She was not afraid to express herself, but this was positive and negative, as I came to realize. We stayed until the place closed and then had a nice hug. Janet was a wedding planner on the side and had a wedding the next day. I said, "Give me a call after your event. I'll be watching football."

The next day Janet called. Larry told her he was cooking dinner. Flirtatiously, she invited herself over.

She said, "What are we having?" I told her and said, "If you want, you can come on by." She was a little more aggressive than

I was used to, but I went with it.

When Janet left after dinner, Larry kissed her goodnight. A few days later he took her out to dinner and spent the night at her place.

There was some petting, but she kept her panties on. It was like we were in high school. We didn't have intercourse for a long time because Janet was very adamant about not having sex before I had an HIV test. I wasn't gonna rush right out and get one; I got one a month later. But she still didn't want to have intercourse. She was very rigid. She said, "Just because you got an HIV test doesn't mean we're going to have sex right away." We'd get to that point and she'd put the brakes on. It was very frustrating but I was trying to respect her.

Whereas some bad girls hook men by having sex on the first date, others keep them panting for sex. Larry suspects that Janet's reluctance to have intercourse may have been more than a ploy. It may also have been connected to the married man she had had a relationship with and still spoke of quite fondly. One day the married man called while Larry was at her house.

I knew who it was immediately by the flirtatious way she was talking with him. He mentioned that he wanted to come over so she could review his 401K since she worked in retirement planning. She made arrangements with him to come over a few nights later. She once told me she didn't believe in having sex with more than one person at a time, which was ironic since he was a married man. I never got the sense that door was completely closed until four or five months later, when she finally agreed to have sex. It was good, but a little more regimented than I've had before. She needs it to be in the same order all the time: oral sex performed on her and then intercourse doggie style. It gets boring after a while, especially because it doesn't satisfy her. When we first started having sex, it was three or four times a week. Now it's down to once every couple of months.

When Larry started dating Janet, he liked that they had a lot in common, and that they also complemented each other. She was more organized and he was more laid back. But as their relationship progressed, he realized that 'organized' became belligerent and controlling. She'd start arguments that became disproportionately intense, considering the issues being discussed and where they were in their relationship.

Her fuse was very short before she got to personal jabs like, "You're no good!" Then she'd say, "I'm sorry. I know I have a bad temper. I have to work on it." She'd go from extreme anger to extreme remorse. Janet and her father had a bad relationship. Growing up, he would spank and beat her past the point of discipline. So she'd say, "I'm not gonna let any man tell me what to do!" She was very defiant when it was just stupid little things couples argue about.

Months into their relationship, Janet arranged for them to meet her friends at a posh restaurant.

She was on me about buying a new shirt and slacks and getting my car washed. I said, "I'm not trying to put on a show." She said, "No man who's gonna be with me is gonna be cheap!" She had complained that her father was very cheap. She felt cheated out of things growing up, even though they could afford them.

When Janet's car broke down, she needed a new one and had always dreamed of driving a Mercedes.

The company was scaling back and cut her bonuses. I warned her, "If you want to live a Mercedes lifestyle on a Honda budget, you'll be very stressed out." But she started leasing one anyway.

Then the company cut Larry's income by more than half. Catching him at this vulnerable moment when he needed emotional support and someone to share expenses, Janet suggested that they move in together. Despite Janet's volatile temper, Larry agreed. Janet's friends planned a group vacation for New Year's. Larry didn't want to go because he didn't think it made sense to spend money on this luxury when money had become tight. But Janet really wanted to go, so she insisted on paying for both of them. Afterwards, it became a source of contention because she kept bringing up how she paid for their vacation. Up to this point, Larry had never let her pay for anything. Then Janet wanted a birthday party lunch at the Ritz for her friends. Larry made sacrifices to make it happen.

Then, not long after they moved in together, Larry got laid off. He still had savings and a 401K, but the power shift had begun. The arguments increased and became more personal.

Janet would say, "You're not making much money, so you can't tell me what to do," or "If you can't do something for me financially, then the least you can do is what I want you to do about this."

Larry found little sales jobs to make ends meet, but he wasn't successful in them because they weren't his passion. When he didn't get a job at the same level he was in when Janet met him, she'd tell him he wasn't trying.

Janet would say, "Who sits around for three months and doesn't get a job?" But I'm not gonna bag groceries. She kept hammering, railing on. She'd say, "You're a failure. Successful people do this and that." We went to counseling a few times. The counselor would give us constructive ways to attack the problem and not each other. But as soon as we'd leave, she'd say, "The counselor isn't here now, so he can't tell me what to say." So things went back to the way it was before.

Larry started following his passion, building a business as an entrepreneur, consulting, and lecturing to companies and groups about mortgages and finance. It was taking time to build. Meanwhile, Janet kept browbeating him.

She'd tell me, "You're useless anyway! You're a loser, a failure! "You can't provide the lifestyle I want! You'll never be successful!" And if I tried to initiate sex, she'd reject me with, "I don't know why you think you can sleep with me if you won't do these other things!"

During the first three years of their relationship there had been some really good times. So, Larry was willing to keep heading towards marriage even though they still had a lot of things to work on.

I said, "We can work on our future even though I can't buy you a ring or a big wedding right now. We could go to the Bahamas with some family and close friends." But for Janet, if it wasn't going to fit her grandiose plans, it wasn't gonna happen. She started a big argument with, "You're trying to downgrade my lifestyle! You want to take me to the courthouse or justice of the peace!" I said, "I'd suggested the Bahamas." It was a wake-up moment for me.

Things came to a head. Larry's business was beginning to flourish, but Janet was still not satisfied.

She was asking, "When are you going to find something in addition to your business?" It struck me as funny because I was making more money than when I had the corporate job. I said, "I'm not gonna stop my business to take a job." I was making more than enough to live our lifestyle and put some to the side for savings. I said, "I'm choosing the path of continuing to build my business. I don't think you'll be satisfied with anything." She said, speaking in the third person, "Janet is never satisfied with the standard. I always have to have the best of the best."

Janet didn't think that being an entrepreneur was real work. To her, Larry was just playing when he traveled the country giving his seminars and consulting.

When I was in Detroit working, she emailed me some ads for bank jobs that her friend had seen. When I wasn't interested, she said, "Why don't you want to work?" She was saying this while I was in Detroit, working!

Although Janet loved having a job in corporate America, she was jealous of Larry's seeming ability to come and go as he pleased.

When she comes home, especially on a Friday if it's a beautiful day, she'll say, "I would've loved to not have to go to work today. I would've loved to sit on the beach." I never did that. If I did, I would really get hell.

Nowadays they still go grocery shopping and have dinner together because they're still living in the same apartment, but there has been no sex because Larry has stopped trying to initiate it.

I told her, "I'm going to look for another place, and then we'll go our separate ways." I don't think she thinks I'm serious because she still talks about what she wants "us" to do in the future. When I tell her it's not really going to be an "us-we" thing, she's quiet, or she brushes it off, or she starts an argument. She says she wants to stay together. But at this point her words don't hold any meaning. If you keep kicking me in the ass and say, "I'm sorry," there's only a certain number of times I'm gonna keep turning around. Professionally, I'm the happiest I've ever been. I'm not gonna be in a relationship that's still negative even when I'm making the most money ever.

Janet planned her whole life when she was a little girl living on a Caribbean Island. Her parents had divorced and left her with an aunt until they established themselves in the United States and called for her, years later. Meanwhile, Janet was left looking at the all the goodies in the world with her nose pressed up against the glass. It was then that she decided on having a big Barbie wedding with a corporate executive husband who would come home for dinner carrying an attaché case. When she met Larry she thought he'd fit in with her plans, but now he didn't.

In arguments, she's brought up many times how things have fallen outside of her expected timeline, how she's had to compromise living a certain lifestyle, and how she was not going to continue to "tolerate" this. She'd say, "Janet is going to live the way that Janet wants to. I'm going to have nice things, the best of the best. I'm going to travel, I'm going to dress nicely, I'm going to drive my Mercedes and no man is going to stand in the way of that!" She's created an image in her mind and since all of those images haven't come to fruition, it's become a problem.

Janet didn't care about Larry's life plan, which involved things more important than material goods. He had been schooled, literally, in having good family values. His mother was a schoolteacher and his father was a middle school principal. Not unlike Janet, they had high expectations and were very demanding of Larry growing up.

My sister and I always had to go to summer school at home. And I've been doing laundry since I was seven years old because, one day, my mother got tired of us throwing our dirty clothes all over the room. My father was even more of a disciplinarian than my mom. He was my hero and role model, but he would give me four-hour lectures, groundings, and spankings, depending on the offense – even though I was only mischievous at best. The worst thing I ever did was get suspended in fourth grade for cursing at the teacher.

Larry's childhood taught him to try to avoid conflict or confrontation because it leads to discipline.

I don't like people being upset or disappointed with me. I walk away from arguments. I sacrifice myself for the sake of placating someone. Neither one of my parents was hesitant to express themselves. They didn't bite their tongue. I bite my tongue rather than rock the boat.

Yet with Janet he brought his 'dirty laundry' with him. He walked right into the same situation that he had with his parents because, even though it made him unhappy, it was familiar. And he's had to do a lot of 'tongue-biting'.

Although it's hard to fault Janet for wanting to make her dreams come true, she was selfishly pursuing them without any regard for Larry's dreams. The one glaring omission from her life plan was love. The Barbie-style life that Janet prearranged in her head was just as plastic as Barbie and all her toys.

Spoiled Little Princess

Elizabeth seemed to have it all. She grew up in the best part of Chicago, had a pretty mom who was an ex-stewardess, a rich daddy, and she ran with the cool kids – the snobby 'in-crowd'. What she didn't have was the feeling that she was loveable.

She was 24, working in public relations, and living in an apartment in town when she kept meeting Louis in the elevator of their building. He was 31 and working in media sales. She could tell he was enthralled with her, and that bored her.

Elizabeth was attractive, with a great sense of style and a great flair with clothes. She wore Gucci and Prada and other designers. She was popular and well known in town. She was invited to the best parties. She seemed like one of the cool kids to get to know. I could tell she wasn't interested, but I did what I could to woo her. I get a lot of tickets because of my work, so I invited her to events. I lent her my car. Once I met her grandmother, who lived nearby, so I started bringing Grandma the newspaper on Sunday mornings.

For almost a year Elizabeth sensed that Louis wanted to be more than her neighbor or friend, but she wouldn't have it. Then one day he happened to meet her mother.

Her mom was very taken with me. Once Elizabeth saw that her mother bought into me, she was more interested. I wasn't like the other guys in her circle, whose parents paid for everything. I was self-made.

Louis and Elizabeth started dating. It became 'official' when she deigned to start going out with him in public as a couple. After three months of dating, she conceded to having sex. She began integrating Louis into her family life, which consisted mainly of going to her parents' country home and going shopping.

Her dad wanted to buy a $150,000 Bentley, so we all went car shopping. He told me, "I'll let you pick the color." Why would I want to pick the color of his car? I'm not 12. He treated us like adolescents.

Then she pushed me to buy an apartment in a trendy new building and moved in with me. Her ex-boyfriend lived there with his wife. It was 'the' address to have. She wanted her ex-boyfriend, who'd made a lot of money as a trader, to know that she was going to have the same lifestyle with or without him. She'd dated him for quite some time and was still dating him when I first met her. She told me she ended it because he was somewhat abusive. He pushed her.

Indeed, trendy apartment or not, Elizabeth needed a man who she could push – not the other way around. And Louis seemed to fit her specifications, so she set her eyes on marriage. They dated for a year and a half before they got engaged. During this time there were plenty of red flags that Louis chose to ignore.

When I was trying to move from the wooing to the dating stage, I bought $100 tickets for her and her friend to go to the House of Blues with me. She ignored me the entire time. Neither she nor her friend said thank you. My friends were appalled.

I sent her a note calling her on the carpet and telling her I was done, but she apologized and I forgave her. Her parents were surprised I continued dating her. They thought I was too nice. I should've taken it more to heart. Then there was the time we were on our way to dinner with another couple. They called and asked if we could pick them up. She threw a shit-fit. It was embarrassing because they could hear her. It wasn't really an inconvenience. She said they were cheaping out of a cab or a valet. All my friends found her inherently difficult. They didn't like her vibe.

So why did a bright guy with a bright future like Louis ignore the warning signs and ask her to marry him anyway?

She was everything I couldn't have in high school. I was not nerdy, but average. I wasn't a part of anything – the cool kids or the nerds. Unlike Elizabeth, I was never the first one to get invited. She represented everything I wasn't and everything I didn't have. She was not drop-dead, stop-traffic gorgeous, but she was very fashionable and always looked good when we went out.

A few days after Louis and Elizabeth got engaged, his mother, who had just recently moved to Chicago, had a bike accident along the running path of Lake Michigan. She was taken in an ambulance and hospitalized with injuries.

When I told Elizabeth that I would need to take care of my mom while she recuperates at home for a few months, her response was that my mother had plenty of money to hire a nurse and it wasn't my responsibility to care for her... and why couldn't my mother just put on a smile for us? I realized my fiancée was jealous, sick, and controlling. I had to sneak off to see my mom because I was scared of Elizabeth. My mother and I had a huge falling out. I was so close to saying, "Fuck you" to my fiancée.

But Louis didn't. Instead he continued on with the engagement and went to therapy because they fought constantly about everything – from his relationship with his mother to decorating their new apartment. But when the therapist started confronting Elizabeth, Elizabeth stopped going to therapy.

Why did I go ahead and marry her? I was already too far down this path and Elizabeth mesmerized me. Planning the wedding was crazy. There were lots of arguments. An obscene amount of money was spent – over $100,000 – so that Elizabeth could claim to have had the wedding of the year, if not the decade. I was on a train I couldn't get off – or I didn't have the balls to get off. The wedding was beautiful, but when she was walking down the aisle I felt dread, like I should not be here. People were making bets for how long our marriage would last.

Every nouveau riche couple in Chicago went to Hawaii for their honeymoon, so of course that's where Elizabeth determined we would go, even though I would have preferred a place with more culture. We stayed in the bridal suite at the best hotel on the beach. It was mindless. The sex was very mediocre. At first it had been good because she was trying to impress me, then it went downhill. She wasn't warm. It was mechanical.

Elizabeth was absolutely certain that once we got married she'd convince me to start a family right away, even though I had told her that, at this point, I couldn't think of children. Right after *we got back, her father tried to lock me into this terrible marriage by offering to buy me a 500 SL Mercedes, worth over $100,000, if I got her pregnant. I didn't take him up on his offer.*

Louis and Elizabeth fought over money. He paid for the apartment, dinners, and all their other expenses. And he put money into a joint account that she could spend as she wished – even for big-ticket items. But Elizabeth still complained, not that there were things she wanted and didn't get, but that she thought Louis was not entitled to what he got for himself. For example, she complained if he went to dinner with his friends at a nice restaurant instead of a hamburger joint.

Elizabeth hated my shopping habits. I'm a huge clotheshorse, as is she. While I had no problem supporting my shopping habit, as well as hers, Elizabeth believed that a guy should not need so much clothing. At one point she started trying to count the number of shirts, ties, suits, and slacks I owned to monitor my shopping. Eventually I turned to buying clothes and bringing them directly to the cleaners, so it would look as though they were already purchased. I also avoided the obvious trail of shopping bags.

Their marriage continued going downhill until Louis reached the breaking point. He was tired of fighting and being scared to come home. He lost friends because they didn't like Elizabeth, and he became very lonely. Then he lost clients because she embarrassed him in front of them by picking fights and being nasty. Finally, Louis told her he wanted a divorce.

Elizabeth ramped up for a fight. She cleaned out the joint account and put the money in her account electronically. She moved out and rented an apartment in the same building. She had a male friend come over and take her jewelry for her. When we saw each other, we either ignored each other or had a fight, as if we were on a Jerry Springer episode. She sought me out and ate up these encounters. I started taking the cargo elevator to avoid her. Since her father was a bigwig attorney, he had his attorney friends do the divorce pro bono, while I couldn't afford to lawyer-up. So I had to move out of our trendy address.

But Louis' losses were far more than monetary when he divorced Elizabeth. His biggest loss was his entrée into the 'in-crowd' that she provided.

I was depressed growing up. I started putting on weight in junior high school. Being a fat kid in junior high wasn't fun. I didn't fit in. I felt alienated.

The reason Louis was depressed was because his sister, who was two years younger, was everything he wasn't, but wanted to be. For one thing, she was their father's favorite.

My sister was in the 'in-crowd'. She was a great athlete, a party girl, and a lot of fun. I married my sister. When I got into fights with Elizabeth, I heard myself calling her by my sister's name. That's when Elizabeth knew I hated her!

Elizabeth had to wonder whether her father hated her, as well.

Her dad used money to manipulate her to do things, such as helping her grandmother. Everything was a negotiation and had a price tag. But the most sadistic was when her father took the family shopping. He'd encourage Elizabeth to say what she liked, such as expensive jewelry, and then he would buy it for her mother instead. Elizabeth's mother married her father for his money and used sex to manipulate him. So Elizabeth played up to her mom because she'd secretly take Elizabeth shopping with her father's money.

It's no wonder that Elizabeth's mother liked Louis when she met him. Just as she colluded with Elizabeth in manipulating her dad, she'd recognized that Louis would be the perfect match for a spoiled little princess who needed to get her way.

The Dog Ate My Balls

David and Joan have been married for 27 agonizing years. They were set up on a blind date by a mutual friend. Before meeting Joan, David had been trying to date another woman, but found her to be too high-maintenance.

She was really difficult. I didn't have any money. She wanted me to take her to French restaurants where it was $50 a person when $50 was my whole net worth!

So David tested Joan by inviting her on a first date that consisted of eating pizza on his coffee table and taking a walk around the neighborhood. She didn't complain and passed with flying colors.

She played the game just right until I married her. That's when the trouble began.

Joan was a vegetarian and did not want meat in the house. She never cooked, so they went out to eat all the time. One night it rained heavily. David didn't want to go out, so he ordered a pepperoni pizza.

When the delivery guy showed up and Joan saw there was pepperoni on the pizza, she screamed, "Oh my God! Take it out of here!" I took it out to the garage and sat in my car and ate it there. After that, I started eating in the car whenever I wanted something that was on the vegetarian hit list.

David admits to being a very isolated, lonely, and miserable man due to years of living under the weight of Joan's constant criticism, complaints and control. His weary voice reflects his hopelessness as he recounts a litany of the problems he's had to endure and hints that these are only the tip of the iceberg.

Joan's very insecure. Everything has to be her way. We're total opposites. She tells me what to say and what not to say, like, "Don't say we're oil and water." She has these impractical ideas for decorating the house, like a freestanding sink or painting the walls black. And there's no discussing it. It has to be her way.

She calls me or texts me 40 times a day for no reason. For example, she'll say, "I'm getting to the mall now." "I'm leaving the mall now." Why do I need to know this? She tells me, "Change that belt, you can't go out like that!" I've never been able to

394

change her mind. *How is it that she has never been wrong in 27 years and I have never been right? What are the odds of that? We even argue about the method we use to argue. She looks away and doesn't look at me when we talk. She micro-manages everything – even telling me where to put a stamp on an envelope. She tells me, "Wear a coat, it's cold." "Those shoes don't look good." I refuse to argue now. I'm fading away. We never make social plans. We don't have friends because she sabotages these relationships. If I tell her something, she refuses to believe me, but if I get a friend to tell her the same thing, she believes them. When I read the newspaper to her, for example, "Ninety-nine percent of scientists in the world believe x," she goes, "No way." Her opinion supersedes ninety-nine percent of scientists. She has opinions about everything, even things she knows nothing about. She'd have an opinion about nuclear isotopes. She's always trying to clean up my desk, and she doesn't care that the effect on me is disruptive since I can't find anything. She complains about having to work on the business we built together. She thinks, "Woe is me!" It only takes a few hours a week of her time. I came out here with two nickels. Now we have enough money and a nice house. We have some nice trees. We have more antiques than we have room for, so some are in the garage. I have gratitude. But she can't relax. She complains non-stop. I keep things stuffed in. I rock in my lazy-boy chair and try to close my ears. We went to counseling, but nothing changes. For over a decade, I was hoping she'd change, but our marriage has just continued to go downhill.*

David is also upset about how Joan has taken over the raising of their three sons.

I never got any one-on-one time with them. She wanted a girl, so every Saturday she took them shopping at the mall for the first 10 years of their lives. They've become metro-sexuals. They talk about how the color of the belt matches the shoes and what stores are best for what items. She continued to spoon-feed and pre-cut their meat for them up to ridiculous ages. She helps them weasel out of school rules, even now that they've started college.

Joan clearly wants to make sure that her sons love her and take her side in arguments with David. So far, it's working.

I've backed off trying to take care of my boys because everything I do, she criticizes. I told them they were watching too much TV and not doing homework. They didn't want to turn the TV off, so I did it through the main switch that controls all the TV screens in the house. Joan pried open the cover of the switch box and turned them on again. I tried to make Wednesday nights "Dad's Night Out with His Sons," but my wife wouldn't let it happen. They're wusses and I'm scared they're going to wind up with Ball-Busters because they won't know that this is not acceptable behavior.

Joan's desperate need to be in control began when she was 11 years old and her mother died of leukemia. Her father, sister, and two brothers fell apart.

Joan became the man of the house. For example, when the electric company shut the lights out at 5:00 P.M. on Fridays because the electric bill hadn't been paid, she had to take care of it. She stepped-up because the others in her family were catatonic.

When Joan's mother died, her brothers started using drugs. Her sister became Pollyanna, telling everyone, "Everything will be okay," but doing nothing to make it happen. Her father went into mourning and never came out.

He was a sweet man, beaten up by his wife's death. After this, he failed at everything he touched. His house was so disorganized I once thought that someone had broken in because it looked like the house had been ransacked. He never remarried.

When the death of Joan's mother spun her young world out of control, it left her with the feeling that her world can collapse at any moment if she is not always in control of it. This perpetual state of insecurity can account for her contacting David 40 times a day and telling him to wear a coat when it's cold. Joan is afraid that something bad will happen to David, just as it did to her mom.

David had his own problems growing up.

I was a latchkey kid. There would be notes like, "Warm spaghetti up for dinner."

His parents were hardworking immigrants who weren't affectionate towards him or each other.

My mother was disappointed with her life. She was very controlling, always telling my father what to do. He got beaten down, relegated to, "Yes, dear." He sat at the kitchen table playing cards... like what I do now.

David choked up as he came to this realization. He had become just like his dad, and Joan was just like his mom. The only difference is that Joan has a barking rottweiler for a ring tone on her cell phone, which David thinks suits her perfectly.

I've lost my balls over the years. I've been emasculated. We stopped having sex 16 years ago. It was the accumulation of all this shit that turned me off. I'm burned out, a shadow of my former self. My friends who knew me before I married Joan don't recognize me. I've lost my zest for life. I keep putting off getting divorced, waiting until the boys are grown or I make a windfall. The truth is if I get my balls back, I'll file for divorce.

But his rottweiler ate his balls....

Famous Ball-Busters

<u>Nurse Ratched</u> – In the book and movie "One Flew Over the Cuckoo's Nest," a sadistic and passive-aggressive Nurse Ratched controls a whole ward full of men by threatening and humiliating them.

<u>Martha Stewart</u> – Named one of America's most powerful women, this multi-millionaire lifestyle guru and CEO is one tough cookie. Between her temper tantrums and single-minded ambition, many men have been afraid to get close to this domestic diva, lest she scour them.

<u>Miranda Hobbes</u> – In the TV show "Sex and the City," Miranda is a successful attorney with a chip on her shoulder towards men, from whom she demands satisfying sexual performances. For

years her cynicism prevents her from treating Steve Brady with anything but condescension, until she eventually marries him.

Bette Davis – Married four times. Bette was known for playing a tough broad on-screen and off. In the book *My Mother's Keeper*, written by Bette's daughter, she described how difficult it was growing up with such an overbearing mother.

Joan Crawford – Known as "Mommie Dearest," after one of her adopted children wrote of her cruelty. Joan was also thought of as a Ball-Buster towards her four husbands. It was her androgynous quality that gave this famous actress her power over men.

Sarah Palin – "The difference between a hockey mom and a pit bull? Lipstick!" This is how Sarah described herself in a speech given at the Republican National Convention.

Amanda Woodward – In the TV show "Melrose Place," Amanda (Heather Locklear) is known as the world's cruelest miniskirt-wearing landlady, boss, and sex kitten. She's as heartless at work as she is with men.

Catwoman – This comic book Ball-Buster is a whip-carrying adversary and love interest of Batman, who keeps him on his toes. Some have speculated that her aggressive exterior has come about because of a childhood history of abuse.

Erin Brockovich – Erin takes on whole companies – not just individual men – and won the largest toxic tort injury settlement in America.

Shania Twain – In, "That Don't Impress Me Much," Shania sings, "You think you're cool, but have you got the touch? Don't get me wrong. Yeah I think you're alright, but that won't keep me warm on the long, cold, lonely night."

Chapter 13
THE BAD GIRL SCORNED

What does a Bad Girl Scorned want?

A Bad Girl Scorned wants her man to cancel his plans to break up with her and promise his undying love. Failing this, she wants to destroy his life by stalking him or extracting sweet revenge.

Why? To soothe her fears of abandonment. Out of all the bad girls, The Bad Girl Scorned has the most profound fears of abandonment from having had a nightmarish childhood that included abandonment and/or abuse. The abandonment can be physical, when a parent is not physically present. Or emotional, when a parent is there physically, but not emotionally because his attention is taken up by work, substance abuse, depression, or other distractions. In a sense, abuse – physical, sexual, emotional, or by neglect – is a kind of abandonment, since the parent abandons the role of a nurturer in order to satisfy his own selfish or sick impulses.

"Hell hath no fury like a woman scorned" paraphrases the line in "The Mourning Bride," written by the British playwright William Congreve in 1697: "Heaven has no rage like love to hatred turned, nor hell a fury like a woman scorned." And indeed, at the slightest hint of her lover's abandonment, a Bad Girl Scorned is ready to unleash her rage and make his life a living hell. Since, to her, it feels as if his abandonment will demolish her, she feels justified in demolishing him – sometimes literally. She is a desperate woman at the end of her rope with nothing to lose because the threatened abandonment of her lover brings unconscious memories to the surface of these same feelings she had in childhood when a parent (usually her father) threatened to abandon her.

The Bad Girl Scorned has a voracious sexual appetite, not just as a means to hook a guy by keeping him in a constant state of arousal and thereby rendering him helpless, but as a means to reassure herself – at least for the moment – that she's loveable. When she feels that she needs more than sex to keep him on her tight leash, she is willing to go to dangerous lengths to keep him or to punish him.

When a Bad Girl Scorned believes there is still hope that her man can be coerced into abandoning his plans to abandon her, she pulls out all the stops to make this happen. But once these manipulations fail, she unleashes her rage and goes into 'destroy mode'. There are two types of Bad Girls Scorned – the stalker and the revenge seeker. If the man is really naughty, or if she is falling off the edge of sanity, she can sometimes become both.

Since The Bad Girl Scorned has a very fragile sense of self, her lover's abandonment threatens not only to make her unhappy, but also to shatter her world and annihilate her. So she feels she needs his love for her very survival. This drives her to resort to malevolent manipulations and outrageous conduct – from ruining his reputation, provoking drug or alcohol abuse, commandeering his cell or computer, or kidnapping him - to threatening suicide. As this bad girl spirals downward out of control, she is capable of causing her lover great bodily harm or even death.

Ever since the 1987 movie "Fatal Attraction" opened the floodgates, more and more Bad Girls Scorned have been goaded to ever-escalating heights of stalking and revenge. Whether it's cooking their lover's pet rabbit or turning in a stained blue dress, they feel validated in stooping to conquer

In "Fatal Attraction," Alex Forrest (Glenn Close) refuses to believe that Dan Gallagher (Michael Douglas), a married man, wants nothing more to do with her after their passionate encounter. The more he ignores her, the more desperate she gets – stalking him, threatening suicide, claiming she's pregnant, boiling the pet rabbit, and intruding into his family's life until tensions explode in an orgy of violence. Like many Bad Girls Scorned, Alex has a borderline personality disorder – with fear of abandonment, volatile moods, impulsivity, a shifting between idealizing him and devaluing him, and self-destructive tendencies.

In a headline-making example of life imitating art, it wasn't long before Amy Fisher, acted on her 'fatal attraction' to Joey Buttafuoco by shooting his wife, Mary Jo, in the head when he refused to leave her. If the lover of a Bad Girl Scorned is married, she may well direct her rage towards his spouse under the delusion that if she just gets rid of his 'ball and chain', he will be free to follow his heart and be with her. Amy, also known as "The Long Island Lolita," had an abusive relationship with her father that fueled the rage she felt when Joey rejected her. Amy wanted their white picket fence and figured if she got rid of Mary Jo, she could have her life.

White House intern Monica Lewinsky was enraged. How dare President Bill Clinton announce to the world, "I did not have sexual relations with that woman, Miss Lewinsky"? She had a blue dress with his semen stain on it to prove that he had! As the president persisted in shattering her romantic fantasies and she realized there was no future with him, this Bad Girl Scorned, who had already been abandoned by her father, tasted sweet revenge by bringing forth the dress as evidence.

Miss Havisham, in Charles Dickens' *Great Expectations*, is another classic example of a Bad Girl Scorned. A spinster who was abandoned by her fiancé on her wedding day, she still wears her frayed wedding gown, and lives amongst the cobwebs that cover her cake and silenced clocks. In her quest for revenge, she teaches her adopted daughter, Estella, to make Pip fall hopelessly in love with her, but to remain cold-hearted towards him, rejecting him like Miss Havisham's fiancé rejected her long ago. She whispers to Estella:

Break their hearts, my pride and hope, break their hearts and have no mercy!

If all bad girls are drama queens, The Bad Girl Scorned is the Oscar-winner! To her, nothing matters except keeping her man. So, she is willing to risk everything – her career, savings, children, health, self-respect, and anything else in her frenzy to keep him or kill him.

And for a drama queen who has always wanted to see her name up in lights, what could be more perfect than a billboard on Broadway advertising to the world that you have been his mistress... until he had the nerve to dump you? This is how Bad Girl Scorned YaVaughnie Wilkins got her revenge when her married lover, CEO Charles E. Phillips, decided to reconcile with his wife. The billboards displayed a beaming "Charles & YaVaughnie" nuzzling each other and quoted him as having sworn to her, "You are my soulmate forever!" They also directed passersby to a Website that was a veritable shrine to their 8 1/2 year affair – with photos of them canoodling around the world, ticket stubs, karaoke renditions, and mushy love notes. In one, Phillips cooed, "I have never met a woman as fascinating as you. You are exactly what I've been looking and waiting for."

Why do men fall for Bad Girls Scorned?

Men who are attracted to Bad Girls Scorned are attracted to high drama. They are intensity junkies either because they were raised in dramatic chaos as a child, where they had to walk on similar eggshells, or because they were raised in Ozzie and Harriet ho-hum boredom.

John Wayne Bobbitt was the product of a chaotic childhood. It has been reported that his father abandoned him as a baby, leaving him and his sickly mother to a crime-infested neighborhood with a babysitter who molested him, all of which turned him into a thrill-seeker. When he threatened to leave his wife, Lorena, she gave him the 'thrill' of his life by cutting off his penis with a kitchen knife while he was sleeping. To add insult to injury, this jealous Bad Girl Scorned then drove away and flung his penis out her car window. It was later found and surgically reattached, but this incident has left both visible and invisible scars. Lorena pleaded self-defense and was found not guilty of "malicious wounding" by reason of temporary insanity induced by her husband's alleged abuse. Copycat crimes of "Bobbittmania" by other Bad Girls Scorned have been reported.

For a man who has had a cautious childhood, a wild child bad girl is like a bright, shiny new toy that his eyes can't help but follow. The problems begin when it's not just his eyes that follow her, but his penis. Because these bad girls are the most intense, a man gets most helplessly swept away and unable to think further than his next orgasm.

With a Bad Girl Scorned, a man doesn't have to worry whether she's 'into' him or not. She unabashedly demonstrates that she is 'super into' him. This is an especially attractive hook for a man who has just been dumped by a woman who he apparently was more 'into' than she was 'into' him. It is also an especially attractive hook for a man who feels he was deprived of attention growing up and is starving for it. Unconsciously, he is drawn to this bad girl who flatters him with her overabundance of attention until he realizes, too late, that he is drowning in her quicksand and is scared to death.

And still other men are lured to The Bad Girl Scorned because unconsciously they are feeling guilty for things they've done in the past, or for having led her on at the beginning. So they believe they deserve whatever punishment she metes out.

Real Stories from Men on the Dating Front

One-Night Stand from Hell

When Kyle's live-in girlfriend, Lauren, agreed to marry him but kept putting off setting a date, he grew increasingly frustrated.

She traveled out of town a lot for business, which gave Kyle time to brood over whether she was ever going to commit.

I wasn't gonna throw my black book away until I felt she'd made a commitment to me. So one time when Lauren was away, I had a one-night stand with Barbara, a woman I met through a classified ad in L.A. Magazine, a mainstream publication. I was attracted to the sexy nature of her ad. Something like, "I like a guy who likes to take long walks on the beach. I'm a fun-loving petite girl, perky in all the ways that count. I never leave men unsatisfied." For men, there's good sex and great sex, so I gave in.

Kyle called her. They chatted and arranged to meet at a nice restaurant in Century City. Barbara appreciated the fine dining, but it was obvious she couldn't wait to leave. She pressed him with, "Let's go back to my place."

Barbara was having her period. I'm not as phobic about this as a lot of men, but it was messy. I had unprotected sex with her because I hate using condoms. It's like washing dishes with rubber gloves. Her period took the romance out of it. When I left, I just felt "eh." It was fun, but if I risk my relationship with Lauren, it had to be better than this. I asked myself if Barbara was really worth it.

A couple of weeks later on a Sunday morning, Lauren and Kyle were lazing in bed after having made love and eaten croissants and cappuccino. Suddenly the phone rang.

I thought "uh-oh" because I had elderly parents and wondered if this morning call could be bad news. It was Barbara. She said, "I'm calling because I just got tested and I have AIDS." Lauren says the look on my face was unbelievable. I was trying to make her think that the caller was just a telemarketer, but my life was passing before me. All I could say was, "Are you sure?" I was thinking, 'I'm gonna die. Lauren has it. I'm gonna have to tell her. And I can't believe I got it from a one-night stand."

When Kyle hung up he sat there in total shock while Lauren stared at him, waiting for him to say something.

I finally told her, "I messed around on you. That was the woman. She told me she has AIDS." I felt I was essentially giving Lauren a death warrant. She said, "If you have it, I have it. Let's just move on." The only thing I could think about was all that blood and how exposed I was. I got tested right away and then every six months. Lauren got tested, too. The waiting was hell. Barbara had given no evidence of craziness.

It was a pivotal point in Kyle's relationship with Lauren, an inadvertent test of her love. He wouldn't have blamed her if she left him, but since she stayed, it reassured him of her love. A year passed and so far they both had tested negative, but knew they were not out of the woods yet. One day sitting in his office, Kyle got a call. It was the Los Angeles Police Department.

The officer asked, "Do you know a girl named Barbara S.?" My mind started racing. Why were the cops calling about her? Did she kill herself and leave a suicide note with my name on it?

Did she die of AIDS alone in her apartment and the police found my name? He asked, "How do you know her?" I admitted I'd had a one-night stand with her. Next the officer said, "For the last year or so, she has been having one-night stands with scores of men around the city, then calling and telling the men that she has AIDS. We arrested her because that's against the law. So far, we've tracked down 34 men." It turned out that some guy she'd been engaged to dumped her. She decided this was the way to get back at men – to use men for sex and then terrify them and destroy their relationships!

The Woman Who Refused to Take "No" for An Answer

Remember Christopher, the Knight in Prison Garb, who tried to rescue Chloe, The Damsel in Distress? After he and Chloe were separated, his ex-mistress, Linda, couldn't wait to get her claws back into him.

I was infatuated with her initially. I was still trying to recover from my inner nerd and Linda had a swagger and was a prominent attorney who wore the right clothes and hung out with the right crowd – just like Chloe had. But she was very controlling. I never wanted to marry her. I was intoxicated with the idea of having sex for the first time after a year. Chloe had never been interested in sex. Sometimes Linda and I had sex seven times a night. I didn't know I could do it. But I could never satisfy Linda because she had a voracious sexual appetite.

During their brief affair, Linda had gotten pregnant. She already had two young sons and didn't want any more children, so

Christopher paid for her abortion.

I broke it off because Linda was crazy. She was playing both sides, telling me that my wife was cheating on me and telling my wife that I was cheating on her, which I was with Linda. I don't think Chloe ever had an affair; it was just a ploy. The first time I broke up with Linda, she was still friends with Chloe and was always trying to get her boys to play with our girls so that she could continue batting her eyelashes at me. After a play-date, Linda would invite herself to stay for dinner. It was too much for me.

Once Linda's strategy for breaking up Christopher and Chloe worked, she thought she would slide into Christopher's heart and be home-free, especially since his world had begun to crumble on all sides.

Her law firm was representing me in my lawsuit against my former employer. I went to her firm after hours, which was the wrong move on my part. We were having sex in her office, but she didn't seem to care that she was risking her career. She'd use my case as an excuse to show up in my office when she knew I'd be alone working late at night. After I was separated, I went on an online dating bender. I was addicted, for sure, with over 1,000 inquiries on Match.com and the other dating sites. When Linda would come over, she'd see my dating spreadsheet. She thought she owned me. She was angry that she wasn't my one and only. I told her I was not interested in being her new husband. How could I get involved with her? I didn't want more scandals than I already had and we were in the same circles. People had begun to talk. When we were at the same kids' birthday parties, for example, I had to try to pretend that she was just another parent. I was an actor in my own life, in my own movie.

Linda's mind was working overtime to figure out a way to make Christopher love her, marry her, have sex with her – or even see her. Since she knew that he scoured the Internet dating sites to buoy his flagging self-esteem by reading the messages from the women who wanted to meet him, she thought it was the perfect spot to bait her hook.

Linda created a fake profile with a photo of her friend, an attractive woman. She knew what to write that would attract my attention: "multilingual world traveler, professional, likes good food, good wine, looking for a funny guy who is a world traveler." She used the screen name "Samantha Jones" from "Sex and the City." Linda liked to think of herself as the character from the show, fashionable, sexually avant-garde. It was her way of suggesting that she was a savvy New York woman, independent and successful.

Christopher took the bait. He emailed "Samantha Jones" and set up a date with her. When he opened the door, there was Linda!

I let her in. We did get it on, but I told her I was not interested in a relationship. She said, "If you just want sex, it's okay." She really wanted a relationship, but she was still trying to get her hooks into me any way she could.

Linda started shadowing Christopher in taxicabs while he walked to his Manhattan apartment. She knew what time he put the kids to sleep at Chloe's place.

I'd be walking back home and I'd see a taxi following me. One time she jumped out. I said, "You can go home now!" I was getting nervous. I was thinking about the movie "Fatal Attraction" and wondering, "Is that how it's going to end?"

Then there was the time she got into my apartment – a doorman building on the Upper East Side. I walked in and there she was. She said, "I'm here to collect." "Collect what?" I asked. "S-E-X," she said. I told her, "You're freaking me out, making me crazy!" The doorman let her in because he'd seen her with me before and thought she was my girlfriend. This time I escorted her out without giving into S-E-X. I told her, "You need to go." After that, she kept showing up in my lobby.

Christopher had told Linda about a girl he had met on an online dating site whose screen name was "Oyster4u." The woman had said she was 5'3" and 105 pounds. She turned out to be 5'9" and 210 pounds. Christopher had wanted to be a gentleman, so he took her out to dinner and talked to her about Chloe and Linda. So Linda looked up the profile for "Oyster4u" and emailed her to suggest that they meet. Linda and "Oyster" went out for drinks and had great fun bad-mouthing Christopher. "Oyster4u" told her, "All he talked about was his soon-to-be-ex-wife and you stalking him."

Then they posted me on websites like dontdatehimgirl.com, dontgooutwithhim.com and hesadog.com, so I became a pariah in the online dating community. They took away my only escape.

And his only way of trying to feel good about himself after his career and marriage imploded. In one final attempt to convince him that he did love her best of all, Linda showed up at his Madison Avenue office.

I was trying to rebuild my professional life. It was the middle of the day. I walked into my reception area and found her talking to a colleague of mine. My mind started racing. I thought, "What is she telling him about me? Is she trying to get me fired?" I took her arm and started walking her towards the hallway. I said, "Let's go outside to have a chat." I argued with her in the elevator and the lobby. She was creating a scene, breaking me down and making my eyes well up with tears. I was on the verge of bawling right in the middle of the lobby, with colleagues and bosses streaming by. I said, "I'm sorry. I can't do this anymore. Please, please stop stalking me!"

Linda stopped for a couple of months, but then started up again, this time stalking him on the Internet. She emailed Christopher from her own email address and from various sites with various identities to intrude on his blog articles, posts, and forums. He didn't answer her.

The last time I heard from her was a few months ago. She commented on my blogspot. I finally wrote her back: "I have no interest in speaking with you. Good luck. I wish you and the boys all the best. I won't respond again."

But Christopher had other demons that continued stalking him and making him sabotage himself in love and business. He'd always felt guilty that he was his mother's golden boy, favored over his brother, who was still jealous. And his father's grumbling about his flashy modeling days still rings in his ears.

One day when I was 18 or 19 yrs old, I was wearing a parachute jumpsuit with big shoulders. I was modeling for a hair products company. My hair was burgundy, in a 'flock of seagulls' haircut, shaved close on the side and outspread on top. My father took one look at me, turned to my mom and said, "Your son's a faggot!"

And ever since, Christopher has been trying to prove him wrong.

Off The Hook

Roger and Nicole had been living together for a year and a half. He promised to marry her. She was a flight attendant with a regular roundtrip route between Los Angeles and Tokyo, two or three times a week. Roger knew her schedule by heart, plus Nicole always called him from the airport when she arrived at LAX to say, "Hi honey, I just landed." He was having some doubts about whether marrying her was still a good idea and was thinking about how he could get out of it. He started having an affair. Then one day Nicole took an earlier flight back to Los Angeles. She wanted to surprise Roger, so she didn't call from the airport. When she opened the door, she was the one getting the surprise.

Nicole walked in and found me in bed with a woman. She started screaming and yelling. I tried turning it around, as men do when they're caught in a compromising situation. I said, "This wouldn't have happened if you hadn't come home early! This was the only time I cheated on you." Finally, I had to admit I was busted. I needed to leave for New York that evening, so I told Nicole, "I want all your stuff out of here when I get back!"

Nicole left crying. She had the key, but nowhere to go, so she killed hours until she saw Roger leave. She thought of throwing his guitar out the window, stealing his stereo, or vandalizing his apartment. Instead, Nicole called the time-of-day service in Tokyo for Japan Standard Time and left the phone off the hook. Meanwhile, Roger was in New York thinking how stupid he was to let her stay in his apartment alone when she was so angry. When he came home four days later, he walked into his apartment and started hearing a voice talking rhythmically to him. He couldn't make out the words.

I finally realized that the sound was coming from the phone that was off the hook. I picked it up, listened, and heard a voice saying in Japanese, "The time is 9:05 and 10 seconds," then, "The time is 9:05 and 20 seconds," "The time is 9:05 and 30 seconds." I didn't understand what was going on, so I hung up the phone and thought no more about it.

That is, until Roger got a phone bill for $1,700. Nicole had purposely left the phone off the hook while he was gone to make him 'pay' for what he'd done to her. He tried explaining to the phone company that it was his stewardess girlfriend who made the call, but they refused to do anything about it.

"Fatal Attraction" Was Just a Disney Movie

Brittany, a woman with a checkered past, licked her lips as she clicked through the photos on an Internet dating site until one of them leapt out at her. She'd later tell Wayne that she chose him because he was cute, but what she didn't tell him was that it was the innocence she saw in his eyes that attracted her even more. Here was a man she could prey upon who wouldn't abuse or abandon her like the others had done. Indeed, her bad girl radar had directed her to the perfect choice.

Wayne grew up in the Northeast in an Ozzie and Harriet family that was too good to be true – except for two alcoholic grandfathers and a spoiled younger sister who took his parents' attention away from him.

My childhood was storybook. My parents married young and have been married for 38 years. I never saw or heard them fight. They have a perfect relationship. I always wondered, "'How am I going to find someone like this?" My first trauma occurred in my senior year of high school when my grandfather had a stroke. I thought, "Holy shit, everything isn't puppy dogs and rainbows!"

That's when Wayne started experimenting with pot and drinking, which gradually led to trying other drugs. Actually, Wayne's realization that life wasn't just "puppy dogs and rainbows" began a little earlier. He attended an all-boys' private high school whose motto was "Developing leadership in young men," but it had developed low self-esteem and lack of confidence in this young man because of their arbitrary rules about who could qualify to play on their teams. Wayne had excelled in sports in junior high, and many of his teammates had gone on to his high school with him.

When I got to high school, I couldn't play sports anymore because the school had decided that only students living within a 12-mile radius could be on their teams. That sucked. My teammates from junior high were allowed to play. They acted as if they didn't even know me when we crossed paths in the halls between classes.

A few years after college, Wayne moved to San Francisco, where he had a great job in sales and began winning awards as top salesman. Although he demonstrated 'leadership' at work, he continued using drugs and drinking. His social life was not anything to write home about. He dated a few girls, but no one special.

I was making good money and partying a lot. I never felt good about myself even though I was getting awards.

When his lease ran out, Wayne left his hard-partying roommates behind and moved in with two other guys. He stopped dabbling in cocaine and Ecstasy and continued with pot and drinking, but at a more manageable level. Then Wayne was introduced to Lily through mutual friends from their same home state. She was a

Pilates instructor and Abercrombie model. They started dating.

This was the first relationship I was excited about. I went out with Lily ten times in two months. Then after having gotten to know each other, we went to dinner and a concert and had sex for the first time. She slept over and we went out for breakfast. She invited me to a black tie event for her modeling agency. I was really looking forward to it. A couple of days later, Lily casually mentioned that a guy friend was coming into town, which apparently was her way of 'disinviting' me because when it came to the date of the black tie event she flaked on me. I was pretty bummed. I really, really liked this girl. I told my friend I wasn't t gonna psycho dial or stalk her, so I let it go. I was into her, but I guess she wasn't into me.

Wayne was sick of the bar scene, so he turned to Internet dating. He was 28 years old and specified that he was looking for a woman who was 24-36. In the first three months, he went on 12 first dates that really didn't amount to much. Then Brittany sought him out. She wrote, "Hey, I'm interested in you. You have a lot of qualities I'm looking for." She had no photos of herself posted on her profile. She said she'd send them and she did. She was very attractive. Her profile said she was 36 years old and divorced with no kids. They spoke on the telephone about a dozen times.

Before we met she sent me a lot of flirtatious texts and racy picture messages. I told my friends, "I'm getting all this crazy stuff from this woman who's trying to hook up with me without even knowing me." My friends were entertained by her texts and photos and encouraged me to hook up with her.

Even though on some level Wayne already recognized that Brittany was "crazy," he kept on going, ignoring these red flags. His recent heartbreak with Lily, a girl who wasn't into him, added to his vulnerability and made him putty in Brittany's hands, a girl who already seemed to be 'super into' him.

Looking back I guess there was something that should have been a warning sign. One time I didn't call her back right away because I was shopping. She got angry and said, "It's okay if you don't want to do this!" I explained why I didn't call her back right away. It seemed like she was overreacting. About a week before we met, she sent pictures of her breasts and told me things she wanted to do to me: perform and get oral sex, masturbate, everything. It was fun and exciting. Obviously, she was looking for a quick hookup. I'd never done this before.

Brittany lived 45 minutes outside of San Francisco. She suggested meeting at Wayne's place on a Sunday evening.

That day I had spent more than a few hours down at a local bar drinking, smoking pot, and watching football, as I did on most Sundays at that time. I was living a carefree lifestyle and was not on good spiritual ground. I was so nervous. I met her at the parking space. She was as beautiful in person as her photos. I walked her to my apartment at the top of the stairs and directly into my room to avoid any uncomfortable introductions to my roommates. I gave her a hug and we started kissing. We hooked up immediately. She was ready to go. One thing led to another. The first time, we had protected sex, but at some point we didn't use protection. I encouraged her to stay, but she left at 2:00 A.M. I was surprised she left.

Brittany was using the tried-and-true bad girl trick of enticing a man and then walking away while he's still panting for more. When Wayne awoke the next morning, he couldn't believe he had had a woman come over whom he didn't know and had had unprotected sex with her. A week later they had a second date. Wayne took her to dinner and then he stayed over at her apartment. He discovered that she did have a child, after all, a 20-year-old daughter. Brittany dismissed this disparity by saying, "It's not like I have a baby." After the second date Wayne was getting to like Brittany.

She seemed like a nice, down-to-earth person. But age was a concern because I wanted to have kids – so 36 was the oldest I would have considered. I thought she was cool, so I tried not to worry about the age.

Wayne went back East to spend the Christmas holidays with his family. He and Brittany either texted or talked every day. On Christmas Eve Brittany sent him a text with news that her period was late and she was afraid she was pregnant.

I was an emotional wreck over the prospect of her being pregnant. I tried to play it cool and assured her everything would be all right. I didn't want her to know how freaked out I was about it. She said she would get an abortion.

As it turned out, Brittany wasn't pregnant. However, she was encouraged by Wayne's reaction. He had not abandoned her. When he got back to San Francisco, Brittany came to his place and, although they had agreed not to buy Christmas presents for each other, she had one for him.

I felt like a jerk because I didn't have anything for her. Brittany took out a Tiffany's box and inside was a surf bracelet. I freaked out because it probably cost at least $500 and I wasn't into jewelry. I told her I appreciated her gift, but I couldn't accept it because it was way too nice. She said, "Okay, then I'll give you cash." When I wouldn't accept that, she said, "How about if I buy courtside seats to a Warriors game?" This is every guy's fantasy. It was harder to refuse, but I tried by saying, "I have a friend coming in for that weekend." She said, "No problem. I'll buy you and your friend tickets." I told her, "Courtside seats are expensive." She said money wasn't an issue. She drove a BMW and claimed that she'd won a big settlement in an auto accident. So even though I kept telling her, "No," she spent about $2,000 and bought four tickets. She explained by saying, "I was thinking you could bring another friend." I told her to give them to her friends instead, but she said she didn't have any friends who wanted to go. I thought it was weird that she couldn't find a friend who'd like a courtside seat. Anyway, we wound up going – Brittany, two of my friends, and me. It was our third date. She stayed over.

Wayne recognized this as a red flag. There was something about the pressing need Brittany felt to hook him with an expensive gift that made him a little uneasy. Then something happened that was fortuitous for Brittany since it helped her get a toehold on him.

Wayne went skiing in Lake Tahoe and broke his wrist. This meant he couldn't drive to make his sales calls for weeks.

Brittany came over and never left my home. I was enjoying her company, but I wondered why she never had anything to do. I asked her, "You've been here for days. Don't you have anything you need to do?" The sex was great, she was taking good care of me, and I liked the attention.

After a month I ended up needing surgery, which would put me out of commission for another few months. When I came home from surgery, Brittany was there waiting for me. She was a saint. She cooked for me, cleaned my room, and did a lot of motherly things. She even did the laundry, carrying it three blocks to the Laundromat and, after spending all day there, folded it when she got home. But after a while it was getting to be annoying. I couldn't get rid of her! I told her, "You don't have to do this." She was over the top – trying to make sure I really liked her and was completely dependent upon her.

Brittany even used to buy my drugs. If I was getting low on pot, she'd say, "Shouldn't we call Phil to get more pot?" She wanted to numb me. She paid for the drugs and she'd fill up the fridge with food. She said she got $1 million from her lawsuit – but later I started to question that when I saw her paying with her mother's credit card. I didn't encourage her to spend money on me, but she would insist. I said, "This might not work out. I don't want you holding it over my head that you spent all this money on me." It was the perfect storm: a lot of pot, surgery for a broken wrist, and her being overly caring – all making it easier for her to get her claws into me.

Then things came to a head. One day after she felt she'd earned enough points nurturing Wayne, Brittany decided it was time to disclose a secret.

She said, "Wayne, I have something to tell you.... I'm not 36. I'm 41." I said, "Oh my God, you've got to be kidding! We have to stop doing this! You lied to me for three and a half months! I'll never be able to trust you ever again!" Brittany dissolved into a blubbering, crying mess. She said, "I'm sorry." I said, "I don't hate you, but this can't go on. I wouldn't have met you in the first place because 36 was already an issue for me because I want to have children."

Wayne was in a Wednesday night skee-ball league and had to meet his buddies in a couple of hours. Brittany was still on his bed blubbering and talking about wanting to marry him.

It broke my heart. I was starting to like her, although the lying and the clinginess had turned me off. I still had a soft spot for her even though it didn't feel quite right. I told her, "I have to go to skee-ball. I'm taking a shower. We can talk later. I'm not saying I'll never see you again."

As Wayne went to leave, he couldn't find his cell phone. Brittany denied taking it, although he suspected it could be her ploy to get him to stay. He looked for it for almost an hour and then finally left to join his skee-ball league buddies. When he got home, Brittany was still there, looking as if she'd been crying the whole time he was gone. She said she hadn't found his phone, but then a few minutes later said she had found it in a bag of groceries. Wayne had looked in this bag before he left.

She'd stolen my phone! We talked for a little bit. I was trying to get her to leave. She was inconsolable. I realized I've got a crazy one on my hands. She was constantly trying to please and constantly trying to have sex.

The sex was not only Brittany's hook, but it also temporarily satisfied her need for reassurance that she was loveable. She had not had good luck with men. Her father was an "emotional flatliner" who was never affectionate with her. A therapist seemed to think Brittany had repressed memories of his sexual abuse. When she was 17, he abandoned her by encouraging her to move out and move in with Don, a boyfriend he knew was abusing her. Brittany had told Wayne that Don jumped out of the bushes, ripped her clothes off, smelled her panties, and beat her up. She'd called the cops. Later when Wayne checked, there was, in fact, a record of Don's domestic violence. Next Brittany married and divorced Billy, an abusive biker. And then there was Sonny, who undoubtedly regrets having met Brittany. He was a married family man who divorced his wife for her and, although next in line to be sheriff, left the state in a hurry after she'd ostensibly caught him cheating. If a soon-to-be sheriff feared her fury, what chance did Wayne have?

It was Thursday and Wayne was still off work on medical leave. He went to get a haircut and asked his barber for advice about Brittany. The barber told Wayne he had to get home and get rid of her immediately. But when he got home, Brittany wouldn't hear of it.

She said, "If we're not gonna be together forever, I just want one more weekend with you. I'll take care of the arrangements and pay for it so we can end things peacefully." She told me that the relationship with her last boyfriend, Sonny, ended suddenly when he took off on a plane and she didn't want the same kind of ending with me. I said, "I don't know about this."

Wayne called his boss to ask if there was some work assignment he could do that weekend so that he could use work as an excuse. Nothing materialized. Despite his protestations, he found himself in Brittany's car on Friday, being driven to a bed and breakfast in a quaint surf town, where she'd booked a room for Friday and Saturday night.

I knew I shouldn't go, that it wouldn't end well, but she made it too tempting to resist. Every weekend she'd been saying she wanted us to have a threesome with her friend Jordan and it never happened. Before we left she swore to me that Jordan would meet us at the bed and breakfast on Saturday night. I'd asked her, "You promise? And there will be no drama?" She promised. I was in the car for only a few minutes when I literally got sick to my stomach and asked her to drop me off, Jordan or no Jordan. She wouldn't.

Brittany and Wayne arrived at the bed and breakfast. On Saturday Jordan never came. They went to the beach and had lunch. It was beautiful, but Wayne couldn't enjoy it. Brittany told everyone that this was their last weekend together, eliciting sympathy from whomever she could.

I couldn't wait for this to be over and done with so that I could be free of this crazy chick. Saturday night Brittany started getting all upset that she had to say good-bye the next day. She'd gotten paranoid that I was sleeping with other women, but they were only friends. She became delusional, screaming that I'd been hooking up the whole time and saying, "Let's just leave right now!"

But they'd had too much to drink to drive the hour and a half back home on curvy roads, so Wayne told her that he wasn't leaving. Every 20 minutes, Brittany would flip the switch. She'd go from jumping up, slamming doors, packing, and screaming she was leaving to lying down in bed. This went on the whole night.

Sunday morning, to Wayne's relief, they packed the car and Brittany started driving. He still couldn't drive because of his broken wrist. Suddenly Brittany started driving in the opposite direction from home and insisted on visiting another coastal town, pleading, "Let's just walk on the boardwalk."

I couldn't hold it in any longer. I told her, "You are driving me out of my head! I can't wait for this to be over! You knew when we began this trip that there wasn't a chance in hell we'd get back together!"

They walked on the boardwalk and when they got back to her car, Brittany conveniently couldn't find her keys. Eventually someone at the lost and found kiosk brought them over. But it was too late to drive all the way home. When they got in the car,

Brittany told Wayne she'd booked the same bed and breakfast for that night. He couldn't believe it. But Wayne had begun smoking more pot and drinking more, as his relationship with Brittany got crazier. He'd wanted to numb himself. Brittany didn't drink much unless she was upset, and Sunday she had been upset and pounded drinks back, so Wayne was again scared to get in the car with her. That night was a repeat of Saturday night's drama.

On Monday morning they drove to Brittany's place so that Wayne could pick up his stuff. They got back in the car to drive to his place. At the entrance to the freeway, she turned towards the opposite direction with some story of having to make a quick stop at a bar to pick up some baseball tickets. When the owner hadn't left the tickets for her, Brittany said, "Let's have a drink and wait for him," knowing that she would pound drinks back again and Wayne wouldn't want her to drive the rest of the way back to his place. When the owner showed up without any tickets, Wayne was so frantic to get home that he said he'd drive. But Brittany had left the car running and the battery was dead. It was now 8:00 P.M.

I knew what she was doing. She was kidnapping me with one delay tactic after another. It was insane. I was only 45 minutes from home. I could've called a taxi or a friend, but I felt sorry for her. She'd had a tough life – abused by her boyfriends and ex-husband, and being a single mom. Early on I wanted to be her knight in shining armor. I thought maybe I could fix her. Every time I was ready to call a cab or a friend, she'd shift gears and say, "Fine, I'll take you." AAA finally got her car jumped, but by then I'd had two or three drinks and painkillers for my wrist. I made another brilliant decision to stay there overnight.

Tuesday morning Brittany came up with another ploy driving back towards her home, claiming she had to get her anxiety medication because saying good-bye to Wayne was too anxiety-provoking. She started driving erratically at 40 miles per hour, all the while rummaging through her purse and talking on her phone. Then she got off at an exit and pulled over, announcing, "I can't do this. I can't take you back! I can't let you go!" Then she switched gears and said, "Take the car with your stuff and I'll have my daughter drive me up later to get my car back." Wayne was thrilled at the idea, but when he tried to open the passenger door Brittany sped away, saying, "No. I'll drive you." She did this three or four more times, breaking down more each time. Brittany pretended to call another guy and have a conversation with him, as if she were going to go see him after she dropped Wayne off.

She was obviously looking for a reaction out of me, but I didn't react. If she was going to meet up with a guy she would be out of my hair, so that sounded just fine with me. Finally I see could see the lights of San Francisco up ahead. Just as I was thinking this was going to end, she swerved over four lanes and went over the Bay Bridge. I shouted at her, "You're kidnapping me! Let me go!" My knuckles were bleeding from punching the dashboard of her BMW because I was so furious. I put 911 into my phone, but I was afraid to put the call through because I didn't want to push her any further off the edge. I was scared for my life. At this moment, dancing through my head, I had visions of O.J. Simpson and his white bronco being chased through the streets. As the last exit came up, Brittany swerved again to keep going in the wrong direction. I was fighting her for the wheel.

Finally, after more swerving and grabbing of the wheel, they reached Wayne's place. He couldn't help laughing to himself, perhaps a little too hysterically, that his favorite storybook had been *Oh, the Places You'll Go!* by Dr. Seuss. Brittany bullied her way upstairs, demanding that he let her retrieve her stuff. Once there she started drinking and talking about killing herself. He lived on the third story of a townhouse, and she claimed to have taken his pain medicine. Wayne didn't know any of her friends to call. He'd met her daughter a couple of times, but didn't have a number for her or their home. At this point he was so frustrated he punched two holes in his wall. After about three hours, Wayne walked her stuff down the steps, grabbed her sweatshirt, pushed her out the front door, locked it, and breathed a sigh of relief. Three minutes later Brittany was walking up the steps. She'd stolen his spare keys. Wayne got her out the front door again, called the cops, and told them she'd stolen his keys and had stolen his phone before.

I found out later she'd been text messaging two of my women friends from my phone as if she were me, saying, "I've never been so in love with any woman as I am with Brittany."

Wayne had a locksmith change his locks. Brittany continued to call, text, and email until he got a new phone number and email address, at which time she resorted to letters. She wrote about how sorry she was, how she never meant for it to be so dramatic, and how she hopes he remembers how happy they were together.

I realize I allowed myself to be manipulated. But over the first couple of months, before I knew she'd lied to me about her age, I thought she had a lot of endearing qualities. She even bought my friend a birthday cake, and the physical chemistry was there. I felt so bad for her. I thought, "How could these guys abuse her? I would never do that. Maybe I could be the one – her knight in shining armor." Brittany had portrayed herself as a victim. I had never felt as sorry for anyone.

Wayne had always had a big heart. As a child he used to find sick baby rabbits and try to nurse them back to health just as he had tried to do with Brittany. Now he was stuck in her web of deceit.

I was freaked out, thinking she'd show back up. I was scared she'd try to hurt me or she'd show up hurt and call the cops and say I hurt her or she'd bring a guy to hurt me. She was crazy.

Then one day Wayne saw her driving down a nearby street. When he opened the entranceway door to his townhouse building, the hall reeked of her perfume. He was terrified she was there, but, in fact, she'd only thrown a ball of socks through the mail slot that she'd sprayed with her perfume. The police had told him to call if he saw her. A few days later while he was on the front porch playing his guitar, he saw her coming down his street. He called the police. They came and told her this was grounds for stalking. She lied and said she'd left her stuff in Wayne's apartment. The next month was relatively quiet – only a letter or two. But it was to be the calm before the storm. Brittany found him on Facebook and sent him this foreshadowing message: "You need to get in touch.

There's something we have to discuss, a decision you should be involved with."

I called her to be a man. We planned to meet to have her take a pregnancy test. We had drinks in an upscale bar in the Marina district. I couldn't walk into the bathroom at this place to watch her pee on a stick. She came out and showed me that an EPT pregnancy test was positive. I thought, "Oh, fuck!" For the first couple of months, even though she insisted on staying with me, I stuck my head in the sand. I did not want to have anything to do with her. We discussed abortion and all the different options. She said, "I know we won't be together if I have this baby, so I might have an abortion." I said I'd help. She called doctors on the speakerphone to set up appointments for an abortion, but then she'd go for an appointment on the spur of the moment while I was at work. I love children and always dreamed of being father – but not this way. She had morning sickness and I heard her vomiting in the bathroom. I only told one friend and my parents.

I wanted her to get an abortion as quickly as possible, but it dragged on. She claimed her appointments got cancelled and there were other delays, until one day she called and said she just got out of a doctor's appointment. "I'm pregnant with twins! So I don't know about having an abortion." She was overjoyed. "We're going to have two babies!" I was a wreck. Ever since she came back into my life, I started smoking more pot, drinking more, and even occasionally using coke and Ecstasy again. I had been a weekend warrior, but now I did whatever I could to mask my feelings. She was putting on weight and announced to her daughter, her parents, and everyone else that she was pregnant with twins.

When Brittany had stolen Wayne's phone, she took down his mother's number. In August she called her and told her that Wayne was using drugs, planting a seed in his mother's mind that he had a worsening problem. She let them know that a week after he'd found out she was pregnant, he combined drinking and Ecstasy and ended up in the ER. Since Brittany was going to be the mother of their grandchildren, his parents came, met her, and did an intervention. The four of them had a picnic in the park. Sitting across from each other, Brittany looked like a slightly younger version of Wayne's mom: Long dirty blonde hair, similar facial features, about the same height – even the same gold hoop earrings, although Brittany's were bigger.

Brittany is real sharp and well-spoken with a superficial charm. My parents were a wreck after they heard about the twins, but they were thankful to Brittany for trying to help with my drug problem. I went into an inpatient residential treatment program for pot and alcohol that was within walking distance from Brittany's home. She was crying to the staff, "I'm pregnant and I need the daddy to be sober." The counselors were going on, "This must be so hard for you." I left AMA (Against Medical Advice) after three weeks and continued going to Alcoholics Anonymous. Somehow I've managed not to use alcohol or drugs again.

When she said she was pregnant, I knew it would never work out for us to be together because she was crazy. But I thought maybe we could work on her insecurity, her baggage, because the babies were coming. I knew, in my heart of hearts, I would be miserable. Still I decided to give it a shot. My parents moved all my stuff to her house. After one week at her place, she wouldn't let me leave unless she was with me. She even demanded to go to my AA meetings. She was getting crazy again. She said she wasn't putting on more weight because of all the stress she was having from me.

She didn't want me to talk with my family. Now that I was sober, I started asking questions. I wanted to see the ultrasound. I begged Brittany to give the babies up for adoption. I went to an adoption clinic, but she refused to go. It was now October. She said her due date had been January 6, but when they discovered she was having twins the date was moved up to December 23. I needed to get out of this madness, so I booked a flight to visit my family for a few weeks. I told her to meet me for dinner. While she was waiting for me at the restaurant, I packed my stuff and went to stay at a friend's place until my plane left the next morning.

During the time that Wayne was visiting his family, Brittany kept him updated with her news, telling him about the baby shower that had been thrown for her, the support group she'd joined for expectant mothers having twins, and the ultrasound that showed they were having a boy and a girl. She told him of all the sympathy she was getting because of how tough it was being pregnant without the father there with her. When Wayne returned to San Francisco, he had decided to move back home with his family permanently, regardless of whether Brittany gave the babies up for adoption or not. He stayed with friends until he could tie up loose ends.

I told her it wasn't gonna work between us. She was totally freaking out, but I made it clear that it was non-negotiable. She'd say, "How are you going to stay sober?"

She moved most of my stuff to a storage unit and gave me the keys. She knew she was running out of runway. I was pissed. I'd told her not to move my stuff because I was concerned about her health. In her twisted, sadistic way, she set me up in case she had a miscarriage. Then it would be my fault and would prove that I was not a good dad. Some things were missing, little things of sentimental value that she kept. She said she didn't have them, but I was welcome to come look myself. Again I was manipulated into a hostage situation. I went to her place. As I was looking for my stuff, I didn't notice any prenatal vitamins, doctors' bills, or baby clothes or toys, like she would have gotten at a baby shower. She said all the shower toys were at her Alanon sponsor's place and the ultrasound was at her parents' house.

She'd been hacking into my email and found out I was moving back home. I waited until the last day. We met for lunch and I told her, "My stuff is packed in my car and I'm leaving tonight." She was devastated. She said maybe she should come with me and have the babies in my hometown. She turned to some people who were sitting nearby and had them take pictures of us so that she could put them up in the babies' room. It was surreal.

Wayne left in early November and drove back home across the country. She kept in touch, asking him what to name the babies and arguing about him not being with her. Then she called and said she was in the hospital and they needed his blood type. She said she might have to have an emergency C-section because she had a placental separation caused by lifting heavy things and not eating well. On November 29 he received an email from Brittany:

This is hard on me as the time draws closer and closer and not having you around.... This is a bit emotional for me, to be honest. I was so interested in having you a part of this through at least the birth.

Brittany had wreaked emotional havoc on me and my family for almost a year. My mom hadn't been able to sleep for months. She was put on anti-depressants. My dad was diagnosed with prostate cancer caused by all the stress. It was an absolute nightmare.

Wayne and his family held their breath as the days ticked by, getting ever nearer to her due date of December 23.

On December 22 at 8:39 P.M. Wayne received an email from Brittany:

Wayne,

I am not pregnant. Please do not contact me. I wish to heal and get on with my life.

Brittany

I didn't know what to believe. Did she have the babies? Miscarry? I started calling her. She wouldn't respond. I finally reached her on Christmas Day. She said, "You don't know the whole story." She was cryptic. Finally Brittany admitted she was never pregnant! She had no remorse for the hell she'd put me through. The pregnancy was a fake, but my emotions were real. She made "Fatal Attraction" look like a Disney movie!

Famous Bad Girls Scorned

Sahel Kazemi – When NFL star Steve McNair decided to end his affair with Sahel instead of ending his marriage, Sahel decided to "end it all." While he was sleeping she blew his brains out and then turned the gun on herself, hoping to die romantically in his lap.

Astronaut Lisa Nowak – Even a NASA astronaut can resort to stalking and revenge when jilted. Lisa drove cross-country wearing diapers and carrying a BB gun and pepper spray. She was charged with the attempted kidnapping and murder of Colleen Shipman, the new girlfriend of fellow astronaut William Oefelein.

Jean Harris – Headmistress Jean had a 14-year affair with Dr. Herman Tarnower, the creator of the Scarsdale Diet, until he prescribed a younger woman for himself. Jean shot and mortally wounded Dr. Tarnower when she saw the 'other woman's' lingerie on his bed.

Carolyn Warmus – Carolyn's parents divorced when she was a little girl, which propelled her towards a string of doomed obsessive relationships. She hoped her affair with fellow teacher Paul Solomon would have a happier ending if she killed his wife, but it landed her in the same New York prison that once housed Jean Harris.

Lisa "Left Eye" Lopes - Known as the "crazy" one in the "CrazySexyCool" girl band TLC, Lisa's abusive past reared its head when, as revenge for NFL star Andre Rison's infidelity and abuse, she set his tennis shoes – and mansion – on fire.

Clara Harris – When Clara, also known as the "Mercedes

Murderess," discovered that her husband, a rich dentist, was having an affair with his receptionist, she steered her Mercedes to the hotel where they were having a tryst, attacked her, and ran over him, killing him at the scene.

Aileen Wuornos – This serial killer claimed the seven men she killed had raped her or tried to rape her while she was working as a prostitute. Her nightmarish childhood filled with 'scorn' is what later caused her to act out her rage on these men, and resulted in her ultimate execution. Her story was popularized in the film "Monster."

Stephanie Lazarus – When detectives opened a 23-year-old cold case, they finally listened to Sherri Rasmussen's family, who tried to tell them about an ex-girlfriend of her husband who'd threatened Sherri right before she was killed. Stephanie, ironically an LAPD Detective, herself, was charged with the murder.

The First Wives – In "The First Wives Club," a movie based on Olivia Goldsmith's novel, three women get revenge on their husbands who have left them for younger women. Ivana Trump makes a cameo appearance with the line, "Remember girls, don't get mad, get everything!"

Elizabeth Kennedy – Former "Brady Bunch" star Barry Williams obtained a restraining order against his live-in girlfriend, Elizabeth, after she allegedly threatened to kill him and then commit suicide because she suspected he was having an affair.

Bernadine Harris – In the movie "Waiting to Exhale," Bernadine (Angela Bassett) sacrifices her catering career to marry and have a family, only to have her husband leave her for another woman. She gets revenge by setting his personal belongings and car on fire.

Juliana Gianni – In the film "Vanilla Sky," Juliana (Cameron

Diaz) is a woman scorned when she realizes that her boyfriend (Tom Cruise) has fallen in love with Sofia (Penelope Cruz) after cooling things with her. To get revenge, Juliana offers him a ride and then crashes their car off a bridge.

Lisa Origliasso – Pop-rock singer/songwriter Lisa (one half of The Veronicas) got her revenge by making "Revenge Is Sweeter (Than You Ever Were)" into a hit song after her boyfriend, Ryan Cabrera, cheated on her. "Do you even know how much it hurt, that you gave up on me to be with her?… You try to make me hate that girl when I should be hating you."

Brooke Hundley – After ESPN analyst Steve Phillips tried to break up their brief affair, Brooke entangled herself with his family. She went to his home, and left a letter for his wife, which described the "big birthmark on his crotch right above his penis," lest the wife not believe that they had been intimate.

Chapter 14

BAD GIRLS' SECRETS TO A MAN'S HEART

Many a woman has had the frustrating experience of loving a man who is oblivious to her because he is swept up in the drama of loving a bad girl, instead. Everyone sees the heartbreak coming and wants to save him from it, but he won't listen. Why not? You've just read about the dozen dangerous damsels and how even successful and savvy men have fallen under their spells and whimpered at their feet.

Ladies, this chapter will dig a little deeper into the bad girls' book of spells to teach you how to become man-magnets, while not encouraging you to become man-eaters. You will discover how to capture the irresistible allure of bad girls without resorting to becoming really "bad" yourself.

Men, you can read this chapter from another perspective – more red flags to watch out for so that you'll be better able to recognize and avoid falling for bad girls instead of having to learn the hard way. Now you'll be able to pause and figure out whether the girl in 'fuck me shoes', licking her lips as she hones in on you from across the room, is a really bad girl or just a good girl trying to get your attention so that you'll give her a chance to show you what a wonderful girlfriend, lover, or wife she would make.

But first, before we go deeper into the bad girls' secrets, let's confront the elephant in the room: fear. Love is the antidote to fear – but what if you're afraid of love? The more you've had your heart broken, the harder it is to believe you will ever find true love and the harder it is to risk your heart on someone new. This is why so many women stop making efforts to look good, lose their confidence, and sit at home moping and seething. And this is why so many men become more vulnerable to bad girls who seem so enamored with them that men are willing to risk taking their heart out of mothballs to try again.

Of course, the fact that you've been reading this book is a positive sign that you haven't given up altogether. So let's take it from here. The secrets in this chapter are culled from hundreds of interviews and therapy sessions with men who have sacrificed their savings, self-respect, and sanity to a bad girl, who has enticed them and kept them enthralled until she got what she wanted – from a gold card to a green card, from sexual bliss to someone else's husband, and from a white picket fence to whatever she tells him to do next.

So ladies, if your heart isn't mended enough to find the backbone or balls, courage or chutzpah to carry off these secrets, find a good psychotherapist to help you get there. In the meantime, fake it 'til you make it. Get out your cauldron, toss in some eye of newt and toe of frog, add water, and stir. Like the witches in Macbeth, start chanting: "Double, double, toil and trouble. Fire burn, and cauldron bubble!" It will put you in the mood to start practicing these new spells on the men you're after.

When the men were asked what attracted them and kept them hooked on a bad girl, their answers fell into the following categories: looks, dress, sex, personality, lifestyle, and the tactics she used to bait and reel them in. Let's call them the "Six Secret Spells of Seduction."

Secret Spell #1: Looks

No one ever told me I was pretty when I was a little girl. All little girls should be told they're pretty, even if they aren't.

Marilyn Monroe

Ninety-nine percent of the men began by saying that they fell for their bad girl because she was: "gorgeous," "hot," "attractive," "sexy-looking," or "beautiful." When asked for the details of these gorgeous broads, it turns out that they came in all different models: blondes, brunettes, redheads; petite, medium, tall; and so on. The features men mentioned most as having enchanted them were her "pretty eyes," "bouncy, shiny hair" and a "great smile."

She was amazingly attractive.

In addition to what number she was, on that intimidating scale of 1-10, men were unconsciously drawn to their bad girls because of the memories the girls triggered. Some men were attracted to bad girls who looked like their mother or the exact opposite of their mother. Other men were attracted to bad girls who looked like a celebrity they lusted after – not necessarily a 'Marilyn Monroe' type, sometimes a 'Helen Hunt' type. And still other men were unconsciously drawn to women who looked like old girlfriends – even those from as far back as elementary school – for whom they had unrequited love.

Now there are some things you can't change about your looks, but there are many things you can change. It's a fact of nature that men are visual creatures, and the media have conditioned them to believe that the stereotypical 'hottie' of Barbie dolls and beer ads is what constitutes a beautiful woman. If we don't look like Barbie or the women in these ads – and 99 percent of us don't – we can start movements and burn our bras, or we can learn how to put on make-up, go on a diet, and follow a nightly skin regimen. Every woman needs to make the decision for herself. Yes, it's important to stand up for 'inner beauty' and try to change the way men think, but you need to realize that it may not happen in your lifetime – or at least your dating lifetime. So it's up to you. It doesn't mean that you need to run out and get plastic surgery to look like Barbie, but it does mean that you need to pay attention to your grooming, be stylish, and portray the image that you respect and care about yourself.

I was and still am in awe of her beauty.

Men who have been besotted by bad girls say, "I don't trust pretty girls, especially the ones who know they're pretty!" Why? Because men know that a pretty girl can turn them into mush, and the ones who know they're pretty can and do use their looks to manipulate them.

Nothing can make a plain girl look more beautiful than self-confidence. But it's a vicious cycle. How do you feel self-confident if you don't feel beautiful? Barbie dolls have done more to lower the self-esteem of little girls than anything else. A little girl looks at Barbie and then looks at herself in the mirror and decides, before the age of 10, that she may not be pretty enough to ever hook a Ken.

Now this is not the time to put this book down and go running for the Rocky Road ice cream for comfort. There is hope. But you have to be willing to be honest with yourself. The first step is to find a full-length mirror and ask it, "Mirror, mirror on the wall, who's the fairest of them all?" If you can't answer, "I am," and believe it, then you need to go from head to toe and write down what you don't like about yourself and then make plans to fix it.

It's just wonderful that someone that gorgeous loves me.

Start with your hair. Men liked "bouncy, shiny hair." Whatever your color or length, bouncy, shiny hair can be yours if you treat yourself to conditioners and other hair products, hair salon services, and vitamins that benefit your hair. When's the last time you changed your hairstyle? Is it out-of-date or does it no longer suit you? Are you letting the gray creep in and pretending to yourself that it's not so bad? Ask a hair stylist for suggestions.

What about your skin? There are countless products and treatments for everything from A to Z, or at least from acne to wrinkles. Facials – performed by an aesthetician or by yourself at home – are vital to revitalizing your skin and should be a regular part of your regime.

Men are captivated by "pretty eyes." Whatever nature gave you can be enhanced by make-up. Eye make-up can make your eyes look bigger and brighter and can lengthen the lashes you'll need to bat. There's make-up to enhance the rest of your face, too, for that matter. If you don't know how to make the best of your features, walk up to any department store cosmetics counter and you will have experts vying to 'do' you. Of course, they're trying to sell their wares and you don't have to buy the lot (at least not all at once), but they will give you some great free tips. You can decide which ones you like best and voila!

If make-up is not enough to make you feel great about yourself and your eyes gravitate to a feature that really taunts you and destroys your confidence when you look in the mirror, then you may consider making an appointment for a consultation with a dermatologist and/or a plastic surgeon. Make sure the doctor is board-certified and check out his or her work, preferably with someone you can see in person and talk to about the experience. Consult with more than one doctor before deciding whom you feel most comfortable with, and then go for it. Know why enhanced pouty lips, lip gloss, and lipstick are such turn-ons to men? Two reasons, whether a man is conscious of them or not. One, it makes them imagine your puffy lips on their penis and, two, your lipsticked lips make them think of your 'lower lips' – and the juicier the better.

She really has the body I was always hoping to find in a woman. I had this pin-up photo of a girl I thought was perfect when I was about 12 or 13 and it was a 1980s version of her.

Weight is a biggie, pun intended. Although some of the bad girls who enchanted their men were overweight, most men spoke of liking women who had a "great body" that was "fit." There's no getting around your needing to get around to the gym or to other exercise like walking, jogging, or sports. A nutritious diet, exercise, and vitamins will not only help you get that "great, fit body," but they will give you that healthy glow that evolutionary theory tells us attracts a mate. Blame evolution while you're sweating on the treadmill, but just make sure you incorporate healthy habits into your lifestyle.

Of course, you need to focus on grooming, as well. Your nails should at least be clean and polished, if not extended by acrylics. Your teeth should be maintained in good hygiene and whitened. Since a "great smile" is an aphrodisiac, consider getting your teeth straightened or having veneers put on if you are embarrassed to smile. Don't forget to tend to body hair as frequently as your body demands. You might want to try a Brazilian bikini wax while you're at it. Men like this because it makes your genital area seem cleaner and less intimidating.

Yes, it all sounds like a lot of work. And women who have been hurt by love are tired of trying and afraid to make all these efforts to look good, only to be hurt again. Instead, they don old clothes, wear no make-up, let their hair roots grow too long, get fat, and do whatever else they can to consciously or unconsciously drive men away. It's akin to hanging a clove of garlic around your neck to keep the vampires away. Yes, men can be like vampires, but you're keeping the good ones away, too.

And then there's that standby rationalization, "beauty is in the eye of the beholder." A man should like me for who I am, and someone will "behold" me as beautiful. Sure, but when? If you keep telling that to yourself as you sit alone at night, not doing anything to make the most of your assets, it will be too late because the rejections will keep eroding your self-confidence. Not all bad girls are '10s.' In fact, many men who fall for bad girls only convince themselves that these girls are "gorgeous" as a rationalization for why they put up with the bad girl behavior. But if they weren't really 10s, they sure did what they could to camouflage this fact and used the rest of the Secret Spells of Seduction to compensate for it.

Darling, the legs aren't so beautiful, I just know what to do with them.

Marlene Dietrich

Secret Spell #2: DRESS

I often think that a slightly exposed shoulder emerging from a long satin nightgown packs more sex than two naked bodies in bed.

Bette Davis

If you believe in the law of attraction, it should be easy for you to understand that if you look schlumpy, you will attract schlumps!

Bad girls know that how you dress is even more important than your God-given looks. Why? Because how you choose to dress conveys a message about how confident you are and how interested you are in attracting men. The more effort you put into looking alluring, the more it tells men that you appreciate yourself and think you're worth going to the trouble of being stylish and well put-together. It tells them you think you're worth a lot of attention and that you want to be approached, appreciated, and adored. It gives them the signal to "come hither." And since men are afraid of rejection, they need this green light to give them the courage.

With this in mind, walk over to your closet and drawers and get ready to make a wardrobe overhaul. Again, you have to be brutally honest with yourself. Make three piles of clothes: one for charity, one for the tailor or your own sewing machine, and one to keep. If you're not sure what goes into each pile, enlist the help of a stylish and caring friend who understands your goal of looking like a bad girl, though not really becoming bad. Give away (or save for when you're just hanging out at home alone) all your big bulky sweaters, big bulky sweatshirts, or anything else that makes you look fatter than you are. Give away anything dingy, or grayish-greenish-brownish clothes that make you fade into the woodwork.

While going through your wardrobe, you probably surprised yourself by finding things that you forgot you bought – like a hat or a feather boa or long dangly earrings or a bustier. When you were in the store, you thought you'd find the spunk to wear it, but somehow it never made it out of your closet. These are the kinds of things you should keep and wear for that very reason – it takes spunk and will convey your devil-may-care attitude.

And now that you've made room in your closet, you can buy more 'props' that get men's attention and convey your new audacity, like push-up bras, tops with low-cut necklines, short skirts or skirts with slits, tight jeans – whatever shows off your assets best. And just say no to those clodhopper shoes. High-heeled 'fuck me shoes' are called that for a reason. They tell the world that the woman is open to being made love to and they usually accomplish their mission.

Yes, this means more effort and more bravado, so what's a busy woman to do? Well, you can sit at home and complain, deny that any of this works, or you can go out and watch what makes men's head turn.

Those of you who are "Sex and The City" aficionados will remember the episodes where Miranda, a Ball-Buster, who usually resents having to pander to men by wearing sexy outfits, occasionally dons one. When she fit into her skinny jeans or rode the motorized bull and her blouse flew open exposing her sexy bra, she got appreciative reactions from men – not just because of the clothes per se but because of the confidence and fun she exuded by wearing them.

Most men who have been lassoed by naughty ladies seem to prefer a combination of sexy and classy – like a classy suit with a low-cut blouse or a slit up the side of the skirt. It's that librarian-lingerie model dichotomy that intrigues them. You can make it your unique style, but make it sexy.

Secret Spell #3: SEX

When I'm good, I'm very good, but when I'm bad, I'm better.
Mae West

Sex sells! A hundred years ago Freud told us that sex is one of our inborn drives. Hollywood and Madison Avenue have been making use of this ever since. If it works to sell soap and movie tickets, it will work to sell you. There's no question that the promise of hot sex is the most powerful secret the bad girl has in her book of spells. Almost unanimously, men described how sexual attraction was what made them think, "Let me check this out!"

The sex was fantastic! She loved to dress up in hot lingerie. She knew how to ring my visual bell.

Men want women to be adventurous and wild in bed and to wear sexy lingerie – matching bras and panties, garter belts, fishnets, crotch-less panties, whatever companies like Victoria's Secret or Frederick's of Hollywood dream up. They especially noted with enthusiasm, "It was like she could read my mind and did what I was hoping for at that very moment." Men want women to be like good mothers taking care of babies and knowing exactly what they want without them having to say it. Paradoxically, men also want to feel like they are taking care of the woman by giving her unparalleled orgasms so that they can reassure themselves they're hot studs who have her under their power. What some men appreciate about bad girls is that they make them feel comfortable about confiding their fantasies and then take pleasure in playing them out, instead of begrudgingly going along with it.

It was awesome that she was willing to understand and fulfill my sexual fantasies! They weren't harmful or overly weird, and it made me feel accepted and loved.

Some men admit they're intimidated by smart, successful, or career-driven women.

I never felt like a good lover with a powerful woman. It's intimidating with a woman who wakes up at 5:00 A.M. to exercise, has the same breakfast and gets on the road, dedicated to being successful. They are very attractive on paper and when I see them, but they are sexually intimidating.

These women need to try harder to let the lingerie model peek through the librarian exterior.

I think the fact that we hit it off sexually and it was obvious that we were clicking kept me from being too intimidated.

Secret Spell #3 can actually be put very succinctly. You simply must get comfortable with sex – especially giving men oral sex. Just like women want to feel beautiful, men want to feel powerful – and having a woman pleasuring their private parts is every man's fondest desire. If you are able to give good head, you'll be in a position of power, too.

The chemistry was just there. We were turning each other on and there was no hiding how much!

If you're not yet comfortable with sex, read books about it, watch sex education videos, and go to psychotherapy to find out what experiences in your past have caused you to be uncomfortable. Look at your vagina in a mirror and use a vibrator to discover what pleasures you the most so you can suggest – verbally or with body language – what the man should do to pleasure you. If you're ready, take tantric sex classes with your partner. As with any technique, practice makes perfect... and sex can be 'perfectly' blissful once you give yourself permission to relax and enjoy. There is nothing like an orgasm to give you perspective on what makes the world go round. If more men were sexually satisfied, there would be fewer wars. So if you still can't get into sex for the pleasure it will bring to you and your partner, then think of it as contributing to world peace.

Guys are suckers when it comes to sex. They love being complimented in and out of bed – especially when the woman is sincere.

There are a couple of caveats that should be mentioned. One is that you should always use a condom unless you are in a committed relationship with a trustworthy man and you have seen his test results for venereal disease. Even then, do you really want to risk accidentally getting pregnant? Yes, some bad girls try this trick as a way to get a man to marry them, or at least stay with them. But as you've read in previous chapters, it doesn't necessarily work. Another caveat is that sex with a man under 21 is risky, even if you do use a condom. You may not get a disease or get pregnant, but you are likely to get your heart broken since these men are usually looking for notches on their belt, not walks into the sunset.

Secret Spell #4: PERSONALITY

I was thought to be 'stuck up' I wasn't. I was just sure of myself. This is and always has been an unforgivable quality to the unsure.
Bette Davis

Bad girls have tons of personality because, in order to get a man to look up from his work or from another woman and follow them, they have to be the shiny new toy that glistens in the sunlight or the spotlight. Men like wit and a good sense of humor. They like a woman who can make her story seem like the most fascinating they've ever heard. Men like an intelligent woman as long as she doesn't make them feel dumb. And you have to be a smart enough cookie to follow these spells and put them to good use.

The key is to be bold and charismatic, if not flamboyant. But how, if you don't really feel that way inside? Remember, brazen bad girls actually have a faux-confidence or pseudo-cockiness, born of rising above their pain, hardening their hearts, and being driven by something they want. So you can muster something that's equally as effective. The law of attraction tells you to "believe" in yourself and act as though you already are or have what you want. So visualize yourself walking into a room, having men's heads turn towards you, and turning these men on. If you follow these secret spells, you will soon start getting attention from men so it will become a self-fulfilling prophecy. Meanwhile, remember that you can fake it 'til you make it.

Men need to feel needed. They don't like risking being hurt, rejected, or abandoned by a woman who is totally self-sufficient. So although they admire some degree of independence in a woman, you should not be emasculating.

Good girls want to know why it doesn't work when they call a guy, walk up to a guy, send him notes, or make other moves that show they're available and interested, when these same moves work for a bad girl. It's all in the attitude. A good girl comes from a needy, hungry, mushy, warm-hearted place that makes men feel uncomfortable, trapped, and scared by the closeness that she seems to be demanding. With a bad girl, he feels more in control. A good girl needs to stop trying to convince herself that a man loves her, but he's not showing it because he's too shy, too self-absorbed, or too busy. She needs more self-love and less self-sacrifice.

Needless to say, to catch a good man one cannot have – or at least should not reveal – a depressed, pessimistic, critical, or ill-tempered personality. If this is you, again the answer is to seek therapy – not just to catch a man, but to be happier and more fun for yourself and the people you care about.

Secret Spell #5: LIFESTYLE

Men want to know that you have a life outside of seducing them, and that it's an exciting one. Though some bad girls have a life filled with chaos, others have a life that's more successful.

It's best to follow your passion. Pursue your education or get a job that you're happier in, preferably one that's socially conscious. Volunteer for charities. You'll feel good about yourself and it will show. Men are attracted to women who demonstrate that they care about others.

Participate in hobbies and sports. Surround yourself with friends. You'd be surprised how much men notice whether or not a woman has good friends. If she doesn't, they wonder why and get uneasy. Plus you need the social support while you're trying to survive in the dating jungle.

Keep a clean, uncluttered, and comfortable home. Decorate it to reflect your personality and good taste. When a man walks into your home, he can't help but think that this is how his home would be if you two got married.

Men are attracted to women who share common interests, whether it's the Philharmonic or fishing, ballet or baseball, crosswords or camping out, Scrabble or skiing, rock concerts or rock climbing. They like having a conversation-starter and someone to share their favorite pastimes.

Bottom line: get a life! And make sure it's a dazzling one.

Secret Spell #6: TACTICS

Now we're down to brass 'tactics' – how to mesmerize your man and put him under your spell. Each of the bad girls you've read about has demonstrated the tactics they used to bait and reel him in. Let's highlight some of them.

First, bad girls are always on the prowl. Their radar hones in on men who are most likely to be hooked. A good guy strolls into her line of vision who has '"sitting duck"' or "vulnerable" or "take me" tattooed on his forehead. She's ready to pounce – lookin' good, dressed to kill, sexually comfortable with herself, bursting with confidence, or at least faux-confidence, and a fascinating life that would be more fascinating if it had him in it. It's a crime of opportunity and she seizes it!

Don't keep a man guessing too long – he's sure to find the answers somewhere else.

Mae West

Many men mentioned that bad girls hooked them by simply making themselves "available" and being "unattached." Now this doesn't work unless you also carry out the other secret spells of seduction – looking sexy, and so on. Otherwise, if you're too available men just think you're desperate.

I want to be left alone.

Greta Garbo

In fact, a key tactic many bad girls use is 'bait and switch'. They make themselves very available at the beginning so it's less work and less risk for the man, and then they become unavailable for a night or a weekend or more with good excuses, such as work or a family matter or simply needing personal time (to get in all that shopping and bikini waxing). They don't let the man feel abandoned exactly because this would be too scary for him. The bad girl is just like a fisherman who lets the bait dangle close to the fish's mouth and then pulls it away a little bit, then lets it dangle, then pulls it away, with the soft to and fro of the current until the next time the fish sees the bait he can't help but swallow it hook, line, and sinker.

A bad girl makes a man feel special without making herself seem less special. For example, she might say, "I don't usually date people I work with or who are not from my ethnic background or (fill in the blank), but you're so special you're making me break my rules." Or, "There's just something about you that draws me deeper and deeper." Similarly, giving a man attention, especially when he didn't get enough attention from his parents, is another useful tactic. Showing him that you're paying attention when he mentions something he would like, and then surprising him with it as a gift, will get you points.

Bad girls move in fast, literally. One of the favorite tactics of bad girls is to claim, true or not, that they desperately need a place to live. They'll say their lease is up or the landlord is throwing them out for some terribly unfair reason. The men they target are too besotted or sleep-deprived from nights of sex to realize that when they let the bad girl in the front door, they won't be able to get her out until it's too late and she's taken what she wants. It's kind of like shutting the barn door after the horse has left, but in reverse. At first men think they've gotten lucky beyond their wildest dreams: "This sexpot, cook, sexpot, companion, sexpot, personal assistant, sexpot... wants to live with me? And be at my disposal 24/7? Wow!" But before they know it, the hidden strings attached are tripping them up beyond their wildest nightmares.

As you've read, some bad girls jump into bed with a man the first chance they get to try to get him hooked on the sex before he can think rationally about whether she's really the right girl for him. This will be left to your discretion and your motives. If you're looking to 'get' something, like a true bad girl, it obviously does work, at least sometimes. But if you're looking for something deeper, you might want to think again.

SOUL MATE SECRETS

At some point after these 'sitting ducks' have had enough drama, they realize that they want a real connection to a woman who 'gets' them in a different way. Bad girls are more effusive so, at first, these men think they have an intense connection. But when they realize that the bad girl wasn't madly in love with them, after all, and that she was exploiting them for her hidden agenda, their bubble bursts and they feel betrayed, disappointed, and in a worse place than they were when they met her. Sometimes this makes these men even more vulnerable to the next bad girl who comes along. Other times the men learn their lesson and look for a real connection with a soul mate.

When men describe the soul mates they went on to marry after their bad girl experiences, it's not with the same ring of breathless excitement and unbridled crazy-making passion, but these good girl relationships were softer and more solid. It's like a woman settling for a 'nice accountant' after she's been on a thrilling roller-coaster ride with a bad boy. The thrills make for good memories and one yearns for them from time to time, but there's also something comforting about the real thing.

Guys are more sensitive than women realize. They remember incredible details of experiences with the women in their life – words said, clothes worn, days, times, places, and so on. Yet even though they were paying attention to details, these men were nonetheless seduced and taken for a ride by bad girls. How? Because they were in denial about some things, notably what it was in them that led to their being vulnerable to a bad girl in the first place. Despite these bad girl stories being in the past – sometimes decades – they are as vivid as yesterday in the retelling, revealing the tremendous impact the bad girls had on their men's lives.

Bad girls leave indelible impressions, but once the seduction is over, the relationship eventually crashes and burns. That's when it's the good girl's chance to step in. The Six Secret Spells of

Seduction are still the way to attract a man, who will then discover that good girls are less damaged and have something deeper to offer.

Here's what some men who have been wounded by bad girls have to say about finding their soul mate:

What attracted me to my soul mate was the first impression I had during our initial phone conversation: she had no guile, no defenses, and she was unguarded. She was very open, honest, and had nothing to hide. On our first date, aside from the physical attraction, it always starts at the physical, she was kind, loving, had a hearty laugh, a good sense of humor, and it was easy to talk with her. She didn't have an agenda. I saw she wasn't like the bad girls I dated previously. For people who have never dated a crazy woman, this doesn't seem like a big deal. But for me, it was extremely significant because I had experienced duplicity and deceit.

My last bad girl relationship was the straw that broke the camel's back. It made me ask myself a bunch of questions. Guys complain about relationships and how messed up the girl is, but the common denominator in all my bad girl relationships was me. I had to ask myself, "Why do I attract these bad girls?" I did a year of celibacy to get in touch with myself. My way of perceiving women was distorted. I realized I had to develop a barrier for entrance: we can get together if you meet certain criteria.

I met my soul mate at a party. I spotted her across the room dancing with her boyfriend. I thought she was really neat. I danced with her and we talked. She was having trouble with her boyfriend. I told my friend, "Someday I'll marry that woman." It was instant love. I kept tabs on her. When I found out she broke up with her boyfriend, we started dating. We went skydiving together. We had a great time – camping, fishing, shooting, and going on wilderness trips. She was my love. We had no problems, no bullshit. Initially there was a big attraction. She admitted she was attracted to me, too. I was attracted to her because of her honesty, her ability to talk openly, and I could trust her. We liked sharing our passions like skydiving. She had a sense of adventure. She was petite, but her heart was bigger than anything. She'd cry after a sky dive because she was scared or because something went wrong, but then she'd get back on the plane and do it again.

She had a family I knew all about. There were no secrets.

I felt an instant love. It was pretty much everything that attracted me, and it hit me hard. I just knew in my soul that she was 'The One'. Nothing like it had ever happened before or since. I simply just knew.

She was into family. She wasn't full of herself. She was really genuine. I could let my guard down. My guard was always up with my bad girl. This was my last shot at a legitimate life or else I would have gone to an island somewhere. I would've become a derelict, a drunk who lives on a shitty little boat because I was done. My bad girl beat me down.

My soul mate treats me with love, consideration, and respect. We share the same basic values about spirituality, family, and money. I like being able to trust her and feeling that she appreciates me. What really clinched it for me was when I saw that she cut all her old love ties. It's totally wrong to string someone along while hoping 'love muffin' comes back – like what my bad girl did to me.

After my bad girl experience I was a bit worried at first that this new woman might be too good to be true. I kept waiting for the hammer to drop for the first few weeks. Thank God none of the fears of my vivid imagination materialized.

Film star Jean Harlow, a Sex Siren, left an indelible memory on the psyche of Batman's creator, Bob Kane, at a young and "impressionable age." He wrote that she "seemed to personify feminine pulchritude at its most sensuous." Years later Harlow served as inspiration when he created Catwoman, a bad girl with some good intentions. Like other bad girls, Catwoman became bad after having been hurt by men in her past. Kane noted:

Cats are as hard to understand as women are.... You always need to keep women at arm's length. We don't want anyone taking over our souls, and women have a habit of doing that. So there's a love-resentment thing with women.

Indeed, lurking in the unconscious mind of every grown man is the indelible impression of the awesome power his mother had over him when he was a little boy. With the bat of an eyelash, she could make him feel loved or destroyed. When a man grows up, this memory makes him fearful of clingy good girls getting too close and "taking over" his soul. A bad girl seems as though she won't take over a man's soul because she's only using him to get what she wants, and she pretends to be madly in love with him – flattering him and fulfilling his sexual fantasies. On some level men know that bad girls can be kept at arm's length because bad girls are cold-hearted. But, paradoxically, these bad girls are the genuine soul-stealers.

A Final Note

The downside to becoming an *awfully* bad girl – one of the dozen dangerous damsels looking only to snatch something for herself – is that you still have a good little girl inside, crushed but not moribund, yearning for true love. When that inner little girl peeks out from behind her hiding place, you realize that you can never truly feel loved by the man you've preyed upon and caught because you'll always wonder if he loves you authentically or was only a 'sitting duck' who you manipulated into loving you.